GERHARD VON RAD

DEUTERONOMY

THE OLD TESTAMENT LIBRARY

General Editors

GERHARD VON RAD

DEUTERONOMY

A Commentary

The Westminster Press
Philadelphia

© SCM Press Ltd 1966
Translated by Dorothea Barton from the German
Das fünfte Buch Mose: Deuteronomium
(Das Alte Testament Deutsch 8)
published 1964 by Vandenhoeck & Ruprecht,
Göttingen

Scripture quotations are from the Revised Standard
Version of the Bible, copyright 1946 and 1952, by the
Division of Christian Education of the National Coun-
cil of Churches, and are used by permission.

Library of Congress Catalog Card No. 66-23088

5 6 7 8 9 10

Published by The Westminster Press₍ᴿ₎
Philadelphia, Pennsylvania

PRINTED IN THE UNITED STATES OF AMERICA

To the Society of Biblical Literature
and Exegesis
and its President for 1960
R. B. Y. Scott
(Princeton, N.J., U.S.A.)
in gratitude

CONTENTS

8 CONTENTS

ABBREVIATIONS

ANET *Ancient Near Eastern Texts relating to the Old Testament*, ed.
James B. Pritchard, 2nd ed., Princeton, 1955
ET English translation
OTL Old Testament Library, London
RSV Revised Standard Version
TLZ *Theologische Literaturzeitung*, Leipzig
TZ *Theologische Zeitschrift*, Basel
VT *Vetus Testamentum*, Leiden
ZAW *Zeitschrift für die alttestamentliche Wissenschaft*, Berlin

TRANSLATOR'S NOTE

In the German edition Professor von Rad provided his own translation of the biblical text. In this English edition the biblical text is that of the RSV, except where a Translator's Note indicates that Professor von Rad's translation has been followed.

INTRODUCTION

THE LITERARY FORM OF DEUTERONOMY

THE NAME Deuteronomy, by which the book is generally known in English, goes back to the Greek translation of the Old Testament, the so-called Septuagint. In Deut. 17.18 in this translation the Hebrew word for 'copy' was mistakenly understood in the sense of 'second law' (beside the law of Sinai). Methodical scholarly research into this book could begin only when it was proved conclusively by De Wette (1805) that this part of the Pentateuch must be considered on its own from the literary point of view and has nothing to do with the great sources of the Pentateuch, the Yahwist, the Elohist and the Priestly Document. As a result of the critical analysis of the sources a number of important facts may be recognized. These include, for example, the peculiar character of the so-called 'Song of Moses' (ch. 32) and of the 'Blessing of Moses' (ch. 33), and also many larger and smaller interpolations, especially several exilic passages which usually stand out in an easily recognizable form from the older literary material. Some interpolations from the literature of the Priestly Writings have also been identified (Deut. 1.3; 4.41–43; 32.48–52; 34.1a, 7–9).

However, this analysis by literary criticism has recently come somewhat to a standstill; yet one cannot say that the questions raised in these matters have been satisfactorily answered. Throughout Deuteronomy, for example, we find sections with 'ye' and sections with 'thou', but the separation of these sections has produced problems which are still unresolved.[1] Beside cases in which the 'ye-sections' are quite clearly recognizable as secondary expansions (9.7b–10; 13.3b–4; 20.2–4; 29.1–29), there are others about which it is doubtful

[1] So the AV are RV; in the RSV 'you' is used throughout. Translator.

11

whether such a distinction can rightly be made.[1] It is very important to note that Deut. 4.44–30.20 forms a book complete in itself, and that therefore the portions 1.1–4.43 and 31–34 must be assigned to other literary contexts, probably to the so-called Deuteronomistic historical work which extends from the Book of Joshua as far as the end of II Kings.[2] But this incorporation of Deuteronomy into that great historical work in about the middle of the sixth century denotes merely the conclusion of a very lengthy process of growth within the development of the historical tradition through which Deuteronomy passed during the stage of its independent existence. It is one of the chief tasks of exegesis to lay bare traces of this process.

Deuteronomy in its narrower sense, that is to say, Deut. 4–30, shows a remarkable arrangement. A predominantly hortatory speech to the people ('exhortation') passes in Deut. 12 into a recital of the 'laws'. This part then ends in Deut. 26.16–19 with the formulation of a covenant. Then there follows, again in elaborate detail, the proclamation of the blessing and the curse. This arrangement certainly cannot be explained as due to literary considerations. On the contrary, we must suppose that Deuteronomy is here following a traditional cultic pattern, probably that of the liturgy of a cultic festival. But we cannot take up until later the question of the meaning of this curious method of arrangement.

If we now turn to the separate sections and the way in which they are arranged, we can indeed recognize that, in fact, the style of a speech by Moses is preserved throughout; but even the inexperienced reader will recognize that he is by no means dealing with a smooth consecutive composition. The account is extraordinarily discontinuous. At frequent intervals the reader comes across interruptions and gaps in the sense. When we consider the form too, we find the style of the speaker changing continually. We must conclude from all this that Deuteronomy and the individual sections of which it is composed must have had an unusually complicated previous history. Here we will content ourselves with the statement that Deuteronomy presents itself to us almost as a mosaic of innumerable, extremely varied pieces of traditional material. But at the same time this is not

---

[1] In a large-scale attempt to solve this problem G. Minette de Tilesse ('Sections "tu" et sections "vous" dans le Deuteronome', *VT* 12, 1962, pp. 29–87) would like to assign the 'ye' parts to the Deuteronomistic editor, that is to say, to the great historical work to which Deuteronomy is closely attached.

[2] M. Noth, *Überlieferungsgeschichtliche Studien*, 1943, pp. 12ff., 27ff.

to deny that the book must nevertheless in the last resort be understood as a unity.

When we examine this traditional material incorporated into Deuteronomy, we are struck by the fact that a large part of the laws or maxims of the sacral code is known already from the Book of the Covenant (Ex. 21–23).

Ex. 21.1–11	= Deut. 15.12–18
Ex. 21.12–14	= Deut. 19.1–13
Ex. 21.16	= Deut. 24.7
Ex. 22.16f.	= Deut. 22.28, 29
Ex. 22.21–24	= Deut. 24.17–22
Ex. 22.25	= Deut. 23.19–20
Ex. 22.26f.	= Deut. 24.10–13
Ex. 22.29f.	= Deut. 15.19–23
Ex. 22.31	= Deut. 14.3–21
Ex. 23.1	= Deut. 19.16–21
Ex. 23.2f., 6–8	= Deut. 16.18–20
Ex. 23.4f.	= Deut. 22.1–4
Ex. 23.9	= Deut. 24.17f.
Ex. 23.10f.	= Deut. 15.1–11
Ex. 23.12	= Deut. 5.13–15
Ex. 23.13	= Deut. 6.13
Ex. 23.14–17	= Deut. 16.1–17
Ex. 23.19a	= Deut. 26.2–10
Ex. 23.19b	= Deut. 14.21b

The number of parallel cases can be reduced. They can also be somewhat increased. In either case it becomes quite obvious what a large stock of legal material Deuteronomy has in common with the Book of the Covenant. However, it is not equally certain that Deuteronomy was therefore actually intended to replace the Book of the Covenant, and that Deuteronomy rather than the Book of the Covenant was now intended to be understood as the authentic revelation at Sinai, as has been urged by Eissfeldt. For if Deuteronomy was derived so directly from the Book of the Covenant, the question would remain unanswered, why so large a part of the ordinances in the Book of the Covenant (amounting in all to about fifty per cent.) were passed over and omitted. Of course, we might also suppose that Deuteronomy goes back to a collection of laws unknown to us, and that this collection had much material in common with the Book of the Covenant, but possibly contained much of what we now find only in Deuteronomy and not in the Book of the Covenant (see below on the material peculiar to Deuteronomy).

But in the majority of cases in which a comparison of the wording is at all possible the wording of Deuteronomy is clearly later and that of the Book of the Covenant is earlier. The 'law of the Hebrew' in Ex. 21.2ff. had assumed the case of the purchase of a slave and had determined the length of his service. Deut. 15.12ff., on the other hand, deals with the enslavement of a man who had previously been free and had probably himself also owned land, but who for economic reasons had been obliged to sell himself into slavery for debt. In this case the initiative came from him and not as in Ex. 21.2 from the slave's master. There is the further difference that in Deut. 15.12ff. it is possible for the wife, too, to sell herself into slavery for debt. This must be connected with changes in the law of property. In the interval the wife had also become competent to inherit property (cf. II Kings 8.3), and so she could find herself in the same situation as a man who owned land.

In the Book of the Covenant the law of the year of release is a sacral ordinance which applies exclusively to agricultural life (Ex. 23.10f.) There it is a matter of letting the land lie fallow temporarily, not from economic or charitable motives, but from religious ones; the custom was intended to demonstrate Yahweh's original ownership of the soil (cf. Lev. 25.23). A custom of this kind could be observed most easily in Israel's early period, when agriculture was not yet the only means of livelihood, but was practised merely as an addition to the pastoral economy. Deut. 15.1ff. is quite different. The old sacral terminology is indeed retained, but there is a decisive change in the custom, inasmuch as the scope of the law of the 're-lease' has been extended to the law of debts. It is now financial values which are subject to the law of release. We can take as an example loans which a man has had to take up in order to carry on his business. Both in the case of the law of the Hebrew slave and in that of the year of release it is quite obvious that Deuteronomy, when compared with the Book of the Covenant, reflects a considerably more advanced stage in economic history. The money economy, in Israel's early period still in its primitive beginnings, had meanwhile become more complicated. If the Book of the Covenant is to be placed in the period between the entry into Canaan and the formation of the State, then this involves bringing the date of Deuteronomy certainly down to the time of the monarchy.

THE MATERIAL PECULIAR TO DEUTERONOMY

The material in Deuteronomy for which no parallel can be found in the Book of the Covenant has many forms, and it is clearly derived from different periods. The law concerning homicide committed by an unknown person (Deut. 21.1–9) bears all the marks of very great antiquity. The original wording of the law of the *qāhāl*, the assembly of the Lord (Deut. 23.1–8), must also go back to the period before there was a kingdom in Israel. But seen as a whole (only the more important points can be mentioned here) this material cannot be very old.

Again, Deut. 13 contains three ordinances which apply to cases of deliberate apostasy from the faith of Yahweh (2–6; 7–12; 13–19). The first assumes that this is initiated by a 'prophet'. But such a suggestion can, after all, have come only from a class of prophets which was already seriously contaminated by the Canaanite syncretism; moreover, the *nebiim* during Samuel's time did not yet possess such a leading position in the people's life. The third ordinance is interesting, for it assumes the apostasy to have been prompted by a city. Such a thing was actually within the bounds of possibility, but of course again not until the period of the monarchy. In this case we must think especially of those cities which lay outside the area originally settled by the earlier tribal union, since these were first incorporated into the kingdom of Israel in the course of the gradual extension of the boundaries under David. In these cities, which were politically independent during the long period of their Canaanite history, the religion of Yahweh had probably never really struck roots. Hence the old spirit of independence could revive in the time of the Israelite kings, particularly in an era in which the cult of Yahweh itself had already become undermined and was lacking in strength.

A particularly characteristic part of the material peculiar to Deuteronomy is the so-called code of laws concerning war, namely regulations about release from military service (20.1–9), two about the siege of cities (20.10–20), and one about keeping the camp clean (23.9–14). This last one is difficult to date; probably it is the oldest of this group. Deut. 20.1–9 has obviously been worked over (vv. 2–4 form the latest stratum); its nucleus lies in the speech of the officers in

vv. 5–7. These officers were royal officials responsible for military affairs and recruitment for military service. The individual regulations by which particular men were excluded from military service certainly originated at a very early period in the conduct of war. Yet just as certainly even the oldest stratum within Deut. 20.1–9 could not have come into being before the period of the monarchy. The same applies to the laws about the besieging of cities which really take for granted an advanced technique of siegecraft (20.20). Deuteronomy also contains a law about the king (17.14–20). The most striking thing about this is its almost exclusively negative trend. For the law endeavours above all to restrict the power and function of the king. It does not draw any positive picture of the kingly office in Israel, only a picture of a king as he ought not to be. Probably the model used for this was the Deuteronomistic picture of King Solomon.

The most important special feature of Deuteronomy, when compared with the Book of the Covenant, has always been considered to be the demand to centralize the cult as 'the place which Yahweh will choose', and certainly at the time of Deuteronomy this demand was something new. Yet, on the other hand, we do not find that all the parts of the book express, or even assume, this demand which was revolutionary for its time. There are not a few laws in Deuteronomy which do not seem to know anything about this demand for centralization. Only six large units are promulgated with this assumption explicitly in mind: the law of the altar, ch. 12; the law of tithing, 14.22–29; the law of the firstlings, 15.19–23; the law concerning the feasts, 16.1–17; the law concerning the tribunal in Jerusalem, 17.8–13; the law of the priests, 18.1–8. To these must be added the law concerning cities of refuge, 19.1–13, which, after the abolition of the plurality of sanctuaries, regulates afresh the system of asylum.

The altar law is divided into three ordinances, and each of them independently includes the demand for centralization (12.1–7, 8–12, 13–19 [20–28]). Of these the third one alone is worded in the singular and is probably the earliest. The new demand for the one altar is contrasted in the first ordinance with the custom of the neighbouring Canaanites, in the second with the custom practised until then by Israel itself. Hence the lawgiver is aware of the fact that he is demanding something quite new in his own time. Nevertheless we must ask whether the centralization of the cult was really something so completely new in the history of Israel. During the period of the judges, when Israel was a sacral tribal union, there was, after all, the ark (finally at Shiloh) as the cultic centre to which the tribes made their way at the great pilgrimage festivals. Centralization was, of course, unknown at that early period in the extreme form demanded by Deuteronomy. For this prescribed that there should be no sacrifice of any kind at all, except those which were offered at the place chosen by Yahweh, and that the firstlings and tithes, too, might be offered only at Yahweh's one place of worship. But at that early period Israel was not, as it was later in the time of Deuteronomy, in extreme danger of losing altogether the special quality of its cult of Yahweh. The immediate result of this demand of Deuteronomy, of course, a great improvement of the religious life of the people. However, the lawgiver faces this secularization. Indeed, he is endeavouring to help the people to lead such a secular life in the conditions of everyday affairs, and even there to keep Yahweh before their eyes. The new arrangements were especially radical as regards the custom of the passover, kept hitherto as a feast of the local family groups. Deuteronomy makes a break with this, too, by transforming the passover into a pilgrimage feast which is to be celebrated at the place of the common sanctuary by the slaying of bulls and sheep. Moreover, this passover arrangement is further complicated by the combination of the old Israelite passover festival with the feast of unleavened bread, which was of Canaanite origin (16.1ff.).

It is evident that Deuteronomy, by including this extremely copious special material, has developed as regards the history of its tradition very far from the Book of the Covenant. But before we begin to enquire into its distinctive theological character itself and its particular place in the long story of Israel's faith and cult, we must first deal with the special characteristics of the form of the material included in Deuteronomy. Unless we are acquainted with the individual items of material and the distinctive form in which they now appear in Deuteronomy, no opinion about the book as a whole is possible.

We must mention first the type of 'conditional laws' which we have already come to know from the Book of the Covenant (Deut. 15.12ff.; 21.15-17, 18-22; 22.13-29; 24.1-4; 25.1-3, 5-10), but which extended also far beyond Israel. It was, in fact, only after the conquest that Israel itself became familiar with the general legal system of the ancient Near East. It took over many of its formulations as well. These laws are introduced by the characteristic word 'if'. Sometimes they define the legal aspect of the case still more narrowly and then end up with another precise legal decision which determines what is to be done; sometimes a rule about the scale of punishment is also added. These laws regulate the broad field of the community's life in Israel; their setting was the legal assembly in the gate (cf. Ruth 4.1ff.; Gen. 23) where the elders were in charge of the administration of justice (Deut. 19.12, 21.1ff.; 22.15; 25.7).[1]

From these we must distinguish the 'apodictic laws' which appear in more general commands, and oftener still in prohibitions. They do not usually define the case with reference to every detail; they are concerned rather to express fundamental prohibitions or commands, taking no account of particular circumstances. Even in those cases in which they include directions for punishments, the important point is the basic issue, 'whoever shall, he who . . .' We know this type especially from the Decalogue (Deut. 5.6–21) and the Dodecalogue (Deut. 27.15–26); it is also not infrequently found elsewhere in Deuteronomy (15.1; 16.19; 16.21–17.1; 23.–17).

As regards setting, it is not only the liturgical construction of the Dodecalogue but also Yahweh's presentation of himself at the beginning of the Decalogue, and the fact that these statutes occur in large series, show clearly that they originated in the realm of the cult, and that their purpose was to form the climax of a sacral ceremonial of some kind. Recently it has been shown to be very probable that these apodictic laws (whose style, it may be remarked, is by no means uniform) belonged originally to the tribal ethos of the great clans. In fact, many parallels to our apodictic commandments, as regards both form and subject-matter, can be found in the collections of wisdom sayings.[2] Thus here, too, more precise distinctions must be made. Not every command formulated in the apodictic manner originated in the cult as a sacral law of Yahweh. This is the explanation of the fact, which has hitherto been difficult to understand, that parallels to some apodictic maxims in Deuteronomy actually occur in the early Egyptian *Instruction of Amen-em-Opet*, which certainly knew nothing of the traditions of the Israelite cult of Yahweh (cf. Deut. 25.13–16 with *Amen-em-Opet* 16 [false weights and measures], Deut. 19.14 with *Amen-em-Opet* 6 [removal of landmark] or the formula 'take care' in Deut. 24.8 with *Amen-em-Opet* 2 and 17).[3]

Undoubtedly we can find plenty of examples of the two types of

---

[1] Cf. on this M. Noth, *Exodus* (OTL), ET 1959, pp. 174f.

[2] E. Gerstenberger, *Wesen und Herkunft des "apodiktischen Rechts"* (Wissenschaftliche Monographien zum Alten und Neuen Testament) 20, 1965.

[3] For a partial ET see *ANET*, pp. 421ff.

law, conditional and apodictic, in Deuteronomy. But this distinction does not yet bring us in sight of what is peculiar to Deuteronomy. For while in the Book of the Covenant the examples of both types are usually stylistically unmodified, larger and more complex units predominate in Deuteronomy. Hence their development and individual type must be determined anew. Thus, for example, the section about the firstlings in Deut. 15.19–23 appears at first as a self-contained unit. It begins with a proposition which can without difficulty be recognized as an apodictic command. On the other hand, vv. 20–23 are an interpretation of the preceding regulation, enabling the old legal principle to be expounded in accordance with the demand for centralization. But this interpretation is not couched in objective legal language. It offers a more personal approach, a kind of sermon. In any case it is instruction for the laity. The section about the year of release in Deut. 15.1–11 is similar, only more complicated. For here after the old apodictic maxim there follows, in v. 2, first a 'legal interpretation', expressed completely in judicial terms. Then from here until the end the preacher again holds the floor. In this case, by a further reinterpretation attached subsequently to the sermon (vv. 4–6), a small body of tradition composed of many strata has come into being. Naturally the situation varies in detail from case to case. Thus for example we also find not a few exhortations which are not connected with any law based on an old tradition. Amongst these should be placed in particular the 'law concerning prophets' (Deut. 13.1–5), the 'law of the king' (Deut. 17.14–20) or the prohibition of Canaanite methods of divination and the promise of a prophet (Deut. 18.9–22). In these units the absence of old laws need not surprise us. For in the sacral traditions of the pre-monarchical period no regulations about kings or prophets could occur.

This trend towards exhortation is the real characteristic of the Deuteronomic presentation of the law. Undoubtedly these sermons include factual explanations and directions for concrete action as well; but they are above all concerned with man's basic attitude towards the will of God. They are concerned to stir up the right spirit. They appeal to the intentions and lay the problem of obedience quite directly on the conscience of each individual. For this reason it is quite appropriate here to speak of the laws being made more spiritual, and it would be equally inappropriate to call Deut. 12–26 a legal corpus. In the separate units the speaker is endeavouring to move from specifically legal formulations towards pastoral exhortation and encouragement. It is true that within Deut. 12–26 the homiletic trend is not developed with equal intensity throughout. The chapters from 23 onwards are perceptibly less and less pervaded by exhortation. The subject-matter consists rather of many small individual precepts strung together, which exhibit only a few, if any, traces of homiletic style. Hence we may conjecture that Deuteronomy soon attracted to itself additional legal material which was no longer filled out to the same extent with exhortations.

A whole block of sermons of a very special kind is found in Deut. 6.10–9.6. They are not linked to precise legal maxims which are cited verbatim. It is all the more tempting to examine them in order to find earlier components of the tradition on which each actual sermon is based, and round which it revolves. The language and style of these, as of all the sermons in Deuteronomy, appear at first sight to be framed in a somewhat conventional way, and the continual repetition of phrases seems almost monotonous. But a closer inspection reveals again and again many formulations which are quite peculiar and out of the common. Theologically these sermons are interesting because in them the preacher was obliged repeatedly (and this happened probably for the first time in the history of Israel's religion) to sum up in one pregnant sentence the essential substance, the heart of the faith of Yahweh (cf., e.g., 10.12; 28.47).

This is, of course, already an advanced era. It is a 'modern' spirit which is occupying itself here with the regulations of Israel's life. For these preachers the ancient traditions from Israel's great past had already almost the validity of canonical law. If anything tends to run counter to the idea that Deuteronomy is derived from Israel's early days, or even from Moses himself, then it is the burden of history and the burden of the immense traditions which speak to us out of every verse of Deuteronomy. How enduring and valid the ancient tradition appeared to these preachers is evident from the fact that they like to adduce not indeed 'proof texts' but yet a proof from tradition. Not only the legal traditions but historical events, too, have significance as a standard for the present day of the preacher (Deut. 4.12; 8.3; 17.16; 18.15f.; 23.4; 24.9). They were scarcely conscious of the great distance which separated them from the ancient times to which they appeal. Hence they were hardly aware of the greatness of their task, which was nothing less than to make the will of God, set before them in the traditions of a distant past, become a matter of urgent importance at a time which had experienced deep-seated changes in politics, in social and intellectual and religious matters. To a large extent quite fresh problems had arisen, and these preachers had to seek their solution in the old traditions. We have already described how they impressed Yahweh's will on the inner life of the individual. Another trait, easily explained by their zeal for interpretation, is an unmistakable trend towards the rational and didactic in these sermons. The old traditions have now become clear, they can be understood and by unceasing repetition they should be learned and remembered.

Another type which cannot be called a sermon, although its hortatory quality is obvious, appears in three passages in Deuteronomy. This is historical narrative, put into the mouth of Moses in the first person singular, as in memoirs (Deut. 1–3; 4.9ff.; 9.6ff.). This Moses certainly thinks, speaks and writes like an Israelite of the later period of the monarchy. Since there is no question of the authenticity of these reports, and moreover the three passages are probably not derived from one single source, it is natural to conjecture that there existed at the period of Deuteronomy a fairly extensive Mosaic literature, composed in the style of memoirs, of which only fragments have been preserved here. We should like to know when it appeared, with which prototypes it was connected, who was responsible for it, and what purpose it served.

Finally we must mention one type of composition used in Deuteronomy which scholars have only recently recognized, namely the formulary used for covenants. The discussion of this has only just begun. It has been known for some time that potentates in the ancient Near East, especially the Hittites, used to draw up their treaties with their vassals according to a definite pattern. But it was astonishing to realize that this treaty pattern can be traced in not a few parts of the Old Testament, and amongst others in Deuteronomy.[1] This pattern consists of the following parts: (1) preamble, (2) previous history, (3) declaration of basic principle, (4) regulations in detail, (5) invocation of the gods as witnesses, (6) curse and blessing. There is no cause for surprise that this pattern cannot be identified completely each time in all its parts; from the outset certain modifications were required when it was transferred from the political field to the relationship of Yahweh to Israel (part 5, invocation of the gods, is an obvious instance). At the time of Deuteronomy this pattern had long

[1] K. Baltzer, *Das Bundesformular*, 1960.

been used freely for literary and homiletic purposes. Even individual units, appearing sporadically (thus, for example, the completely stereotyped 'description of the land' in Deut. 6.10f.; 8.7–9), place it beyond all doubt that they are modelled on the full form already mentioned. Longer sequences depending on the regular formulary for covenants occur in Deut. 10.12–11.32 and in 29.1–30.20. However, the question is still quite open how and when Israel came to understand its relationship to God in the form of these early Near Eastern treaties with vassals.

We find admitted into Deuteronomy several other types of composition, or at least reminders of them. (See below for the 'war sermons'.) Yet Deuteronomy is more than a repository of separate traditions. All this material has now been fitted into a definite framework which is itself by no means neutral. Exegesis must therefore go on to understand the book in this, its characteristic final shape. At this point it is advisable (see above) to leave on one side Deut. 1.1–4.40. We should start by noting the striking fact that Deuteronomy is composed in the style of a farewell speech by Moses, whilst elsewhere in the Pentateuch the will of God to be declared to Israel is made known as a speech by Yahweh.[1] But outside the Pentateuch, too, we meet with quite a number of farewell speeches, or speeches made when laying down an office, by men who have undertaken a very definite task of leadership in Israel, especially, for instance, in Josh. 23, I Sam. 12 and I Chron. 22 and 29. Now we are surprised to discover that in the plan of these speeches, too, we can recognize the pattern of the 'regular covenant formulary', of course with differences in each case, as Baltzer explains. This is nothing extraordinary; for just as in the affairs of high politics the existing legal arrangement required a fresh confirmation on the death of a vassal-prince, so Israel, too, held the view that at a change of leadership the particular form of its relation to Yahweh required a special settlement. Thus when an office was laid down, this took place entirely within the range of ideas concerning the covenant ordinances, which were old, yet ever to be understood anew. A testament of this kind is no personal arrangement by a will. The personal aspect recedes completely into the background behind that of the institution.

All this means that the form of Deuteronomy must be regarded as

---

[1] This is hardly affected by the fact that this stylistic form in Deuteronomy is interrupted only very seldom and obviously inadvertently: 7.4a; 11.13–15; 17.3(?); 28.20b; 29.5–6.

that of a farewell speech, but in a wider context, that is, as a variant of the type of such 'testaments' of office-bearers. Much of the detail is not yet elucidated. Is what was formerly described as 'exhortation' (Deut. 4–11) to be understood as a 'declaration of basic principle', elaborated into many sermons?[1] At any rate, Deut. 12–26 would have to be understood as 'regulations in detail', followed by 'blessing and curse'. If we now ask what *Sitz im Leben* is demanded by the pattern in accordance with which Deuteronomy is arranged, it can have been taken only from a cultic celebration, perhaps from a feast of renewal of the covenant. This conjecture is supported by the insertion of a formal covenant-making (Deut. 26.16–19). Thus the classical pattern of the regular covenant formulary appears in Deuteronomy in any case only in a mutilated form. Its setting in the cult, in which the form of Deuteronomy was originally rooted, has, in fact, been already abandoned in the book as we now have it. That is because its contents now appear in the form of a homiletic instruction for the laity.

THE ORIGIN AND PURPOSE OF DEUTERONOMY

All these considerations lead us to the conclusion that the question concerning the authors of Deuteronomy can be asked only in the following terms: On whom devolved this practice of preaching which, from the first sentence to the last, gave to Deuteronomy this distinctive stamp? The task which these preachers set themselves is clear. They are concerned to make the old cultic and legal traditions relevant for their time. The urgent tone of these sermons conveys the feeling that the people to whom they were addressed had almost outgrown those old ordinances of Israel. This is the explanation of the pressing, sometimes even imploring, way of speaking, and the endeavour to grip the hearers personally in order to bind the divine commands on their conscience. In this respect a certain monotony has rightly been noted in Deuteronomy, at least in its phraseology. Yet on the other hand the wide range of its contents, the diversity of the subjects on which sermons are preached, must not be overlooked. Beside the homilies presenting the apodictic laws there stand others which bring to mind the conditional ordinances. These preachers concern themselves with the arrangement of the feasts, with the institution of the monarchy, as well as with the maintenance

[1] N. Lohfink, S.J., *Das Hauptgebot. Eine Untersuchung literarischer Einzelfragen zu Dt. 5–11*, 1963.

of the priests, with the rules about the holy war and with marriage and family law.

Who were those men who had equally at their disposal the whole sacral and the legal traditional material and who could lay claim to the authority to interpret this old material so much in accordance with their own wishes? They could not have been laymen; they must have been holders of a religious office. The ease with which they move amongst material of the most varied origin implies from the start a comparatively advanced period in the history of Israel's traditions. The only passage within the historical tradition of the Old Testament which can give us further help is the description of the reading of the law of the God of heaven which Ezra organized (Neh. 8.1ff.). For the Chronicler reports that on this occasion the Levites instructed the people by giving the sense of what was read aloud. The reference is no doubt to a later historical period than any which can be seriously considered for the first appearance of Deuteronomy. But if such interpretative activity as we are looking for in the case of Deuteronomy is known for the fifth century, the possibility certainly exists that the Levites carried out this work earlier as well.

But there is yet another indication that we must look for the Deuteronomic preachers in priestly and Levitical circles. According to the law of warfare (Deut. 20.1ff.), a priest must make a speech before the battle begins. Now, the outline of the address placed in his mouth (vv. 3–4) corresponds precisely to the war sermons which occur elsewhere in the book (cf. especially 7.16–26; 9.1–6; 31.3–8). But the passages which refer to war are not merely one part of Deuteronomy alongside others. On the contrary the whole of the book is marked by a pronounced warlike spirit which pervades the hortatory part (ch. 6–11) as much as the legal part (ch. 12–26) (cf. 6.18f.; 7.1f.; 11.23ff.; 12.29; 19.1; 20.16, etc). It is just in this respect that Deuteronomy differs so strikingly from the Book of the Covenant, from the Law of Holiness and from the Priestly Document. So to ask about the origin and the authors of Deuteronomy is again equivalent to asking who were the representatives of this militant piety. It is natural at first to think of Deuteronomy as the expression of a mainly intellectual and literary movement; that is to say, as a theoretical, theological scheme by a group with a literary interest. But surely we ought also to raise the question whether it cannot, after all, be explained, just by reason of its characteristically warlike stamp, as arising out of a particular political situation in Israel's history.

Whilst in the pre-monarchical period Israel carried on its wars by means of a general summons to arms, by a levy of the free peasants, the kings turned increasingly to mercenaries, and so to professional soldiers for fighting their wars. Around 701 Judah's political existence was, however, destroyed by Sennacherib. Not only were large areas of the old kingdom of Judah assigned to the Philistines; the Assyrians must also, in accordance with their custom in dealing with subjugated peoples elsewhere, have taken into their own army the mercenaries and specialized fighting charioteers. After this catastrophe, when Josiah wished to regain his political independence, he was obliged to return to the old method of the levy of the free peasants. It was much too expensive for the empty coffers of the State to establish a force of mercenaries ready for action. In fact, it can be proved by a number of statements in the historical work of the Deuteronomists and the Chronicler, that Josiah, in his efforts towards political expansion, returned to this old-fashioned form of military organization.[1] Since it is necessary in any case to connect Deuteronomy with the events under Josiah, it is certainly very natural to connect the warlike spirit of Deuteronomy, which breaks out so spontaneously, with this reorganization.

Until this time politics and the conduct of war had been the business of the king, his officials, his officers and his mercenaries. With the putting into operation of the general levy, forces which had for centuries been excluded from the centre of the stage suddenly take their place there. Old traditions concerning the holy wars, as they had been conducted in the pre-monarchical era came to life and were made to fit, as makeshifts, the needs of the new times. We must assume that the Levites in particular were responsible for this warlike movement of renewal. Perhaps the prophetic circles had a share in it also, for Deuteronomy here and there shows prophetic influence, too. Probably, however, the prophetic element in Deuteronomy is to be ascribed rather to the general ideas and conceptions characteristic of the religious life and thought of this whole period. Those who represented, declared and interpreted the old traditions collected in Deuteronomy were scarcely the prophets; the Levites would be more likely. It was they who set themselves the task, especially in their war speeches, of awakening the spirit of the old religion of Yahweh (e.g. Deut. 7.16–29; 9.1–6). They can hardly have been conscious of the fact that in this enterprise they remained, after all, children of their

[1] E. Jung, *Der Wiederaufbau des Heerwesens des Reiches Juda unter Josia,* 1937.

time and dependent on the problems of their time. The opponent against whom they called up Israel with such great eloquence was in the last resort the Canaanite religion which was irreconcilable with the faith of Yahweh.

Although Deuteronomy in this way really took effect in the Kingdom of Judah under Josiah, yet this does not imply that it must therefore be considered a specifically Judean tradition. On the contrary, we find indications pointing to an origin in the Northern Kingdom, as was rightly emphasized by A. C. Welch some time ago and more recently by A. Alt. The striving for distinctness from the Canaanite cult of Baal and the fight against religious syncretism which pervade Deuteronomy throughout fit much better, according to all that we know, into the circumstances of the Kingdom of Israel than into those of Judah. Moreover, Deuteronomy certainly addresses itself to Israel as a whole, and this tradition concerned with Israel has its home in the Northern Kingdom, while in Jerusalem and Judah, as we can learn, for example, from Isaiah, traditions about Zion and about David were fostered. The Deuteronomic law concerning the king, too, because it speaks of a free choice of the king and even considers the choice of a foreigner to be possible, from the constitutional point of view indicates rather the Kingdom of Israel. The correspondence between Deuteronomy and the prophet Hosea is especially significant. Hosea's attack on the kingship agrees with Deuteronomy's negative attitude (Deut. 17.14ff.; Hos. 3.4; 8.4, 10; 13.11). Then, too, the demand to love Yahweh (Deut. 6.5 etc.) is probably more or less closely connected with Hosea's message, although, of course, we must not think of any direct, possibly literary, derivation. Further, the Shechem chapter (Deut. 27), although its place in Deuteronomy is in any case open to question, would perhaps not appear as an inexplicably alien element in Deuteronomy if the book were thought to be connected with the Northern Israelite tradition. If these considerations are well grounded, then we shall suppose one of the sanctuaries of Northern Israel (Shechem or Bethel?) to be Deuteronomy's place of origin, and the century before 621 must be its date. There are no sufficient reasons for going farther back.

We could make a considerable advance if we knew in what shape and at which stage in the history of its tradition Deuteronomy reached Judah from the Northern Kingdom. Was it actually already in the shape in which we have Deut. 4.44–30.20 before us today? It would certainly be rash to take it for granted that the laws concerning the centralization, for example, which in indeed any case occupy a special position (see the exegesis of Deut. 12.1ff.), could be understood merely by reference to the situation in Jerusalem at the time of King Josiah. The demand for a uniform cult can equally well have been made earlier and elsewhere, too. But what about the war ideology, which is inseparable from the spirit of the present book? In the stratification of the laws concerning war in Deuteronomy there is no doubt that in 20.1–9 the preaching priest does not appear until the last stratum. But this, too, provides us merely with a relative, not an absolute, chronology. Was there ever an earlier Deuteronomy without sermons? If so, we must consider that it was not until a later stage that the material was presented in the sermonlike form so characteristic of Deuteronomy for the first time. Perhaps this took place during the Judean stage of the transmission process. The only conjecture which we may allow ourselves to accept is that the internal growth of the book in essence came to an end when it was incorporated into the great Deuteronomistic historical work, that is to say, at least fifty years after the death of King Josiah.

King Josiah and Deuteronomy

The study of Deuteronomy began with the discovery of its close connexion with the reforms of King Josiah. For a long time II Kings 22–23 was taken to be the point of connexion. But the closeness of the relationship was undoubtedly overestimated, and it would be making a short circuit if Deuteronomy were simply explained by Josiah and Josiah by Deuteronomy. The book is a product of the theology of the time. Accordingly, in spite of all its bias towards the practical, it nevertheless has an unmistakably theoretical character. Hölscher was not entirely wrong to call it plainly utopian. On the other hand, King Josiah was certainly not stimulated to take action by Deuteronomy alone. The rapid decay of the Assyrian world-empire must have encouraged him to throw off his vassalage and in consequence to abandon the cult of the official Assyrian gods. It can hardly be true that all the measures taken for this purpose were provoked by Deuteronomy. If Josiah was thinking of restoring the kingdom of David, then a connexion with Deuteronomy, which is so far removed from Jerusalem's sacral traditions of kingship, is even more remote. On the other hand, the steps taken by Josiah against the Yahweh sanctuaries in the country, and against those of the Canaanite deities, cannot be explained by the political demands of this period (II Kings

23.8, 10, 13f., 15), nor can the special celebration of the passover (II Kings 21–23). It is obvious, however, that a document like Deuteronomy could not be used just as it stood as a programme for the reform of the cult by a king of Judah. It was inevitable that, in the measures he adopted, the king would in some ways go beyond Deuteronomy, in others fall short of it. The actual account of the reform mentions one case in which it was not practicable to carry out the regulation prescribed in Deuteronomy (II Kings 23.9).

The sermons in Deuteronomy are addressed to Israel in the form of words of Moses, now hear to his death, when they arrived in the land of Moab after their wanderings. This fiction is maintained consistently throughout the whole of Deuteronomy. But it really is a fiction. In fact, these sermons are addressed to the Israel of the later period of the monarchy. We need only consider what is said about the possibility of whole towns falling into apostasy (13.13ff.), the appearance of false prophets, the introduction of the money economy, which compelled the old rules concerning the year of release to be reinterpreted (15.1ff.), the sad experiences underlying the law concerning the king and much else. It is surely a very interesting fact that the Israel of the later period of the monarchy saw itself in the guise, which had be-become almost canonical, of the Israel of the Mosaic period. This is far removed from a freely chosen literary artifice. It is the form in which Israel presented itself before God, in which it understood itself as the recipient of his plan of salvation and of his instructions. The great cultic festivals had already taught Israel to realize that they were present at the redemptive events of the past. That is sufficiently remarkable. For the Israel addressed by Moses in Deuteronomy was situated in all respects at a time prior to the fulfilment of the promise, especially that concerning the land, while on the other hand for the Israel of the later period of the monarchy their entry into the land from the desert was an event lying in the remotest past. As an event of political history this no longer had any repercussions on the life of the nation of six centuries later. The conception of the Israel called in the person of their forefathers, addressed solemnly at Sinai, and then led through the desert with fulfilment in view, had already become 'canonical'. Thus every subsequent generation (and the recent generation especially), if it wished itself to be understood as Israel and as the 'people who were Yahweh's possession', entered quite of its own accord into this conception and thought of itself as strictly analogous to the Mosaic Israel. If Moses is envisaged as addressing through the imaginary audience of his contemporaries the actual Israel of the period of the kings, then this signifies that this recent Israel should understand itself as being still between the promise and the fulfilment, but yet already very near to the fulfilment. Although the conquest had taken place long ago, this Israel, too, had not yet seen the complete realization of these promises, as, for example, the promise of rest, which is so definitely Deuteronomic (12.9; 25.19). Just because it is recognized that even immediately before the divine fulfilment a great deal may still occur, including even apostasy, we must appreciate the unprecedented urgency of this appeal. This appeal is indeed made explicitly to the Israel of the period of the monarchy. This becomes evident from the fact that the latest strata of Deuteronomy adapt their instructions even so far as to fit the quite new situation of God's people in exile (e.g. 28.25ff., 47ff.; 30.1ff.). Thus there is certainly no wish for Deuteronomy to be a timeless, unalterable 'law'. On the contrary, it is an appeal to Israel at a quite definite moment in its history, an appeal of such a nature that all the actual happenings, problems and dangers of this one moment are visualized and taken seriously. On the other hand, it cannot be overlooked that, for the times to which it is speaking, Deuteronomy is intended to be at least something in the nature of a 'complete course of instruction', an attempt to embrace the sum total of the revelation of Yahweh's will with all that this involved. It is unnecessary to emphasize that behind this attempt (it was the first in Israel), beside the well-known practical and hortatory concern, there was also at the same time a strong effort toward theoretical and theological comprehension.[1] With this awakened interest in the entirety of Yahweh's revelation, Deuteronomy is unmistakably on the way towards working out a canon, towards delimiting those traditions which possess authoritative significance for Israel. Deuteronomy does indeed still think of itself as a free, a very flexible, and above all an oral interpretation of Israel's early traditions, making them relevant for the present. Thus these ancient traditions, provided for it from the time of the forefathers and of Moses, nevertheless already possess almost canonical validity. Yet it is also very significant that in the latest amplifications of the book it is itself understood as 'Scripture', that is to say, as the will of Yahweh, established in writing (17.18;

[1] The theology of Deuteronomy is discussed in greater detail in G. von Rad, *Old Testament Theology* I, ET 1962, Part Two B, ch. IV, section 5.

28.58, 61; 29.20f.). By this change the characteristic quality of those old traditions, that is, their status as a standard, has been transferred to the book itself, which now begins to become authoritative, if not precisely as a canon, yet as a *regula fidei* laid down in writing.[1]

[1] On the so-called 'canonical' formula ('You shall not add to the word . . . nor take from it'), see below on Deut. 4.2; 12.32.

CHAPTERS 1.1 – 3.29

1 ¹These are the words that Moses spoke to all Israel beyond the Jordan in the wilderness, in the Arabah over against Suph, between Paran and Tophel, Laban, Hazeroth, and Dizahab. ²It is eleven days' journey from Horeb by the way of Mount Seir to Kadesh-barnea. ³And in the fortieth year, on the first day of the eleventh month, Moses spoke to the people of Israel according to all that the LORD had given him in commandment to them, ⁴after he had defeated Sihon the king of the Amorites, who lived in Heshbon, and Og the king of Bashan, who lived in Ashtaroth and in Edrei. ⁵Beyond the Jordan, in the land of Moab, Moses undertook to explain this law, saying, ⁶"The LORD our God said to us in Horeb, "You have stayed long enough at this mountain; ⁷turn and take your journey, and go to the hill country of the Amorites, and to all their neighbours in the Arabah, in the hill country and in the lowland, and in the Negeb, and by the sea-coast, the land of the Canaanites, and Lebanon, as far as the great river, the river Euphrates. ⁸Behold, I have set the land before you; go in and take possession of the land which the LORD swore to your fathers, to Abraham, to Isaac, and to Jacob, to give to them and to their descendants after them."

9 'At that time I said to you, "I am not able alone to bear you; ¹⁰the LORD your God has multiplied you, and behold, you are this day as the stars of heaven for multitude. ¹¹May the LORD, the God of your fathers, make you a thousand times as many as you are, and bless you, as he has promised you! ¹²How can I bear alone the weight and burden of you and your strife? ¹³Choose wise, understanding, and experienced men, according to your tribes, and I will appoint them as your heads." ¹⁴And you answered me, "The thing that you have spoken is good for us to do." ¹⁵So I took the heads of your tribes, wise and experienced men, and set them as heads over you, commanders of thousands, commanders of hundreds, commanders of fifties, commanders of tens, and officers, throughout your tribes. ¹⁶And I charged your judges at that time, "Hear the cases between your brethren, and judge righteously between a man and his brother or the alien that is with him. ¹⁷You shall not be partial in judgment; you shall hear the small and the great alike; you shall not be afraid of the face of man, for the judgment is God's; and the

case that is too hard for you, you shall bring to me, and I will hear it." [18]And I commanded you at that time all the things that you should do.

19 'And we set out from Horeb, and went through all that great and terrible wilderness which you saw, on the way to the hill country of the Amorites, as the LORD our God commanded us; and we came to Kadesh-barnea. [20]And I said to you, "You have come to the hill country of the Amorites, which the LORD our God gives us. [21]Behold, the LORD your God has set the land before you; go up, take possession, as the LORD, the God of your fathers, has told you; do not fear or be dismayed." [22]Then all of you came near me, and said, "Let us send men before us, that they may explore the land for us, and bring us word again of the way by which we must go up and the cities into which we shall come." [23]The thing seemed good to me, and I took twelve men of you, one man for each tribe; [24]and they turned and went up into the hill country, and came to the Valley of Eshcol and spied it out. [25]And they took in their hands some of the fruit of the land and brought it down to us, and brought us word again, and said, "It is a good land which the LORD our God gives us."

26 'Yet you would not go up, but rebelled against the command of the LORD your God; [27]and you murmured in your tents, and said, "Because the LORD hated us he has brought us forth out of the land of Egypt, to give us into the hand of the Amorites, to destroy us. [28]Whither are we going up? Our brethren have made our hearts melt, saying 'The people are greater and taller than we; the cities are great and fortified up to heaven; and moreover we have seen the sons of the Anakim there.' " [29]Then I said to you, "Do not be in dread or afraid of them. [30]The LORD your God who goes before you will himself fight for you, just as he did for you in Egypt before your eyes, [31]and in the wilderness, where you have seen how the LORD your God bore you, as a man bears his son, in all the way that you went until you came to this place." [32]Yet in spite of this work you did not believe the LORD your God, [33]who went before you in the way to seek you out a place to pitch your tents, in fire by night, to show you by what way you should go, and in the cloud by day.

34 'And the LORD heard your words, and was angered, and he swore, [35]"Not one of these men of this evil generation shall see the good land which I swore to give to your fathers, [36]except Caleb the son of Jephunneh; he shall see it, and to him and to his children I will give the land upon which he has trodden, because he has wholly followed the LORD!" [37]The LORD was angry with me also on your account, and said, "You also shall not go in there; [38]Joshua the son of Nun, who stands before you, he shall enter; encourage him, for he shall cause Israel to inherit it. [39]Moreover your little ones, who you said would become a prey, and your children, who this day have no knowledge of good or evil, shall go in there, and to them I will give it, and they shall possess it. [40]But as for you, turn, and journey into the wilderness in the direction of the Red Sea."

41 'Then you answered me, "We have sinned against the LORD; we

will go up and fight, just as the LORD our God commanded us." And every man of you girded on his weapons of war, and thought it easy to go into the hill country. ⁴²And the LORD said to me, "Say to them, Do not go up or fight, for I am not in the midst of you; lest you be defeated before your enemies." ⁴³So I spoke to you, and you would not hearken; but you rebelled against the command of the LORD, and were presumptuous and went up into the hill country. ⁴⁴Then the Amorites who lived in that hill country came out against you and chased you as bees do and beat you down in Seir as far as Hormah. ⁴⁵And you returned and wept before the LORD; but the LORD did not hearken to your voice or give ear to you. ⁴⁶So you remained at Kadesh many days, the days that you remained there.

2 ¹"Then we turned, and journeyed into the wilderness in the direction of the Red Sea, as the LORD told me; and for many days we went about Mount Seir. ²Then the LORD said to me, ³"You have been going about this mountain country long enough; turn northward. ⁴And command the people, You are about to pass through the territory of your brethren the sons of Esau, who live in Seir; and they will be afraid of you. So take good heed; ⁵do not contend with them; for I will not give you any of their land, no, not so much as for the sole of the foot to tread on, because I have given Mount Seir to Esau as a possession. ⁶You shall purchase food from them for money, that you may eat; and you shall also buy water of them for money, that you may drink. ⁷For the LORD your God has blessed you in all the work of your hands; he knows your going through this great wilderness; these forty years the LORD your God has been with you; you have lacked nothing." ⁸So we went on, away from our brethren the sons of Esau who live in Seir, away from the Arabah road from Elath and Ezion-geber.

'And we turned and went in the direction of the wilderness of Moab. ⁹And the LORD said to me, "Do not harass Moab or contend with them in battle, for I will not give you any of their land for a possession, because I have given Ar to the sons of Lot for a possession." ¹⁰(The Emim formerly lived there, a people great and many, and tall as the Anakim; ¹¹like the Anakim they are also known as Rephaim, but the Moabites call them Emim. ¹²The Horites also lived in Seir formerly, but the sons of Esau dispossessed them, and destroyed them from before them, and settled in their stead; as Israel did to the land of their possession, which the LORD gave to them.) ¹³"Now rise up, and go over the brook Zered." So we went over the brook Zered. ¹⁴And the time from our leaving Kadesh-barnea until we crossed the brook Zered was thirty-eight years, until the entire generation, that is, the men of war, had perished from the camp, as the LORD had sworn to them. ¹⁵For indeed the hand of the LORD was against them, to destroy them from the camp, until they had perished.

16 'So when all the men of war had perished and were dead from among the people, ¹⁷the LORD said to me, ¹⁸"This day you are to pass over the boundary of Moab at Ar; ¹⁹and when you approach the frontier of the sons of Ammon, do not harass them or contend with

them, for I will not give you any of the land of the sons of Ammon as a possession, because I have given it to the sons of Lot for a possession." [20](That also is known as a land of Rephaim; Rephaim formerly lived there, but the Ammonites call them Zamzummim, [21]a people great and many, and tall as the Anakim; but the LORD destroyed them before them; and they dispossessed them, and settled in their stead; [22]as he did for the sons of Esau, who live in Seir, when he destroyed the Horites before them, and they dispossessed them, and settled in their stead even to this day. [23]As for the Avvim, who lived in villages as far as Gaza, the Caphtorim, who came from Caphtor, destroyed them and settled in their stead.) [24]"Rise up, take your journey, and go over the valley of the Arnon; behold, I have given into your hand Sihon the Amorite, king of Heshbon, and his land; begin to take possession, and contend with him in battle. [25]This day I will begin to put the dread and fear of you upon the peoples that are under the whole heaven, who shall hear the report of you and shall tremble and be in anguish because of you."

26 'So I sent messengers from the wilderness of Kedemoth to Sihon the king of Heshbon, with words of peace, saying, [27]"Let me pass through your land; I will go only by the road, I will turn aside neither to the right nor to the left. [28]You shall sell me food for money, that I may eat, and give me water for money, that I may drink; only let me pass through on foot, [29]as the sons of Esau who live in Seir and the Moabites who live in Ar did for me, until I go over the Jordan into the land which the LORD our God gives to us." [30]But Sihon the king of Heshbon would not let us pass by him; for the LORD your God hardened his spirit and made his heart obstinate, that he might give him into your hand, as at this day. [31]And the LORD said to me, "Behold, I have begun to give Sihon and his land over to you; begin to take possession, that you may occupy his land." [32]Then Sihon came out against us, he and all his people, to battle at Jahaz. [33]And the LORD our God gave him over to us; and we defeated him and his sons and all his people. [34]And we captured all his cities at that time and utterly destroyed every city, men, women, and children; we left none remaining; [35]only the cattle we took as spoil for ourselves, with the booty of the cities which we captured. [36]From Aroer, which is on the edge of the valley of the Arnon, and from the city that is in the valley, as far as Gilead, there was not a city too high for us; the LORD our God gave all into our hands. [37]Only to the land of the sons of Ammon you did not draw near, that is, to all the banks of the river Jabbok and the cities of the hill country, and wherever the LORD our God forbade us.

3 [1]Then we turned and went up the way to Bashan; and Og the king of Bashan came out against us, he and all his people, to battle at Edrei. [2]But the LORD said to me, "Do not fear him; for I have given him and all his people and his land into your hand; and you shall do to him as you did to Sihon the king of the Amorites, who dwelt at Heshbon." [3]So the LORD our God gave into our hand Og also, the king of Bashan, and all his people; and we smote him until no survivor was left to him. [4]And

we took all his cities at that time—there was not a city which we did not take from them—sixty cities, the whole region of Argob, the kingdom of Og in Bashan. 5All these were cities fortified with high walls, gates, and bars, besides very many unwalled villages. 6And we utterly destroyed them, as we did to Sihon the king of Heshbon, destroying every city, men, women, and children. 7But all the cattle and the spoil of the cities we took as our booty. 8So we took the land at that time out of the hand of the two kings of the Amorites who were beyond the Jordan, from the valley of the Arnon to Mount Hermon 9(the Sidonians call Hermon Sirion, while the Amorites call it Senir), 10all the cities of the table-land and all Gilead and all Bashan, as far as Salecah and Edrei, cities of the kingdom of Og in Bashan. 11(For only Og the king of Bashan was left of the remnant of the Rephaim; behold, his bedstead was a bedstead of iron; is it not in Rabbah of the Ammonites? Nine cubits was its length, and four cubits its breadth, according to the common cubit.)

12 'When we took possession of this land at that time, I gave to the Reubenites and the Gadites the territory beginning at Aroer, which is on the edge of the valley of the Arnon, and half the hill country of Gilead with its cities; 13the rest of Gilead, and all Bashan, the kingdom of Og, that is, all the region of Argob, I gave to the half-tribe of Manasseh. (The whole of that Bashan is called the land of Rephaim. 14Jair the Manassite took all the region of Argob, that is, Bashan, as far as the border of the Geshurites and the Maacathites, and called the villages after his own name, Havvoth-jair, as it is to this day.) 15To Machir I gave Gilead, 16and to the Reubenites and the Gadites I gave the territory from Gilead as far as the valley of the Arnon, with the middle of the valley as a boundary, as far over as the river Jabbok, the boundary of the Ammonites; 17the Arabah also, with the Jordan as the boundary, from Chinnereth as far as the sea of the Arabah, the Salt Sea, under the slopes of Pisgah on the east.

18 'And I commanded you at that time, saying, "The LORD your God has given you this land to possess; all your men of valour shall pass over armed before your brethren the people of Israel. 19But your wives, your little ones, and your cattle (I know that you have many cattle) shall remain in the cities which I have given you, 20until the LORD gives rest to your brethren, as to you, and they also occupy the land which the LORD your God gives them beyond the Jordan; then you shall return every man to his possession which I have given you." 21And I commanded Joshua at that time, "Your eyes have seen all that the LORD your God has done to these two kings; so will the LORD do to all the kingdoms into which you are going over. 22You shall not fear them; for it is the LORD your God who fights for you."

23 'And I besought the LORD at that time, saying, 24"O LORD God, thou hast only begun to show thy servant thy greatness and thy mighty hand; for what god is there in heaven or on earth who can do such works and mighty acts as thine? 25Let me go over, I pray, and see the good land beyond the Jordan, that goodly hill country, and Lebanon."

²⁶But the LORD was angry with me on your account, and would not hearken to me; and the LORD said to me, "Let it suffice you; speak no more to me of this matter. ²⁷Go up to the top of Pisgah, and lift up your eyes westward and northward and southward and eastward, and behold it with your eyes; for you shall not go over this Jordan. ²⁸But charge Joshua, and encourage and strengthen him; for he shall go over at the head of this people, and he shall put them in possession of the land which you shall see." ²⁹So we remained in the valley opposite Beth-peor.'

[1.1–5; 12.1] Both the large number of headings (cf. also 4.44ff.) and also the shapelessness of some of these headings give us an idea of the complicated history through which the book of Deuteronomy passed before it reached the final form in which we have it today. Thus the heading in vv. 1–5 is itself already a small but thoroughly complicated body of traditions similar to that in Deut. 4.44–49. If only we could analyse it unambiguously! To begin with, we can easily distinguish between the heading about the 'words' of Moses (vv. 1–4) and the heading about an explanation of 'this law' (v. 5). But the contents of vv. 1–4 are themselves still far from homogeneous. Thus v. 4 is no doubt an addition which defines more precisely in historical terms the point of time when the speech was delivered; v. 3 describes it only chronologically by the year, the month and the day. But we cannot discover in Deuteronomy as a whole any particular interest in chronology. On the other hand, this method of dating (the numbering of the months according to the spring calendar) represents an important element in the so-called Priestly Document, the fourth of the great sources of the Pentateuch. Hence we must regard v. 3 as an addition out of the Priestly Document from the time when Deuteronomy was already combined in a literary way with the P source.

The remaining heading, vv. 1f., contain a remarkable difficulty, in that it contains statements about places which cannot be reconciled with each other. If the event took place in the Arabah, then only the Jordan valley, or possibly its edges, can be meant, for Arabah is the geographical technical term for the Jordan valley. Or did it happen in the 'wilderness'? In that case we must suppose it to be the high plateau of Moab, and the places named in v. 1b also point in that direction, namely to a district a little east of the Madeba of today.¹ It was here, according to the original heading, that Moses

¹ Further details in M. Noth, *Überlieferungsgeschichtliche Studien*, p. 28 n. 3.

delivered his speech. This indication of the place was supplemented later by the words 'in the Arabah', because it was supposed then that the speech was delivered here, i.e. near Beth-peor, and therefore on the eastern edge of the Jordan valley, opposite Jericho (cf. Deut. 3.29; 34.6). Verse 5 understands the speech which follows as leading up to the announcement of the law: thus it regards all subsequent matter from the standpoint of the 'law'. It is therefore a later addition, for the speech which now begins has nothing whatever to do with the 'law', as will soon appear. The law does not start until Deut. 4.44ff. Hence the essential part of the heading (vv. 1–2) applies only to the speech in 1.6–4.40. But many items, some of them quite alien to the subject-matter, have attached themselves to this speech, too, and to it we shall now turn.

Before we turn to the detailed exposition we must consider the distinctive character of 1.6–3.29. This speech of Moses (ch. 4 will have to be taken by itself) contains an account, a recapitulation, of the historical events which took place between Israel's departure from Horeb and its arrival in the country east of the Jordan. The following incidents are mentioned:

Moses' task is lightened by the appointment of judges, 1.6–18;
the story of the spies, 1.19–46;
the passage through the land of the Edomites, 2.1–8;
the passage through the land of the Moabites, 2.9–25;
the defeat of King Sihon of Heshbon, 2.26–37;
the defeat of King Og of Bashan, and the transfer of both regions
    to the tribes of Reuben, Gad and half of Manasseh, 3.1–22;
Moses' request and its refusal, 3.23–29.

If we compare this description, quite generally in the first instance, with that in the pre-Deuteronomic sources (and we are compelled to do so by the fact that we already find there most of the narrative material of Deut. 1–3), it strikes us at once how much more primitive the material still appears to be in JE. There it is strung together loosely; thus it is easy to perceive that we are dealing with separate, originally independent traditions which were incorporated as well as might be into a great literary composition. In our description, on the contrary, the older material is incorporated much more freely into an uninterrupted narrative. Here, too, the old outlines can indeed still be recognized, but they are now fused more definitely into the whole structure and style of the Deuteronomistic narrative. Thus the picture of the events in Deut. 1–3 produces an effect of much greater homogeneity than the earlier sources of the Pentateuch, and in consequence reads much more easily. Actually the technique used to give a general shape to the whole narrative is, in fact, quite simple in Deut. 1–3 as well; namely, the writer has linked together the stories of the seven separate events by means of connecting passages. It is because of these passages in particular that the reader has an impression much less of a series of separate individual narratives than of a continuous complete story. These (to be recognized by the first person plural, which is hardly used at all elsewhere) are in 1.6–8; 1.19; 2.1, 8, 13b–15; 2.26–3.13abα; 3.29.

All this naturally impels us to ask the further question: from whence could our comparatively late narrator have obtained these separate pieces? Most of this material, as we have said, is also found in JE, the early sources of the Pentateuch. We must therefore first examine the relationship of Deut. 1–3 to this tradition. The passages which approximately correspond are as follows:

Deut. 1.9–18 and the narrative in Num. 11 and Ex. 18.
Deut. 1.20–46 and the narrative in Num. 13–14.
Deut. 2.2–7 and Num. 20.14–21.
Deut. 2.26–33 and Num. 21.21–31.
Deut. 3.18–22 and the narrative in Num. 32.
Deut. 3.23–28 and the note in Num. 20.12; 27.12.

We can understand that in view of so many examples of correspondence the earlier commentators could explain the relationship of Deut. 1–3 to the older traditions only as an indication of literary dependence. Our narrator must have known the earlier sources and elaborated them. Yet there are weighty considerations against this hypothesis even today, though it cannot simply be rejected out of hand. In Deut. 1.9–18 our chronicler has welded together into a fresh whole two stories—or rather one half of one story and the other half of another story. Could he first have cut up the stories, which are far apart from each other in the earlier sources, and then combined them? This hypothesis is not quite impossible, as we have said. Again the account of the passage through Edom in Deut. 2.2–7 corresponds to the older tradition merely the problem it poses; it really differs decisively from it because it is unaware that the passage was refused (see below). Nor is there anything in the earlier tradition to correspond to the passage through Moab in Deut. 2.9ff., nor to the account of the defeat of King Og of Bashan in Deut. 3.1ff. The reason given for Moses' death outside the promised land in Num. 20.12 differs completely from that in Deut. 3.23–28.

Still, all this does not yet provide conclusive evidence that our narrator is altogether independent of JE. He could have revised and supplemented his prototype in each case. Yet in my opinion the more probable conjecture is that he relies on an account not preserved for us, which gave a considerably shorter description of the events between Horeb and the arrival in the country east of Jordan. Is he really likely to have slected only a small part out of the abundance of material offered in JE? However, it is above all the homogeneity of the narrative in Deut. 1.9–18 which supports the hypothesis of an independent prototype and calls in question the hypothesis, which in this case is, in fact, very complicated, of an extract taken from each of two stories which are quite independent of each other. In any case, whoever supports the former of the two hypotheses must explain the striking divergence from the tradition of the Pentateuch; whoever supports the second one, the equally striking correspondence.

[1.6–8] This section is one of the connecting links mentioned on p. 38. It is, in fact, not a narrative, but a presentation of the situation into which the following narrative can be inserted. On the strength of a divine command Israel has departed from Horeb towards the country of the 'Amorites'. The name of Amorite for the inhabitants of Canaan is not rare in the Old Testament. It is an example of a very generalized usage of a word—it means 'west'—used in Assyrian inscriptions to designate Palestine and Syria. The summons in v. 8 sounds like a legal formula of conveyance. The perfect tense 'I have set . . . before you' is the perfect used in contracts.

[1.9–18] The first part of the short narrative telling of Moses' complaint about his excessive burden and how this was lightened by the appointment of military assistants recalls Moses' complaint in Num. 11.14ff.; the second part corresponds to the description in Ex. 18.13ff. If we assume a direct literary dependence on the older sources by our narrator, we are faced by the strange fact that he has omitted in the first case the rest of the story told there (the commissioning of seventy elders), and in the second case its beginning in Ex. 18 (the visit to Moses of his father-in-law Jethro), and that he has made a new story out of the two 'torsos'. If the account which we have here were all that had been handed down to us, who would even have supposed that this narrative, which appears so homogeneous, had been pieced together out of two traditions? In Num. 11 Moses' complaint is directed to Yahweh. It actually borders on blasphemy in its vehemence. But here it is addressed to the people, and by this means it is toned down. Besides, the men in question are selected by the people themselves and not by Yahweh or Moses. In Ex. 18 the military leaders of the thousands and hundreds are at the same time appointed as judges. We are no doubt concerned here with a reform of the legal system in the early period of the monarchy.[1] It is strange that in our account the military and judicial functions are again divided between different persons, for the judges are admonished separately in vv. 16ff. As we meet with the same separation of duties in Deut. 16.18 as well, we must conclude that the old tradition had to be made to fit a new situation (see the commentary on 16.18). On the retention of a central court of justice for the serious cases, see on Deut. 17.8ff.

[1.20–46] Now follows the departure from Horeb (discussed in a link passage) and the account of the story of the spies, told by Moses. In contrast with the preceding narrative this corresponds in all essentials to the description in Num. 13f. Admittedly in our narrative the whole undertaking is initiated by the people and not by Yahweh. Whilst the older narrative in Num. 13f. is clearly still based on an old aetiological tradition (how did the Calebites get to Hebron?), in our account that earlier basis is no longer to be found. The name Hebron no longer occurs at all in our narrative. Probably Caleb was not mentioned in it originally either, for vv. 36–38 are a later addendum from the older account. In our form of it the prerequisites for the note about the preferential treatment of Caleb are lacking. In comparison with the older description the twelve spies, too, recede into the background, apart from the mention of their route and their short report in vv. 24f. What happens is between Moses and the people, and, in fact, it is now transferred more definitely to the speeches of the two parties.

In view of this the actual narrative portion is reduced to a minimum. Note how quickly the despatch of the spies and the reconnaissance of the land is passed over in vv. 23–25. The report of the spies, too, compared with the older account, is much plainer: 'It is a good land.'

[1] R. Knierim, 'Ex. 18 und die Neuordnung der mosaischen Gerechtsbarkeit', *ZAW* 73, 1961, pp. 146ff.

This makes the behaviour of the people appear in a different light. Their protests are bound to be understood by the reader as an incredible reaction of ingratitude. Not until we read the retort of the agitated people in v. 28 can we perceive that the spies did after all say something about the impending dangers as well. The Israelites even allow themselves to be driven to a 'wrongful accusation' against Yahweh, and to declare that he had led Israel into such a precarious situation out of hatred (v. 27). Now, only just before the fulfilment of the ancient promise, is it dawning upon them to what they had committed themselves when they entrusted themselves to this God! It is true that nothing is said here about the demand to return again to Egypt (cf. Num. 14.3f.). It is noteworthy, too, that there is lacking in our account the great intercessory speech of Moses in Num. 14.13–19, which is usually considered to be a later insertion, resembling more closely the spirit of Deuteronomy. Instead, Moses encourages the people in one of his characteristic warlike sermons. The divine reprimand, which orders Israel to turn back again southwards, and prohibits the present generation of adults from entering the promised land, also the change-over from the disobedience of passivity to a disobedience of a self-chosen act—all this corresponds in its essentials to the earlier narrative.

[2.2–7] After 2.1, one of those brief passages which serve to bind two others together, there follows the story of the turn northwards and of the passage through the territory of the Edomites. The older narrative about the meeting of the wandering Israelites with Edom in Num. 20.14–21 is hardly derived from early days either, since it lacks all the peculiarities of an early local tradition. It is on the contrary a touching tale of Israel's humble request, made twice over, to be allowed to cross the foreign land, a request which was hardheartedly rejected. Our account is quite different. It tells nothing of an embassy to the King of Edom. Instead it relates a severe warning by Yahweh to Israel to refrain from interfering in any way with the Edomites and their country and of the ensuing journey across it. But in spite of the differences a relationship implying correspondence as regards the history of the tradition (cf. the themes in both of paying for food and water) undoubtedly exists between our account and the earlier one. It is, of course, less probable that the earlier account was available to our narrator in a literary form. It is also open to question whether the divergence of our narrative from the earlier account should be brought into connexion with certain tendencies in

Deuteronomy which are well disposed to the Edomites (cf. Deut. 23.7). In our version the Edomites themselves do not appear at all: they neither forbid nor consent.

[2.9–24a] The next section, containing Moses' great speech from v. 9 to about v. 25, differs from what precedes it in being strikingly uneven in form and overloaded in content. As a result the reader gains no clear picture of the course of events from the individual historical and geographical statements. We must no doubt assign vv. 13b–15 to the group of those 'we' passages which provide connexions and summaries. Possibly at an earlier stage of the form of the text it followed directly on vv. 8–9a*a*. Probably the warning against touching the territory of the Moabites (v. 9aβ–b), and indeed that of the Ammonites (2.18f., 37), was added only by a later hand. The interpolator could not succeed in producing a real narrative as in 2.2–7; he could only apply to Moab and Ammon in a similar way some of the stock material from 2.2–7. In fact, when Israel had crossed the Zered, an eastern tributary at the southern part of the Dead Sea, and had crossed the Arnon, they had reached the frontier of the area which was to belong to them later. The period of their wanderings was at an end. The conquest was now to begin.

In this context there occurs also the statement about the duration of the whole wandering. This is its rightful place, for the period of the actual wandering is concluded at this point of the narrative's recapitulation. With the conquest of the promised land, which our narrator pictures to himself as a warlike affair, there begins a new stage, the last one, in the history of salvation. Since the exodus from Egypt forty years had elapsed (Deut. 1.3; 2.7; 8.4), since the departure from Kadesh thirty-eight years. How and where Israel had spent this long time our narrator cannot indeed describe clearly to the reader, any more than can his earlier predecessors. This note of time had long since been traditionally connected with Israel's wandering (cf. Amos 2.10; Ps. 95.10 etc.); but the relevant traditional material is completely insufficient to fill up this period adequately.

Apart from the interpolations already mentioned (prohibition to enter the territory of the Moabites and the Ammonites), a still later hand has now amplified this original form of Moses' narrative by means of the insertion of various antiquarian notes about the earliest inhabitants of these regions (Deut. 2.10–12, 20–23). Our only information about the Emim is that in one other passage they are assumed to have lived in about the same area (Gen. 14.5). Possibly they are a people who had entered it from the west.[1] The Rephaim are mentioned more often, as for example in a list of the pre-Israelite inhabitants of Palestine in Gen. 15.20; cf. Josh. 17.15. Our passage seems to understand the word as a somewhat indeterminate collective description comprising several separate nations. The Anakim are named quite frequently as the original inhabitants, but nowhere do we obtain very clear historical conceptions of them. Judges 1.20 assumes them to be in the neighbourhood of Hebron. Remnants of them are said to have maintained themselves for some time longer in the towns of the Philistines (Josh. 11.22). The idea that they were of gigantic stature occurs only in Num. 13.33; Deut. 2.21. The Horites are known to us as the Hurrians, an important people which in the second millennium lived in northern Mesopotamia. If in the Old Testament the name is attached to the original inhabitants of the Edomite area (Gen. 14.6; 36.20ff.), it can only refer to a detached part of the great nation which it had shed it there. The Avvim (v. 23) were a group of the Canaanite population who lived in the south-western coastal plain, but were then destroyed by the Caphtorim, that is, the Philistines. Caphtor, the original home of the Philistines (Amos 9.7), is usually identified with Crete; but Cappadocia has also been suggested. In any case, all these learned notes added at a later date bear witness to Israel's asonishing interest in history and in individual historical movements, even in those which did not in any way touch directly its immediate surroundings.

[2.24b–37] At v. 24b ('behold, I have . . .'), which probably followed directly on vv. 16f., we presumably return to the course of Moses' original speech. Its continuity from now on until 3.29 is not disturbed by any very large literary intrusions. The only point worth noting is that the narrative concerning the meeting with the Kings Sihon and Og (2.26–3.12) is in the first person plural, which so far has been the characteristic mark only of short connecting passages. Verse 24b marks a major break in the speech. The behaviour of Israel towards the other nations changes from now on, because Israel is at this point entering upon the conquest of the promised land. Into this theoretical and theological conception there is fitted what is, in fact, the earlier tradition, taken up again here of the encounter with Sihon, King of Heshbon (Num. 21.21ff.). But the tradition is only partly reproduced, for the existing narrative reports the request to grant a peaceful passage, which is comparable

[1] See von Rad, *Genesis* (OTL), ET 1961, p. 172.

throughout with the account of the crossing through Edom (vv. 2–7). War did not break out until it was caused by Sihon's refusal. (We can avoid this difficulty if we reckon vv. 24b–30 to be still part of the later supplementary interpolations and do not let Moses' original speech start until v. 31, which could be understood—perhaps like v. 2—as the beginning of the whole Sihon pericope.) It can hardly be doubted that this tradition preserves the memory of an actual warlike clash, perhaps of a more or less local dispute between the tribe of Gad and the population which they found in the area. Later bands then fitted it into the large continuous narrative of the entry of all Israel into the promised land. Our description differs from the earlier one in that it states in full with the correct procedure for 'putting the enemy under the ban'. This action was originally a sacrifice, and was equivalent to a formal acceptance of Yahweh and of his guidance (I Sam. 15.10ff.). Since Deuteronomy is concerned to re-create somewhat theoretically the sacral ordering of the hold war, it shows a particular interest in the command to place under the ban, which was taken to be a demand for separation from everything heathen.

[3.1–7] With the victory over Sihon the whole southern part of the land east of the Jordan was conquered. Now, with the clash with Og of Bashan, Israel's sphere of action shifts towards the north. No earlier tradition reports this event, for the mention of it in Num. 21.33 is no doubt itself a later supplementary addition. Our account, too, is very colourless. In addition to the note about the sixty cities in the region of Argob (v. 4), it cannot say anything except what was said before about Sihon as well. Nevertheless, here, too, there has no doubt been preserved a reliable early memory of a comparatively large region ruled by a king named Og.

[3.8–17] The following paragraph sums up in its original form (vv. 8, 10, 12–13abα in the first person plural) the result of what has been achieved so far. With the defeat of both the kings, all the land east of the Jordan had passed into the possession of Israel. This and the fact of the conveyance of this region to the tribes of Reuben, Gad and half of Manasseh is recapitulated here with almost official objectivity. All kinds of separate learned notes have become attracted to this paragraph also; for example, there is one about the name of Hermon (v. 9). Og of Bashan is described here as the last of Rephaim. The object which was shown in Rabbah of the Ammonites as the 'bed', probably the coffin of the king, can hardly have been originally a sarcophagus in view of its length (about fourteen feet), for it is more than double the length of the famous sarcophagus of Ahiram of Byblus. The mention of the tribe of Manasseh provides the occasion to add something about Jair and his 'Havvoth Jair' and about Machir. Jair was a grouping of families within the tribe of Manasseh which had finally settled in the region east of the Jordan (according to Num. 32.30–41 actually in Gilead, not in Bashan). To the north it bordered upon the Geshurites and the Maacathites, who were Aramean tribes (Josh. 13.13; II Sam. 15.8). The tribe of Machir is understood here as that part of Manasseh which had turned aside into the land east of Jordan, i.e. Gilead (Num. 32.39f.).

[3.18–29] After the tribes east of Jordan had had their future homes assigned to them, they were solemnly bound by Moses to take their part in the conquest of the land west of the Jordan as well. Here, too, Moses' speech in Deut. 1–3 has taken up an older piece of the tradition which in the earlier account of Num. 32 occupies considerable space (cf. on this also Josh. 1.12ff.). During the conquest an attack was made by the Transjordanian tribes, i.e. certainly Manasseh, and probably Gad as well, but in fact it was made in the opposite direction, that is, from west to east. Hence the question arises as to what purpose was served by the conception which later became traditional? Was it merely an inference drawn from the dominating idea of Israel's unity?

Finally Moses reports a request addressed to Yahweh on his own behalf that he might enter the promised land. Since in the preceding account the final preparations to conquer the land west of Jordan had been made, this scene, of which the older sources appear to know nothing, follows in logical sequence. The reason given, namely that Moses dies outside the promised land as a substitute for the people (v. 26, 'on your account') is an important characteristic of the conception of Moses in Deuteronomy (cf. on this 1.37; 4.21f.). The Priestly Document treats this incident as the result of a sin on Moses' part (Num. 20.12; Deut. 32.51). It is not clear how Pisgah is related to Nebo. Was it one of the peaks of the Nebo *massif* (Deut. 34.1)? Perhaps the mountain on which Moses died is called in the one tradition Pisgah, in the other Nebo. But is it credible that an account in which Moses is commanded to climb Pisgah, and before doing so to instal Joshua as his successor, could include an extended proclamation of the law as well? Here Moses' great retrospective historical summary breaks off. Hence everything supports the conjecture that at an earlier stage Deut. 31.1ff. followed immediately after this.

CHAPTER 4.1-43

4 ¹'And now, O Israel, give heed to the statutes and the ordinances which I teach you, and do them; that you may live, and go in and take possession of the land which the LORD, the God of your fathers, gives you. ²You shall not add to the word which I command you, nor take from it; that you may keep the commandments of the LORD your God which I command you. ³Your eyes have seen what the LORD did at Baal-peor; for the LORD your God destroyed from among you all the men who followed the Baal of Peor; ⁴but you who held fast to the LORD your God are all alive this day. ⁵Behold, I have taught you statutes and ordinances, as the LORD my God commanded me, that you should do them in the land which you are entering to take possession of it. ⁶Keep them and do them; for that will be your wisdom and your understanding in the sight of the peoples, who, when they hear all these statutes, will say, "Surely this great nation is a wise and understanding people." ⁷For what great nation is there that has a god so near to it as the LORD our God is to us, whenever we call upon him? ⁸And what great nation is there that has statutes and ordinances so righteous as all this law which I set before you this day?

9 'Only take heed, and keep your soul diligently, lest you forget the things which your eyes have seen, and lest they depart from your heart all the days of your life; make them known to your children and your children's children—¹⁰how on the day that you stood before the LORD your God at Horeb, the LORD said to me, "Gather the people to me, that I may let them hear my words, so that they may learn to fear me all the days that they live upon the earth, and that they may teach their children so." ¹¹And you came near and stood at the foot of the mountain, while the mountain burned with fire to the heart of heaven, wrapped in darkness, cloud, and gloom. ¹²Then the LORD spoke to you out of the midst of the fire; you heard the sound of words, but saw no form; there was only a voice. ¹³And he declared to you his covenant, which he commanded you to perform, that is, the ten commandments; and he wrote them upon two tables of stone. ¹⁴And the LORD commanded me at that time to teach you statutes and ordinances, that you might do them in the land which you are going over to possess.

15 'Therefore take good heed to yourselves. Since you saw no form on the day that the LORD spoke to you at Horeb out of the midst of the fire, 16beware lest you act corruptly by making a graven image for yourselves, in the form of any figure, the likeness of male or female, 17the likeness of any beast that is on the earth, the likeness of any winged bird that flies in the air, 18the likeness of anything that creeps on the ground, the likeness of any fish that is in the water under the earth. 19And beware lest you lift up your eyes to heaven, and when you see the sun and the moon and the stars, all the host of heaven, you be drawn away and worship them and serve them, things which the LORD your God has allotted to all the people under the whole heaven. 20But the LORD has taken you, and brought you forth out of the iron furnace, out of Egypt, to be a people of his own possession, as at this day. 21Furthermore the LORD was angry with me on your account, and he swore that I should not cross the Jordan, and that I should not enter the good land which the LORD your God gives you for an inheritance. 22For I must die in this land, I must not go over the Jordan; but you shall go over and take possession of that good land. 23Take heed to yourselves, lest you forget the covenant of the LORD your God, which he made with you, and make a graven image in the form of anything which the LORD your God has forbidden you. 24For the LORD your God is a devouring fire, a jealous God.

25 'When you beget children and children's children, and have grown old in the land, if you act corruptly by making a graven image in the form of anything, and by doing what is evil in the sight of the LORD your God, so as to provoke him to anger, 26I call heaven and earth to witness against you this day, that you will soon utterly perish from the land which you are going over the Jordan to possess; you will not live long upon it, but will be utterly destroyed. 27And the LORD will scatter you among the peoples, and you will be left few in number among the nations where the LORD will drive you. 28And there you will serve gods of wood and stone, the work of men's hands, that neither see, nor hear, nor eat, nor smell. 29But from there you will seek the LORD your God, and you will find him, if you search after him with all your heart and with all your soul. 30When you are in tribulation, and all these things come upon you in the latter days, you will return to the LORD your God and obey his voice, 31for the LORD your God is a merciful God; he will not fail you or destroy you or forget the covenant with your fathers which he swore to them.

32 'For ask now of the days that are past, which were before you, since the day that God created man upon the earth, and ask from one end of heaven to the other, whether such a great thing as this has ever happened or was ever heard of. 33Did any people ever hear the voice of a god speaking out of the midst of the fire as you have heard, and still live? 34Or has any god ever attempted to go and take a nation for himself from the midst of another nation, by trials, by signs, by wonders, and by war, by a mighty hand and an outstretched arm, and by great terrors, according to all that the LORD your God did for you in Egypt

before your eyes? [35]To you it was shown, that you might know that the LORD is God; there is no other besides him. [36]Out of heaven he let you hear his voice, that he might discipline you; and on earth he let you see his great fire, and you heard his words out of the midst of the fire. [37]And because he loved your fathers and chose their descendants after them, and brought you out of Egypt with his own presence, by his great power, [38]driving out before you nations greater and mightier than yourselves, to bring you in to give you their land for an inheritance, as at this day; [39]know therefore this day, and lay it to your heart, that the LORD is God in heaven above and on the earth beneath; there is no other. [40]Therefore you shall keep his statutes and his commandments, which I command you this day, that it may go well with you, and with your children after you, and that you may prolong your days in the land which the LORD your God gives you for ever.'

41 Then Moses set apart three cities in the east beyond the Jordan, [42]that the manslayer might flee there, who kills his neighbour unintentionally, without being at enmity with him in time past, and that by fleeing to one of these cities he might save his life: [43]Bezer in the wilderness on the tableland for the Reubenites, and Ramoth in Gilead for the Gadites, and Golan in Bashan for the Manassites.

The break between what has gone before and the beginning of this chapter is very complete. Who would expect Moses, after he had just reported the command to go up to Pisgah in order to die there, now to launch out into a detailed introduction to his recital of the law? If the speech in ch. 4 is really intended to be a direct continuation of the preceding one, ought not the transition to this completely new subject of his speech be more clearly marked? But in other respects also the analysis of this chapter presents a number of difficulties.

[1–8] Verses 1–4 can be described as an exhortation introducing a recital of the law. In it the preacher underlines the seriousness of the situation by giving a terrifying example from 'salvation history' as a warning; the disobedient who deserted Yahweh at Baal-peor received their punishment. The so-called canonical formula (v. 2, 'you shall not add to the word . . . nor take from it') has a long history. It appears as an injunction for scribes as early as in ancient Egypt (Ptah-hotep, *c.* 2450 BC),[1] and later in fuller and shorter forms in Deut.

---

[1] The question has recently been raised whether the phrase in Ptah-hotep has this meaning. See S. Morenz, *Ägyptische Religion* (Die Religionen der Menschheit 8), 1960, pp. 235f.

12.32; Jer. 26.2; Prov. 30.6; Eccles. 3.14. But it did not come to have its full meaning until it occurred in sub-apostolic writings and in the Church Fathers.[1] Deuteronomy is not in fact very far from the idea of a complete course of doctrine with binding force.

There are some difficulties in the section vv. 5–8. For the verb in v. 5 can surely be rendered only in the past tense, and this indicates that our passage looks back to a recital of the law which has already taken place. This is supported, too, by the praise of 'all this law' in v. 8, which makes sense only if the people can themselves confirm this verdict and are not merely looking forward to the announcement of the law. The eloquent words which place the revelation at Sinai as the embodiment of all wisdom above the truths possessed by all other nations (vv. 6–8) can surely be understood only as an exhortation to reinforce a recital of the law which has already been made. Hence the sections vv. 1–4 and 5–8 are hortatory formulae such as are collected in large numbers in Deut. 6–11.

[9–24] This section is also hortatory. But the alternation between the use of the second person singular and the second person plural immediately indicates certain breaks in homogeneity. In fact, the contents do not make a perfect whole, for the admonitions proceed oddly along a double track. On the one hand the law revealed by Yahweh at Horeb is mentioned in comprehensive and general terms (vv. 9–14); but beside it there runs an exhortation which revolves round a single concern, namely that of making the prohibition of images compulsory (vv. 15–20, 23–24). This cannot be the original form (cf. the clear break between vv. 14 and 15). The explanation of the text must be that it dealt originally with the revelation at Horeb as a whole; then secondarily the warning against the worship of God in an image was attached to v. 12, which says that at Horeb Israel only heard Yahweh's voice, but saw no form with their eyes.[2] From the standpoint of theology it is just this later stratum that is interesting, because here 'evidence from tradition' is adduced. The preacher takes up the statement contained in the tradition that at Horeb Israel merely heard Yahweh, but did not see him, in order to press its meaning theologically. For he has made the comparatively insignificant passage in the tradition the basis for a comprehensive attack on the worship of Yahweh in images (for the evidence from

---

[1] J. Leipoldt and S. Morenz, *Heilige Schriften*, 1953, pp. 56ff.
[2] A detailed analysis in M. Noth, *Überlieferungsgeschichtliche Studien*, pp. 38f.

tradition see the Introduction, pp. 20f.). There is a remarkable contrast between the uncompromising enforcement of the prohibition of idols for Israel and the tolerance towards the worship of idols by the other nations. Nowhere else in the Old Testament is the idea that Yahweh himself allotted the stars to the nations for their worship (v. 19) expressed with such broadmindedness. We might ask whether the prophetic passage in vv. 25–28 is not a continuation of the sermon against the worship of idols. The explanation that Israel was condemned to be scattered because of its worship of idols occurs also in the Deuteronomistic historical writings, as well as in later strata of Deuteronomy (31.16). Hence this section could belong also to the general admonition to obey the laws. It gives a clue for dating the whole, since this preacher knows already of the exile of 587.

[25–40] If we allowed ourselves to be guided by the internal evidence alone, it would be natural to follow earlier commentators in taking by itself the section in vv. 25–31 about the future rejection and reacceptance of Israel, and then to turn back and connect the section vv. 32–40 with v. 24. However, the section vv. 29–40, apart from a few interruptions, appears to be a continuous passage employing the second person singular and is complete in itself. This fact carries so much weight that in spite of all that precedes it vv. 29–40 ought to be taken separately. The preceding 'prophecy' had ended with the gloomy picture of an Israel rejected and sunk in the heathen worship of idols. Nevertheless the last section of this shapeless accumulation of discourses begins with the prophecy of a quite fresh initiative on the part of Israel to 'return' (v. 30) to Yahweh. The saying that at every time of judgment the way stands open for Israel to return to Yahweh appears like the theme of a fugue in each climax of the Deuteronomistic history. This work is concerned to introduce variations on this theme with such great urgency because just at this time, i.e. in the situation after God's judgment in 587, it is endeavouring to show to its contemporaries this one and only way to salvation.[1] The preacher in ch. 4 is stirred by the same motive. What is understood by this return, by this seeking of Yahweh, is not explained more precisely in either passage. Evidently it is a matter of a very spiritual process, and not of a return to correct cultic forms. Moreover, the wording of the saying about seeking and finding Yahweh (v. 29) resembles that in Jer. 29.13 so closely that a con-

[1] H. W. Wolff, 'Das Kerygma des deuteronomistischen Geschichtswerk', *ZAW* 73, 1961, pp. 171ff.

nexion must exist. But is it so certain that the well-known letter of Jeremiah is quoted here? Is not the hypothesis just as likely that Jeremiah adopted a contemporary phrase used in sermons? The saying too in Jer. 29.13, 'with all your heart', also sounds very Deuteronomic. A quite similar admonition (Isa. 55.6) occurs also in the preaching of Deutero-Isaiah. They all speak out of the same situation and try to make the people understand that the door through which they may return to Yahweh is still standing open.

This basic idea also enables us to understand the section vv. 32–40: Yahweh's relationship to Israel, which he created by such great deeds and maintained for so long, cannot have been in vain! The speaker with his summons to search into earlier times is clearly standing at the end of a long stretch of history. It is possible to look back on a period filled with acts of God, and during the long interval since the events the aura of the miraculous has grown even brighter. Indeed, Israel as the actual object of such great happenings has in the process become miraculous to itself. Meanwhile the intellectual horizon has become so much wider that what befell Israel can be compared quite rationally with what other nations experienced in their relationship with their gods. Nothing even remotely analogous occurs elsewhere. (The same passion for comparing Yahweh and the gods is found with the same negative result in Deutero-Isaiah in Isa. 41.1ff., 25ff.; 43.8ff.; 44.6ff.). To make this comparison Israel has at its disposal the longest possible span of history (from the creation of man) and the widest possibly area (from one end of heaven to the other). The view of history offered here for acceptance shows an element of crudity. Reference is made only to the miraculous, indeed specially to the spectacular nature of the individual events (God's voice was heard out of the fire; God has come to choose a nation for himself). This and much else has brought Israel to know Yahweh as the true God (v. 35). In v. 38 the preacher has forgotten the fiction of Moses' speech before the conquest.

[41–43] The note about the cities of refuge set apart by Moses for unintentional manslayers differs in style from the speech. Since Deut. 1.5 there has been no further mention of Moses in the third person. This section is certainly an addition. It is due to an interpolator who knew both Num. 35.9–15 and Josh. 20, and who was puzzled that Moses was not said to have appointed at least the cities east of Jordan before he died. He took the names from Josh. 20.8. The establishment of cities of refuge is usually considered to have resulted from the centralization of the cult and the secularization of the arrangements for the system of asylum connected with it. However, this is not quite certain. It is possible that there were already cities of refuge in Israel earlier as well. (On the right of asylum itself see Deut. 19.1ff.)

CHAPTERS 4.44 – 6.3

4 ⁴⁴This is the law which Moses set before the children of Israel; ⁴⁵these are the testimonies, the statutes, and the ordinances, which Moses spoke to the children of Israel when they came out of Egypt, ⁴⁶beyond the Jordan in the valley opposite Beth-peor, in the land of Sihon the king of the Amorites, who lived at Heshbon, whom Moses and the children of Israel defeated when they came out of Egypt. ⁴⁷And they took possession of his land and the land of Og the king of Bashan, the two kings of the Amorites, who lived to the east beyond the Jordan; ⁴⁸from Aroer, which is on the edge of the valley of the Arnon, as far as Mount Sirion (that is, Hermon), ⁴⁹together with all the Arabah on the east side of the Jordan as far as the Sea of the Arabah, under the slopes of Pisgah.

5 ¹And Moses summoned all Israel, and said to them, 'Hear, O Israel, the statutes and the ordinances which I speak in your hearing this day, and you shall learn them and be careful to do them. ²The LORD our God made a covenant with us in Horeb. ³Not with our fathers did the LORD make this covenant, but with us, who are all of us here alive this day. ⁴The LORD spoke with you face to face at the mountain, out of the midst of the fire, ⁵while I stood between the LORD and you at that time, to declare to you the word of the LORD; for you were afraid because of the fire, and you did not go up into the mountain. He said:

6 ' "I am the LORD your God, who brought you out of the land of Egypt, out of the house of bondage.

7 ' "You shall have no other gods before me.

8 ' "You shall not make for yourself a graven image, or any likeness of anything that is in heaven above, or that is on the earth beneath, or that is in the water under the earth; ⁹you shall not bow down to them or serve them; for I the LORD your God am a jealous God, visiting the iniquity of the fathers upon the children to the third and fourth generation of those who hate me, ¹⁰but showing steadfast love to thousands of those who love me and keep my commandments.

11 ' "You shall not take the name of the LORD your God in vain: for the LORD will not hold him guiltless who takes his name in vain.

12 ' "Observe the sabbath day, to keep it holy, as the LORD your

53

God commanded you. ¹³Six days you shall labour, and do all your work; ¹⁴but the seventh day is a sabbath to the LORD your God; in it you shall not do any work, you, or your son, or your daughter, or your manservant, or your maidservant, or your ox, or your ass, or any of your cattle, or the sojourner who is within your gates, that your manservant and your maidservant may rest as well as you. ¹⁵You shall remember that you were a servant in the land of Eygpt, and the LORD your God brought you out thence with a mighty hand and an outstretched arm; therefore the LORD your God commanded you to keep the sabbath day.

16 ' "Honour your father and your mother, as the LORD your God commanded you; that your days may be prolonged, and that it may go well with you, in the land which the LORD your God gives you.

17 ' "You shall not kill.

18 ' "Neither shall you commit adultery.

19 ' "Neither shall you steal.

20 ' "Neither shall you bear false witness against your neighbour.

21 ' "Neither shall you covet your neighbour's wife; and you shall not desire your neighbour's house, his field, or his manservant, or his maidservant, his ox, or his ass, or anything that is your neighbour's.' "

22 'These words the LORD spoke to all your assembly at the mountain out of the midst of the fire, the cloud, and the deep gloom, with a loud voice; and he added no more. And he wrote them upon two tables of stone, and gave them to me. ²³And when you heard the voice out of the midst of the darkness, while the mountain was burning with fire, you came near to me, all the heads of your tribes, and your elders; ²⁴and you said, "Behold, the LORD our God has shown us his glory and greatness, and we have heard his voice out of the midst of the fire; we have this day seen God speak with man and man still live. ²⁵Now therefore why should we die? For this great fire will consume us; if we hear the voice of the LORD our God any more, we shall die. ²⁶For who is there of all flesh, that has heard the voice of the living God speaking out of the midst of fire, as we have, and has still lived? ²⁷Go near, and hear all that the LORD our God will say; and speak to us all that the LORD our God will speak to you; and we will hear and do it."

28 'And the LORD heard your words, when you spoke to me; and the LORD said to me, "I have heard the words of this people, which they have spoken to you; they have rightly said all that they have spoken. ²⁹Oh that they had such a mind as this always, to fear me and to keep all my commandments, that it might go well with them and with their children for ever! ³⁰Go and say to them, 'Return to your tents.' ³¹But you, stand here by me, and I will tell you all the commandment and the statutes and the ordinances which you shall teach them, that they may do them in the land which I give them to possess." ³²You shall be careful to do therefore as the LORD your God has commanded you; you shall not turn aside to the right hand or to the left. ³³You shall walk in all the way which the LORD your God has commanded you, that you

may live, and that it may go well with you, and that you may live long in the land which you shall possess.

6 ¹'Now this is the commandment, the statutes and the ordinances which the LORD your God commanded me to teach you, that you may do them in the land to which you are going over, to possess it; ²that you may fear the LORD your God, you and your son and your son's son, by keeping all his statutes and his commandments, which I command you, all the days of your life; and that your days may be prolonged. ³Hear therefore, O Israel, and be careful to do them; that it may go well with you, and that you may multiply greatly, as the LORD, the God of your fathers, has promised you, in a land flowing with milk and honey.'

[4.44–49] This section consists of two headings (v. 44 and vv. 45–49) both of which introduce the Torah announced by Moses to the Israelites. From the standpoint of its syntax it is something of a monstrosity. The place of the recital of the law which now follows is fixed with precision: it is beyond Jordan (that is, the standpoint of the writer is again in the land west of Jordan!) in the valley opposite Beth-Peor. The range of a work with so elaborate a title cannot be determined by the wording of the headings alone. Yet there is some support for the hypothesis that this is the heading of Deuteronomy proper, which starts here and ends at ch. 30.20.

[5.1–5] Moses' speech, which begins in Deut. 5.1, and after this has no further interruptions, directs our attention at once to God's revelation at Sinai. In view of Deut. 2.14ff. we are surprised by the remark that this covenant was made not with an earlier generation but with those who are now alive. Even though the death of the Sinai generation had occurred meanwhile and lay outside the speaker's view, his intention is clear enough. He wants to bring the event of the covenant-making which already belongs to the past vividly before the eyes of his contemporaries (cf. a similar procedure in Deut. 29.13f.). These are the words of a generation which must begin by providing itself with an explanation of its relation to the 'saving event' (*Heilsereignis*). The following description of the events at Sinai emphasizes from the start Moses' function as a mediator ('I stood between the Lord and you', v. 5). Verse 5 seems to assume that Moses first received the revelation of the decalogue alone and that he then handed it on to Israel. According to vv. 22f. Yahweh addressed the whole of Israel (cf. 4.12f., 15; 9.10). On the abrupt transition in the style of God's speech in v. 6, see below on v. 22.

[5.6–21] The decalogue is the best known of those series of commandments whose form must be explained by the custom of solemnly reciting the law within the framework of the cult (see the Introduction, p. 18). In the case of the individual items in these series, a careful distinction must be made between the separate prohibitions on the one hand and on the other the very varied explanatory additions, which became necessary in course of time if they were to be understood correctly. In the first half these amplifications exercise a very strong influence on the presentation of the decalogue, whilst in the second half of it, from v. 17 on, the original extremely concise form of the commandments has been preserved.[1] Since these amplifications, except for the reason given for the commandment about the sabbath, occur in the same form in the other setting of the decalogue (Ex. 20.2–17), they must be derived from a considerably earlier time in the history of the tradition than that of Deuteronomy.

The decalogue begins with the formula of self-introduction, which demonstrates at the outset its origin in the cult.[2] In this form, which is widespread throughout the Old Testament, the divine 'I' enters into the presence of the cultic community and addresses it as his own possession. It is of great importance for the correct understanding of the decalogue that it begins with an appeal to the intimate relationship between Yahweh and Israel which existed since the deliverance from Egypt. The God who is speaking now had long ago manifested his will to save in a 'saving event' acknowledged by the whole community. It may be asked whether this opening precept, including the first commandment, ought not to be understood as the 'declaration of basic principle', followed by the 'regulations in detail'. This hypothesis would be supported by the fact that the dodecalogue of Shechem begins with the second commandment (Deut. 27.15; on the covenant formulary see the Introduction).

[5.7–10] The prohibition on serving any other divine powers is in any case the commandment par excellence for Israel, and its stringency —there is nothing else like it in the whole history of religion—influenced to a greater or lesser degree all vital utterances on the faith of Yahweh. It is chiefly concerned not with the general idea that there is only one god (monotheism) but rather with the fact that Yahweh

---

[1] J. J. Stamm, *Der Dekalog im Lichte der neueren Forschung*, Bern, 1958 (ET in preparation); H. Graf Reventlow, *Gebot und Predigt im Dekalog*, 1962.

[2] More details about this formula of self-introduction in W. Zimmerli, in 'Gottes Offenbarung', *Gesammelte Aufsätze*, 1963, pp. 11ff.

is to be the only God for Israel. Strictly speaking, the commandment even takes for granted a polytheistic situation amongst those who are addressed. But it is Yahweh's zeal which insists on his being the only one for those who belong to him. The prohibition of idols must be understood with the purpose of the idols in mind, namely to manifest the deity. This prohibition, rejecting the idea that Yahweh can be portrayed in any kind of shape (animals, stars, human form, etc.), expresses an understanding of the world different from that of the religions of the ancient Near East. It was impossible for Israel to identify God with one of the mythical world powers or world orders. It could not understand the world more or less as a form in which the deity itself became apparent, as an 'emanation'. God could not become present for Israel in the cult by means of an earthly image. The world was a created thing, and as such had its own glory; but a created thing could not represent Yahweh himself. The prohibition in v. 8 has already been altered from its original form, and to it has been added in v. 9 a further amplifying sentence which applies the prohibition particularly to the worship of Yahweh in the likenesses of strange gods. (There might also, of course, be the possibility of dedicating to Yahweh images of himself.) In this way the addition refers back to the first commandment and understands the portrayal of Yahweh in the likeness of strange gods as a sin against that commandment.[1] Israel is fond of speaking in connexion with the first commandment about Yahweh's zeal, that is, about God's holiness which forces itself upon man (cf. 6.14f.; Ex. 34.14; Josh 24.19). But Yahweh's will to punish is far outweighed by his will to save.[2]

[5.11] The third commandment protects from every kind of harm the name of Yahweh, the knowledge of which Yahweh has entrusted to his people (Ex. 3.13ff.; 6.3). It is probable that the word which we translate as 'in vain' might at a very early period have meant 'magic', as Mowinckel suggests. Israel has been assailed at all periods by the temptation to use the divine power with the help of the divine name in an anti-social manner and to place it at the service of private and even sinister interests.

[5.12-15] The Old Testament nowhere gives an explanation of the real significance of celebrating the sabbath. If the sabbatical year was kept as a sacral fallow period in order to demonstrate Yahweh's

---

[1] W. Zimmerli, op. cit., pp. 234ff.
[2] For fuller treatment of the first and second commandments see G. v. Rad, *Old Testament Theology* I, Part Two B, ch. IV, sections 3-4.

right of ownership over the cultivated land (see on Deut. 15.1ff.), the same principle would require the day to be kept undisturbed by any use for the benefit of man; it is the day which really belongs to God and sets a standard undefiled by any kind of human business. No mention is made of a cultic celebration of any sort on this day. Hence it must be assumed that the celebration of the sabbath, at least in Israel's earlier period, was discharged by abstaining demonstratively from productive labour, and symbolically handing the day back to God. When giving the reason for the commandment concerning the sabbath, our decalogue follows quite a different line from that in Ex. 20.11, where the custom is explained by the creation, by God's rest on the seventh day. Our decalogue bases this commandment on Israel's bondage in Egypt, which it ought to remember, and on the need of toiling man and beast for rest. These various reasons are intended to make the commandment intelligible without claiming to be an exhaustive explanation. Thus it is not surprising to see the argument ranging freely. The reason given in Ex. 20 is thoroughly theological; our decalogue argues more psychologically and sees particularly the beneficial aspect of the sabbath. The fact that it is a 'sabbath to Yahweh' (v. 14a) is no longer fully brought out.

[5.16] When considering the commandment concerning parents, we must not think of the modern family, but of the society of antiquity organized in extended families, of the 'fathers' houses', that is to say, the group of grown-up sons subordinated to the father and living in a settled community with their wives and children. Here there were enough possibilities of slighting the authority of parents, especially of the aged ones. The negative wording of the commandment concerning parents in Ex. 21.17; Lev. 20.9 (prohibition of cursing) is much more primitive. By the change into a positive commandment its meaning has been drastically enlarged. It differs from the commandment about the sabbath by having no explanation attached to it, but a promise instead. According to Old Testament ideas, the promise of life is attached not only to this commandment but to all of them (Deut. 4.1; 8.1; 16.20; 30.15ff.). Hence the later interpreters took a liberty when they emphasized this promise here particularly, perhaps with the family's own smallholding in mind.

[5.17] The verb in the sixth commandment (*rāṣaḥ*) cannot be translated strictly as 'kill'; it does not denote just any killing, for example in war or in the administration of justice. In these cases more usual words are available. On the other hand, it conveys something different from our 'murder', because it is, of course, used also for accidental homicide. Hence it means anti-social killing.[1]

[5.18] The prohibition of adultery was based originally on a conception of marriage which cannot indeed be described as monogamous in the modern sense, but even less as simply polygamous. It is true that a man was free to have sexual intercourse with the female slaves of his household as well, but this type of marriage, too, was protected by strict legal concepts, the disregard of which was considered to be adultery.

[5.19] It is today regarded as certain that the prohibition of stealing referred originally to the kidnapping of a free person (Ex. 21.16; Deut. 24.7).[2] Thus the prohibition of theft, like that of adultery, has experienced changes of meaning with the passage of time.

[5.20] The prohibition of false witness was so important because according to the early Israelite legal usage a very great significance was attached to the testimony of the witness. The burden of proof in legal proceedings was placed to a large extent on the accused. He was obliged to prove his innocence in face of the accusation.

[5.21] If in the last commandment the translation of the verb as 'covet' were correct, it would be the only case in which the decalogue deals not with an action, but with an inner impulse, hence with a sin of intention. But the corresponding Hebrew word (ḥāmad) has two meanings, both to covet and to take. It includes outward malpractices, meaning seizing for oneself (Josh. 7.21; Micah 2.2 etc.). To sum up, the decalogue displays a distinct arrangement; it speaks of duties towards God and towards man. In the second part the commandment to honour parents comes first, then follow the commandments which protect the life, the marriage, the freedom, the reputation and the possessions of fellow men.

[5.22–6.3] If we compare the course of events at the revelation on Sinai in Ex. 19f. with that given here, we see at once that Deuteronomy had a different understanding of an important aspect of it. While the account in Ex. 19f. contains a circumstantial preparation for Yahweh's coming and speaking, which is then described in detail with all the accompanying phenomena, the report here begins with a summons to hear statutes which Moses is about to impart to the

---

[1] J. J. Stamm, 'Sprachliche Erwägungen zum Gebot "Du sollst nicht töten" ', *TZ* 1, 1945, pp. 81ff.

[2] A. Alt, 'Das Verbot des Diebstahls im Dekalog', *Kleine Schriften* I[2], 1959, pp. 333ff.

people. During the great revelation of God, Moses occupied a position between Yahweh and Israel in order to hand on Yahweh's words to Israel. But this has very little connexion with the announcement in vv. 6ff. of ten commandments to all Israel (v. 22), which follows immediately. As we have said, a speech by God is not expected at this point, and the transition to it with its terse 'He said' in v. 5b is unusually abrupt. It may therefore be asked whether the whole passage, vv. 6–22, must not be considered as a later interpolation. In any case, in our account in Deuteronomy the earlier tradition has been superseded by a concept in which the appeal to the senses and above all the directness of Yahweh's manifestation of himself was modified in favour of a message transmitted through Moses. This is shown especially clearly by the narrative which now follows concerning Israel's request to Moses to remove from them the risk of direct speech with God. This passage occurs also in the older account in Ex. 20.18–21, but it has now grown to twice the length. With a wealth of detail and of words the people adduce reasons for their refusal to listen any more to Yahweh (for the almost proverbial statement that he who has seen God face to face must die, cf. Ex. 33.20; Judg. 6.22f.; Isa. 6.5 etc.). In contrast with the account in Ex. 20.18ff., Yahweh himself replies to this desire. The solemn manner in which Yahweh expresses his approval of this cry for a mediator, and praises Israel's attitude as a proof of the true fear of God, leads us to conjecture that all this is told for a special purpose. Here Yahweh himself is shown to be giving authority for the transmission of his will to be mediated through Moses, that is, through a man. The authority for this mediatorial proclamation then passed from Moses to others and was finally claimed by the Deuteronomic preachers (cf. also the commentary on Deut. 18.15ff.). Thus the report of these events is far from being an historical report in our sense; instead it is a complete theological statement. This applies in a certain sense to the earlier account also. For if God's descent on Sinai could be understood as an act to test Israel and their fear of God (Ex. 20.20), this indicates that the traditional material had already been permeated to a large extent by interpretation.

Verse 31 brings Moses' narrative of what happened at Sinai to an end. Verses 32f. refer back to the exhortation in vv. 1–5, that is, they lead the hearers back from contemplating the past to the present time, i.e. to the situation in the land of Moab, which is, of course, the place where Moses' whole speech in Deuteronomy is delivered. Here at last we discover the meaning of this very discursive retrospect on the events at Sinai. What Moses is now about to announce to his people is no other than what he had already learnt at Sinai from Yahweh when he had presented himself on the mountain to speak with Yahweh apart from the people (v. 28). Thus the purpose of the entire section, 4.45–5.30 (6.3) is to represent Moses' whole speech in Deuteronomy as a communication to Israel, not really of the Decalogue, but of that conversation on the mountain with Yahweh. Owing to the 'and',[1] Deut. 6.1a is probably not to be regarded as a fresh title, and therefore vv. 6.1–3 had best be understood simply as a continuation of 5.33.

[1] Chapter 6 begins with 'and' in the German text, and not with 'now', as in the RSV. Translator.

CHAPTER 6.4–25

6 ⁴ 'Hear, O Israel: The LORD our God is one LORD; ⁵and you shall love the LORD your God with all your heart, and with all your soul, and with all your might. ⁶And these words which I command you this day shall be upon your heart; ⁷and you shall teach them diligently to your children, and shall talk of them when you sit in your house, and when you walk by the way, and when you lie down, and when you rise. ⁸And you shall bind them as a sign upon your hand, and they shall be as frontlets between your eyes. ⁹And you shall write them on the doorposts of your house and on your gates.

10 'And when the LORD your God brings you into the land which he swore to your fathers, to Abraham, to Isaac, and to Jacob, to give you, with great and goodly cities, which you did not build, ¹¹and houses full of all good things, which you did not fill, and cisterns hewn out, which you did not hew, and vineyards and olive trees, which you did not plant, and when you eat and are full, ¹²then take heed lest you forget the LORD, who brought you out of the land of Egypt, out of the house of bondage. ¹³You shall fear the LORD your God; you shall serve him, and swear by his name. ¹⁴You shall not go after other gods, of the gods of the peoples who are round about you; ¹⁵for the LORD your God in the midst of you is a jealous God; lest the anger of the LORD your God be kindled against you, and he destroy you from off the face of the earth.

16 'You shall not put the LORD your God to the test, as you tested him at Massah. ¹⁷You shall diligently keep the commandments of the LORD your God, and his testimonies, and his statutes, which he has commanded you. ¹⁸And you shall do what is right and good in the sight of the LORD, that it may go well with you, and that you may go in and take possession of the good land which the LORD swore to give to your fathers ¹⁹by thrusting out all your enemies from before you, as the LORD has promised.

20 'When your son asks you in time to come, "What is the meaning of the testimonies and the statutes and the ordinances which the LORD our God has commanded you?" ²¹then you shall say to your son, "We were Pharaoh's slaves in Egypt; and the LORD brought us out of Egypt with a mighty hand; ²²and the LORD showed signs and wonders, great

and grievous, against Egypt and against Pharaoh and all his household, before our eyes; [23]and he brought us out from there, that he might bring us in and give us the land which he swore to give to our fathers. [24]And the LORD commanded us to do all these statutes, to fear the LORD our God, for our good always, that he might preserve us alive, as at this day. [25]And it will be righteousness for us, if we are careful to do all this commandment before the LORD our God, as he has commanded us." '

[4-9] The exhortation which starts in Deut. 6.4 with such solemnity, or at least those parts of it which employ the second person singular in Hebrew, belongs to the original stratum of Deuteronomy which later had such varied accretions woven into it or appended to it. This speech, as the commentary will demonstrate, is composed largely of several separate sermons strung together without artificial links. The first of these begins at Deut. 6.10. Verses 4-9 are not themselves a sermon but one single appeal, although expressed in a great variety of ways, a chain of very forceful imperatives, prefacing the subsequent sermons in order to draw attention to their unique importance. The words 'Hear, O Israel' are evidently a stereotyped formula in Deuteronomy (5.1; 9.1; 20.3; 27.9). Since this is so, the hypothesis that this summons is merely a literary coinage can hardly be accepted and we must therefore enquire into the setting in which it originated. Probably it was the traditional summons with which in the old days the assembly for worship of the tribes, the qāhāl, was opened (cf. especially 20.3). From the point of view of its syntax the meaning of v. 4 is debatable. For instance, it might be translated: 'Yahweh is our God, Yahweh alone!' But it might also be translated: 'Yahweh, our God, is one Yahweh' (and there are still other possibilities). In the first case the passage is a confession set in opposition to the temptations of the Canaanite cult of Baal; in the other case it is a confession of the oneness of Yahweh in face of the multiplicity of divergent traditions and sanctuaries of Yahweh. Both interpretations can claim support from Deuteronomy.

So far as the demand to love God is concerned, we must bear in mind that the covenant-relationship established by Yahweh had always allowed for a variety of feelings, and not for one alone (certainly not only that of fear!). In spite of this there seems to be something new in the unequivocal manner based on fundamental principle in which stress is laid on love for God as the only feeling worthy of God. It can hardly be doubted that the realization of this is due in part to the prophecy of Hosea. But it is important that the experience of Yahweh's love for Israel had already preceded this demand. Although for Hosea the idea of love was determined by the concept of conjugal love, no trace of this background can any longer be perceived in Deuteronomy. It understands Israel's relationship to Yahweh rather as that of a son (Deut. 8.5; 14.1). The statement in vv. 4–5, with its programmatic emphasis, stands somewhat by itself at the head of the section. It does not become quite clear whether 'these words' in v. 6a refer merely to the basic confession in vv. 4f. or to the whole subsequent sermon. The demands made in vv. 6–9 attract attention by the intensity of their spirituality, and also by a certain intellectualization. For here the concern with Moses' words appears already almost as an end in itself, as something which ought to claim the whole of a man's mental and spiritual powers and to occupy him completely. It is not clear what significance is attached to the tokens which were to serve as reminders and so forth. Probably we still have to do here with a figurative mode of expression, which was then later understood literally and led to the use of the so-called phylacteries.

[10–15] The sermon in vv. 10–15 starts from the now imminent situation when the divine promises will be fulfilled. Anxiety is expressed lest the great and sudden change to affluence might entice Israel into forgetting God. A warning is given to adhere to the worship of Yahweh (v. 14 is an expansion in the plural) and is followed by a threat of God's zeal which will not let disobedience remain unpunished. An interesting detail is the stereotyped list of 'real estate' in vv. 10f. (cf. Josh. 24.13; Neh. 9.24f.). Its form is derived historically from the legally binding list, like a land-register, contained in the section 'previous history' in ancient Near Eastern treaties. (Introduction, pp. 21f.)

[16–19] This sermon begins by addressing the people in the plural, but then passes into the singular. From this we might suppose that a very general and undifferentiated exhortation to behave well towards Yahweh was subsequently particularized and deepened by the exhortation not 'to put God to the test'. Putting God to the test means letting his worship depend on a test, and this would be equivalent to a complete failure to appreciate God's claim, and hence a defiance of God. Evidently the sermon assumes that the hearers already possess a good knowledge of biblical history. Exodus 17.1–7 mentions the place Massah (amongst the oases of Kadesh?) and tells what happened there.

[20–25] This sermon begins with the question to be expected later, that is, from the succeeding generation, about the significance of the divine statutes. It assumes therefore that a certain break between the generations has taken place (cf. Judg. 2.6f., 10). The question which is asked gives the father an opportunity to recite the chief items of the credal salvation-history (cf. on 26.5ff.). It is a remarkable fact that this text, which is based upon tradition, contains actually no reference at all to the revelation of the commandments. Of course, at such an advanced period mention of the departure from Egypt and of the history until the entry into Canaan could also obviously be interpreted as having a bearing on the Sinai event, which was originally rooted in another tradition. With these ordinances Yahweh had offered his people life (on the theologically important co-ordination of commandments and life, cf. Deut. 5.16). The acceptance and observance of the commandments is reckoned as righteousness (similarly Deut. 24.13). It is characteristic, too, that this concept appears in connexion with the divine commandments (cf. Ezek. 18.5–9). The Hebrew word, for which the translation 'righteousness' can only be an approximation, denotes a man's correct attitude towards claims which others or another—in this case God—have upon him. He who accepts the commandments or who 'believes' (cf. Gen. 15.6) is regarded by God as 'righteous', that is to say, his relationship with God is in order; of course, this does not mean that he is sinless; but, on the ground of his intention to be associated with God, God is willing to recognize him.

CHAPTER 7.1–26

7 ¹'When the LORD your God brings you into the land which you are entering to take possession of it, and clears away many nations before you, the Hittites, the Girgashites, the Amorites, the Canaanites, the Perizzites, the Hivites, and the Jebusites, seven nations greater and mightier than yourselves, ²and when the LORD your God gives them over to you, and you defeat them; then you must utterly destroy them; you shall make no covenant with them, and show no mercy to them. ³You shall not make marriages with them, giving your daughters to their sons or taking their daughters for your sons. ⁴For they would turn away your sons from following me, to serve other gods; then the anger of the LORD would be kindled against you, and he would destroy you quickly. ⁵But thus shall you deal with them: you shall break down their altars, and dash in pieces their pillars, and hew down their Asherim, and burn their graven images with fire.

6 'For you are a people holy to the LORD your God; the LORD your God has chosen you to be a people for his own possession, out of all the peoples that are on the face of the earth. ⁷It was not because you were more in number than any other people that the LORD set his love upon you and chose you, for you were the fewest of all peoples; ⁸but it is because the LORD loves you, and is keeping the oath which he swore to your fathers, that the LORD has brought you out with a mighty hand, and redeemed you from the house of bondage, from the hand of Pharaoh king of Egypt. ⁹Know therefore that the LORD your God is God, the faithful God who keeps covenant and steadfast love with those who love him and keep his commandments, to a thousand generations, ¹⁰and requites to their face those who hate him, by destroying them; he will not be slack with him who hates him, he will requite him to his face. ¹¹You shall therefore be careful to do the commandment, and the statutes, and the ordinances, which I command you this day.

12 'And because you hearken to these ordinances, and keep and do them, the LORD your God will keep with you the covenant and the steadfast love which he swore to your fathers to keep; ¹³he will love you, bless you, and multiply you; he will also bless the fruit of your body and the fruit of your ground, your grain and your wine and your oil, the

increase of your cattle and the young of your flock, in the land which he swore to your fathers to give you. [14]You shall be blessed above all peoples; there shall not be male or female barren among you, or among your cattle. [15]And the LORD will take away from you all sickness; and none of the evil diseases of Egypt, which you knew, will he inflict upon you, but he will lay them upon all who hate you. [16]And you shall destroy all the peoples that the LORD your God will give over to you, your eye shall not pity them; neither shall you serve their gods, for that would be a snare to you.

17 'If you say in your heart, "These nations are greater than I; how can I dispossess them?" [18]you shall not be afraid of them, but you shall remember what the LORD your God did to Pharaoh and to all Egypt, [19]the great trials which your eyes saw, the signs, the wonders, the mighty hand, and the outstretched arm, by which the LORD your God brought you out; so will the LORD your God do to all the peoples of whom you are afraid. [20]Moreover the LORD your God will send hornets among them, until those who are left and hide themselves from you are destroyed. [21]You shall not be in dread of them; for the LORD your God is in the midst of you, a great and terrible God. [22]The LORD your God will clear away these nations before you little by little; you may not make an end of them at once, lest the wild beasts grow too numerous for you. [23]But the LORD your God will give them over to you, and throw them into great confusion, until they are destroyed. [24]And he will give their kings into your hand, and you shall make their name perish from under heaven; not a man shall be able to stand against you, until you have destroyed them. [25]The graven images of their gods you shall burn with fire; you shall not covet the silver or the gold that is on them, or take it for yourselves, lest you be ensnared by it; for it is an abomination to the LORD your God. [26]And you shall not bring an abominable thing into your house, and become accursed like it; you shall utterly detest and abhor it; for it is an accursed thing.'

[1–11] This sermon deals with the future relationship of Israel to the Canaanite population of the country. The list of the seven nations is traditional and with certain changes appears frequently in the Old Testament (Gen. 15.20f.; Ex. 3.8, 17; 13.5). With these nations Israel may not enter into any kind of association; on the contrary they are to be utterly 'banned'. The banning (*ḥerem*) is a kind of sacrifice of dedication, at any rate a sacral proceeding. It is the final act in the ritual conduct of the Holy War, the handing over of the captive enemies and the booty to Yahweh. Deuteronomy, being late, has, as a result of its theological viewpoint, a much more radical attitude on this matter than Israel had in the early days. Thus there may be no intermarriage, no *connubium* between Israel and the native population. This rule is derived from the sacral right of God and hence would need no reasoned explanation. Nevertheless, a clear reason is supplied: the Israelite spouse concerned might be tempted to forsake Yahweh (on the rule in Deut. 21.10ff., which evidently did not yet worry about this, see below). The other reason, which now follows in v. 6 after an intensifying interpolation in the plural, sounds much more primitive: Israel is a holy nation, that is, a nation set apart for Yahweh, and must abstain from everything which might prejudice its subordination to Yahweh's sole authority. This statement about Israel as the holy people and a people for Yahweh's own possession is now followed by a particularly forceful comment in the plural (vv. 7–8a), which at the same time guards against an obvious misunderstanding: this choice was not made because Yahweh might have allowed himself to be impressed by Israel in any respect, but simply from an impulse of love. With this explanation of the choice of Israel as an act of paradoxical divine love Deuteronomy arrived at a perception of a truth which had not been seen so clearly in the earlier days. The use, too, of the quite secular verb *ḥāšaq*, 'to hang on someone', in v. 7 for this basic theological fact about Israel is characteristic of the linguistic versatility of the Deuteronomic sermon. In v. 9 the preacher passes over into the diction of hymns (the Hebrew participial style): Yahweh is faithful and watches over the covenant relationship, but he allows the evil set in motion against him to 'fulfil' itself.[1]

[12–16] The opening words, in which the almost stereotyped 'if' is lacking, already make it doubtful whether this section can be considered a self-contained sermon. Even more significant is the fact that it is not constructed in the usual way with a central admonition. The section is one single promise of blessing, the wording of which is clearly seen to be modelled on cultic formulae (cf. on this Deut. 28.1ff.). Thus it is better to consider it as the ending of the great sermon which begins at 7.1.

[17–26] This sermon on the contrary shows all the characteristics of the series. It begins with an outline of the psychological condition of those who are addressed, namely the access of despondency in face of the superior strength of their enemies. In opposition to this the preacher recalls Yahweh's earlier demonstrations of power against the Egyptians; Yahweh will give the same proof of his help

---

[1] On this remarkable conception see von Rad, *Old Testament Theology* I, pp. 262ff., 383ff.

once again. At v. 21 the sermon (it is again a war sermon) reaches the main exhortation. Israel must not be afraid, for Yahweh is waging war with the help of miraculous phenomena: a mysterious discouragement, a divine terror, a kind of paralysing confusion, will descend upon the foe. Among these revived ideas of the holy war, an all too modern impression is given by the direction that this expulsion had better take place only by stages, since otherwise dangerous animals would increase too much. But it shows that these preachers were already obliged to reckon with a very enlightened way of thinking (similar rationalizing considerations appear in Judg. 2.21f.; 3.1f.). The sermon ends with a warning on no account to appropriate what has been banned (cf. Josh. 7). In v. 25a, which is in the plural, we meet again the interpolator of v. 5.

CHAPTERS 8.1–9.6

8 [1]'All the commandment which I command you this day you shall be careful to do, that you may live and multiply, and go in and possess the land which the LORD swore to give to your fathers. [2]And you shall remember all the way which the LORD your God has led you these forty years in the wilderness, that he might humble you, testing you to know what was in your heart, whether you would keep his commandments, or not. [3]And he humbled you and let you hunger, and fed you with manna, which you did not know, nor did your fathers know; that he might make you know that man does not live by bread alone, but that man lives by everything that proceeds out of the mouth of the LORD. [4]Your clothing did not wear out upon you, and your foot did not swell, these forty years. [5]Know then in your heart that, as a man disciplines his son, the LORD your God disciplines you. [6]So you shall keep the commandments of the LORD your God, by walking in his ways and by fearing him. [7]For the LORD your God is bringing you into a good land, a land of brooks of water, of fountains and springs, flowing forth in valleys and hills, [8]a land of wheat and barley, of vines and fig trees and pomegranates, a land of olive trees and honey, [9]a land in which you will eat bread without scarcity, in which you will lack nothing, a land whose stones are iron, and out of whose hills you can dig copper. [10]And you shall eat and be full, and you shall bless the LORD your God for the good land he has given you.

[11] 'Take heed lest you forget the LORD your God, by not keeping his commandments and his ordinances and his statutes, which I command you this day: [12]lest, when you have eaten and are full, and have built goodly houses and live in them, [13]and when your herds and flocks multiply, and your silver and gold is multiplied, and all that you have is multiplied, [14]then your heart be lifted up, and you forget the LORD your God, who brought you out of the land of Egypt, out of the house of bondage, [15]who led you through the great and terrible wilderness, with its fiery serpents and scorpions and thirsty ground where there was no water, who brought you water out of the flinty rock, [16]who fed you in the wilderness with manna which your fathers did not know, that he might humble you and test you, to do you good in the end. [17]Beware

lest you say in your heart, "My power and the might of my hand have gotten me this wealth." ¹⁸You shall remember the LORD your God, for it is he who gives you power to get wealth; that he may confirm his covenant which he swore to your fathers, as at this day. ¹⁹And if you forget the LORD your God and go after other gods and serve them and worship them, I solemnly warn you this day that you shall surely perish. ²⁰Like the nations that the LORD makes to perish before you, so shall you perish, because you would not obey the voice of the LORD your God.

9 ¹'Hear, O Israel; you are to pass over the Jordan this day, to go in to dispossess nations greater and mightier than yourselves, cities great and fortified up to heaven, ²a people great and tall, the sons of the Anakim, whom you know, and of whom you have heard it said, "Who can stand before the sons of Anak?" ³Know therefore this day that he who goes over before you as a devouring fire is the LORD your God; he will destroy them and subdue them before you; so you shall drive them out, and make them perish quickly, as the LORD has promised you.

4 'Do not say in your heart, after the LORD your God has thrust them out before you, "It is because of my righteousness that the LORD has brought me into possess this land"; whereas it is because of the wickedness of these nations that the LORD is driving them out before you. ⁵Not because of your righteousness or the uprightness of your heart are you going in to possess their land; but because of the wickedness of these nations the LORD your God is driving them out from before you, and that he may confirm the word which the LORD swore to your fathers, to Abraham, to Isaac, and to Jacob.

6 'Know therefore, that the LORD your God is not giving you this good land to possess because of your righteousness; for you are a stubborn people.'

[8.1–6] This sermon begins with a revision in the plural (by the same hand as in 7.7f.?). This opening, and especially the ending in v. 6, show clearly that it is an admonition to obey the commandments. But the way in which it argues is all its own. For it urges the listeners to consider the hardships of the wanderings in the wilderness which lie behind them. In itself this period of history could be regarded, especially at such an advanced period, from very different points of view. This preacher saw in it, above all, the fatherly guidance of God, the working out of a wise divine discipline which trained the people sometimes through scarcity, sometimes through blessings, to reach a mature understanding. According to v. 16 this was not only a question of humbling Israel, but of a divine process of testing.

In this context the giving of the manna receives an interpretation which distinguishes it from the older conception in Ex. 16. There the occurrence was understood on the one hand as a simple feeding miracle (JE). On the other hand it was represented in a mysterious concatenation of events in such a manner that the thoughtful reader might have an inkling of deeper truths behind what actually happened (P). Here, however, it is bluntly stated that the direct purpose of the feeding was to teach Israel that man does not just live on earthly bread alone, but that he also depends on the word addressed to him by God. The statement that man lives 'on all that is created by God's command' or 'what proceeds out of the mouth of God' is reminiscent of an early Egyptian formulation and (perhaps for that very reason) is not completely unambiguous. Should it be understood to mean that Yahweh has many possibilities of keeping men alive, and in this case the means is manna?[1] But within the range of Deuteronomic theology it seems after all more natural to think of it as Yahweh's word, which means life to Israel (Deut. 30.15; 32.47). If so, the passage would therefore have to be understood as an interesting example of an intentional fresh interpretation of the early tradition concerning manna. (In Ps. 78.24f. manna is understood to be 'the bread of angels' and 'the grain of heaven'. This is probably yet another interpretation of the old tradition. Cf. with this also I Cor. 10.3.) The other miracle, the preservation of their clothing and shoes, is never mentioned anywhere else in the Old Testament.[2] We see once again that these preachers had at their service many other traditions in addition to those which we still possess. This fatherly guidance of which Israel had such a long experience should now induce Israel for its part also to remain obedient to its divine Instructor. This is a particularly fine example of this style of preaching.

[8.7–20] This sermon looks forward to the future, to the situation when Israel is settled in the promised land. It begins by praising the wealth of this land in unmistakable imitation of the style of a hymn (cf. the fivefold 'a land' followed each time by a statement arranged in parallel phrases). Everything is described here by asserting sheer perfection, almost as though it were describing a paradise (see also Deut. 11.10–12). If we do not want to suppose that the Deuteronomic preacher has passed of his own accord into the style of a hymn, we may conjecture that there really were such hymn-like poems about the land which the preacher took as his model, or even quoted. A

---

[1] H. Brunner, ' "Was aus dem Munde Gottes geht" ', *VT* 8, 1958, pp. 428f.
[2] Cf. the Gilgamesh epic XI, 244ff., *ANET*, p. 96.

difficulty is presented by the reference to the wealth of iron and copper. In Palestine, at any rate west of Jordan, no such things are to be found (cf. Deut. 33.25).

Because this very superabundance might become a danger to Israel, the preacher hastens on to his main admonition not to forget Yahweh in this profusion of blessings and in a possible satiety (v. 11) or even to become self-confident and arrogant (v. 17). No sooner has the preacher mentioned Yahweh than his pen runs away with him and he adopts the hymn-like style ('who brought you out', v. 14; 'who led you', v. 15; 'who fed you', v. 16). It is evident that he had at his disposal in the tradition plenty of material for him to exploit. To this generation, already grown somewhat soft in the cultivable country, the great wilderness appeared to be a terrible region, waterless and full of serpents and scorpions. The situation would be even worse if afterwards Israel wanted to attribute its wanderings and its endurance to its own strength. For the strength to wander came from Yahweh, who in this way demonstrated his faithfulness to his covenant. Verse 17 seems to recall the type of arrogant soliloquy probably created by the prophets (cf. Isa. 10.8ff.; 14.13f.; Ezek. 28.2 etc.). It is open to question whether vv. 19f. were originally part of the sermon, because the warning against serving strange gods does not really fit in with its theme. In v. 20 there are traces of a revision using the plural.

[9.1–6] This sermon likewise looks forward to the occupation of the promised land which is now immediately ahead or, to be more precise, to the psychological situation after the conquest. This situation is marked by the fact that Israel with the help of its God will have overcome nations much more powerful than itself (the Anakim are looked upon here as a generally well-known and much-feared nation, see on Deut. 2.11). But this event might suggest to Israel a misunderstanding with serious consequences: it might conclude that the intervention of Yahweh was due to its own good behaviour. This interpretation of what had happened would be wrong. For Yahweh had been moved to act by quite different motives, namely, the depravity of the indigenous population and his own faithfulness to the covenant which he had made. The idea that the Canaanites driven out by Israel must blame themselves for their defeat because of their wickedness was expressed comparatively early by Israel (Gen. 15.16). Like the sermon in 6.10–15 or 8.7–20, this sermon, too, places itself in the situation immediately after the victorious conquest. But here the psychological effect which the preacher fears is a different one. It is not the danger that Israel in its satiety will forget Yahweh, nor the danger that in its boastfulness it will attribute what has happened to itself and to the vigorous onslaught of its fighting men, but it is the danger of pious self-deception. What Yahweh had done for Israel might lead Israel to have a false idea of the true divine motive. In any case, Israel's good behaviour had no influence in this matter, for Israel was and is a stubborn people.

CHAPTERS 9.7-10.11

9 [7]'Remember and do not forget how you provoked the LORD your God to wrath in the wilderness; from the day you came out of the land of Egypt, until you came to this place, you have been rebellious against the LORD. [8]Even at Horeb you provoked the LORD to wrath, and the LORD was so angry with you that he was ready to destroy you. [9]When I went up the mountain to receive the tables of stone, the tables of the covenant which the LORD made with you, I remained on the mountain forty days and forty nights; I neither ate bread nor drank water. [10]And the LORD gave me the two tables of stone written with the finger of God; and on them were all the words which the LORD had spoken with you on the mountain out of the midst of the fire on the day of the assembly. [11]And at the end of forty days and forty nights the LORD gave me the two tables of stone, the tables of the covenant. [12]Then the LORD said to me, "Arise, go down quickly from here; for your people whom you have brought from Egypt have acted corruptly; they have turned aside quickly out of the way which I commanded them; they have made themselves a molten image."

13 'Furthermore the LORD said to me, "I have seen this people, and behold, it is a stubborn people; [14]let me alone, that I may destroy them and blot out their name from under heaven; and I will make of you a nation mightier and greater than they." [15]So I turned and came down from the mountain, and the mountain was burning with fire; and the two tables of the covenant were in my two hands. [16]And I looked, and behold, you had sinned against the LORD your God; you had made yourselves a molten calf; you had turned aside quickly from the way which the LORD had commanded you. [17]So I took hold of the two tables, and cast them out of my two hands, and broke them before your eyes. [18]Then I lay prostrate before the LORD as before, forty days and forty nights; I neither ate bread nor drank water, because of all the sin which you had committed, in doing what was evil in the sight of the LORD, to provoke him to anger. [19]For I was afraid of the anger and hot displeasure which the LORD bore against you, so that he was ready to destroy you. But the LORD hearkened to me that time also. [20]And the LORD was so angry with Aaron that he was ready to destroy him; and

75

I prayed for Aaron also at the same time. 21Then I took the sinful thing, the calf which you had made, and burned it with fire and crushed it, grinding it very small, until it was as fine as dust; and I threw the dust of it into the brook that descended out of the mountain.

22 'At Taberah also, and at Massah, and at Kibroth-hattaavah, you provoked the LORD to wrath. 23And when the LORD sent you from Kadesh-barnea, saying, "Go up and take possession of the land which I have given you", then you rebelled against the commandment of the LORD your God, and did not believe him or obey his voice. 24You have been rebellious against the LORD from the day that I knew you.

25 'So I lay prostrate before the LORD for these forty days and forty nights, because the LORD had said he would destroy you. 26And I prayed to the LORD, "O LORD God, destroy not thy people and thy heritage, whom thou has redeemed through thy greatness, whom thou hast brought out of Egypt with a mighty hand. 27Remember thy servants, Abraham, Isaac, and Jacob; do not regard the stubbornness of this people, or their wickedness, or their sin, 28lest the land from which thou didst bring us say, 'Because the LORD was not able to bring them into the land which he promised them, and because he hated them, he has brought them out to slay them in the wilderness.' 29For they are thy people and thy heritage, whom thou didst bring out by thy great power and by thy outstretched arm."

10 1'At that time the LORD said to me, "Hew two tables of stone like the first, and come up to me on the mountain, and make an ark of wood. 2And I will write on the tables the words that were on the first tables which you broke, and you shall put them in the ark." 3So I made an ark of acacia wood, and hewed two tables of stone like the first, and went up the mountain with the two tables in my hand. 4And he wrote on the tables, as at the first writing, the ten commandments which the LORD had spoken to you on the mountain out of the midst of the fire on the day of the assembly; and the LORD gave them to me. 5Then I turned and came down from the mountain, and put the tables in the ark which I had made; and there they are, as the LORD commanded me.'

6 (The people of Israel journeyed from Beeroth Bene-jaakan to Moserah. There Aaron died, and there he was buried; and his son Eleazar ministered as priest in his stead. 7From there they journeyed to Gudgodah, and from Gudgodah to Jotbathah, a land with brooks of water. 8At that time the LORD set apart the tribe of Levi to carry the ark of the covenant of the LORD, to stand before the LORD to minister to him and to bless in his name, to this day. 9Therefore Levi has no portion or inheritance with his brothers; the LORD is his inheritance, as the LORD your God said to him.)

10 'I stayed on the mountain, as at the first time, forty days and forty nights, and the LORD hearkened to me that time also; the LORD was unwilling to destroy you. 11And the LORD said to me, "Arise, go on your journey at the head of the people, that they may go in and possess the land, which I swore to their fathers to give them." '

The series of sermons which we have followed from Deut. 6.10 onwards breaks off in a remarkable way at Deut. 9.7. We reach a separate unit of the text which must be defined quite differently from the form-critical point of view. Moses narrates in the first person an event in history, namely the episode of 'the golden calf'. The reader of Deuteronomy will remember that in another place, in Deut. 1–3, a much longer unit of text occurs, which (apart from short connecting passages in the first person plural), shows exactly the same form-critical characteristics. It is also an historical narrative by Moses in the first person. On the other hand, we cannot succeed in bringing the passage here into an organic connexion with the other one, for our historical account goes back in time beyond the preceding one, which has, in fact, already told of the settling of the two and a half Transjordanian tribes into their territories. Correctly speaking, this historical account ought to be placed before Deut. 1–3, because the narrative there does not actually begin until after Israel's departure from the mount of God. So unless we suppose that both passages really belonged at an earlier stage to a large unit, which appears here merely in fragments, we must be satisfied with the statement that we possess several historical narratives taken from the method of preaching in later Israel, which have been composed with the same literary characteristics. For the exhortation in 4.9ff. should also still be included in this class. Towards the end our account is distorted by some more extensive interpolations. The announcement that the request has been granted, which concludes the whole section, and finally relieves the great tension (10.10f.), stood originally directly after the great intercessory prayer in 9.26–29. In other respects, too, the narrative is also probably not all of a piece. The account of the intercession and its resulting fulfilment in 9.18f. runs parallel to the one in 9.25–10.10f. The second account gives us the wording of the prayer. The alternation between the singular and the plural in the mode of address also points possibly to a rather complicated origin and development of the present text.

[9.7–20] The comprehensive narrative of the events connected with setting up the golden calf is intended to serve a quite definite purpose. Unlike the account given in Ex. 32, the instructive and didactic trend of the description, with its 'Remember and do not forget', is evident from the start. The Israel which faces its God today with the same rebelliousness as it did then must learn from past events and become conscious of its own threatening situation. Without such a powerful intercessor Israel would have been lost even then. So our description differs considerably from the older one in Ex. 32. Certainly with regard to the external sequence of events both accounts are almost in agreement. Only in a few points concerning the incidents themselves does our report go its own way. But now Moses himself is speaking, that is to say, everything is presented from his point of view, and his experiences in all that has happened are placed in the foreground. In consequence the episode is now seen from a completely fresh standpoint. In the earlier account Moses' struggle with God (if we neglect the long interpolation in Ex. 32.9–14 because it is primarily Deuteronomistic), was only one incident among many. Here on the contrary the struggle is at the centre of events. Thus our account does not relate what happened in chronological order, but it begins at the point when Moses is on the mountain without an inkling of what is going on down below amongst the people. He received the first indications that something serious was afoot from the lips of God when he was handed the two tables on which Yahweh had written with his own finger. The expression 'Tables of the covenant', vv. 9, 11, 15, used in Deuteronomy in this context alone, has no doubt a long previous history. For it assumes that the word 'covenant' could be used for 'decalogue' (on this cf. the expression in Deut. 4.13). The breaking of the tables was, of course, more than an act of emotional disturbance. Moses (in his office as mediator of the covenant?) regards as broken the covenant which has only just been made, so that the tables handed to him have become meaningless. Here, just between the breaking of the tables and the destruction of the cultic image, our account makes Moses offer his first intercessory prayer. This is not very skilful, for the result is that the destruction of the golden calf is delayed for forty days. We would like to know something more precise about the mental images formed by our narrator of the idol itself which Moses first burned and then crushed into dust.[1] Verses 22–24, which interrupt the narrative, have long been considered as a later insertion enumerating other additional cases of such rebellions on the part of Israel.

The intercession in 9.26–29 differs from that in the earlier account chiefly by the absence of the main idea of the earlier form of the prayer, namely that if God refuses to forgive his people then he ought also to blot his, Moses', name out of his book (Ex. 32.32). In other re-

---

[1] On the 'calf', which was originally understood merely as the pedestal for an invisible deity standing upon it, see M. Noth, *Exodus*, pp. 247ff.

spects it corresponds more or less precisely to the prayer given there, which however was probably first taken from our text and written into the earlier account. Moses appeals to the act of deliverance in leading the people out of Egypt, and then quite generally to the patriarchs, and finally even to Yahweh's honour. This, too, is, of course, endangered, since the other nations would explain Yahweh's deliberate destruction of Israel quite differently, saying that it was a proof of Yahweh's lack of power.

[10.1-5] The account of making the ark and two new tables might have formed a conclusion to 9.18f., where a kind of pause in the story had already been reached with the mention of Yahweh's hearkening to Moses. The story that an ark and tables were both to be constructed immediately after the sentence of annihilation upon Israel had with difficulty been revoked does not agree with the older report in Ex. 32 and 34. Perhaps a fragment of the earlier tradition has, after all, been preserved here. Commentators have always pointed to the fact that behind Ex. 33.6 there must once have stood originally an account of the making of an ark. In our text the ark is understood rather prosaically as a container for the safe custody of the tables (I Kings 8.9). This conception differs considerably from the earlier one which saw in it the place of Yahweh's throne (Num. 10.35f.; I Sam. 4.4.; Jer. 3.16f. etc.).

[10.6-7] There is hardly any doubt that these verses are a secondary interpolation, and indeed one that has been inserted into the text rather clumsily. The style of address to Israel has been dropped; the barest list is made of some places to which the Israelites had come during their wanderings in the desert. Thus we have the fragment of an itinerary before us. In view of the scantiness of the material it is not possible to work out its connexion with the great itinerary in Num. 33. There seems to be a relationship between the two texts; yet obvious differences exist in their spelling and their order, and particularly with regard to their idea of Aaron's death. Probably at some point in their early history they are derived from a common source— the last witnesses to a literature of which merely fragments have reached us.

[10.8-9] The passage about the authority given to the Levites is also interpolated and its isolated position makes it hard to explain. The very loose temporal link had probably some reference to what is said in vv. 1-5. The short text contains four important statements about the office of the Levites. (1) They were appointed by Moses to carry the ark. It is hard to say how and when this tradition arose. Possibly the Levites still acted as bearers in processions of the ark during the period of the monarchy. According to the view expressed in the historical work of the Chronicler, David had already entrusted the temple singing to the bearers of the ark (I Chron. 16). Exodus 32.25–29 seems to follow another tradition with regard to the special cultic duties with which Moses charged the Levites. (2) They have to attend to the service of Yahweh, which includes the offering of sacrifices as well as the reception of oracles and divine decisions. (3) The authority to bless is a great privilege, because all blessing presupposes an association with God's holy name; the priests. when they bless put Yahweh's name on Israel (Num. 6.27). (4) The Levites receive their livelihood from definite portions of the cultic dues which are theirs by right. That is the meaning of the phrase 'Yahweh is his inheritance' (cf. Num. 18.20). They do not live by cultivating the land and have no landed property at all, but live, so to speak, from Yahweh's table. The Old Testament contains nothing else about a promise to Levi, such as the one to which the narrator in v. 9 alludes.

[10.10–11] Here now at last (removed by several interpolations from its original position immediately after the intercessory prayer in 9.26–29) comes the announcement that Yahweh had granted the prayer. The forgiveness vouchsafed is expressed still more effectively by the order to Moses to prepare for departure and for a journey towards the promised land.

CHAPTERS 10.12-11.32

10 12'And now, Israel, what does the LORD your God require of you, but to fear the LORD your God, to walk in all his ways, to love him, to serve the LORD your God with all your heart and with all your soul, 13and to keep the commandments and statutes of the LORD, which I command you this day for your good? 14Behold, to the LORD your God belong heaven and the heaven of heavens, the earth with all that is in it; 15yet the LORD set his heart in love upon your fathers and chose their descendants after them, you above all peoples, as at this day. 16Circumcise therefore the foreskin of your heart, and be no longer stubborn. 17For the LORD your God is God of gods and Lord of lords, the great, the mighty, and the terrible God, who is not partial and takes no bribe. 18He executes justice for the fatherless and the widow, and loves the sojourner, giving him food and clothing. 19Love the sojourner therefore; for you were sojourners in the land of Egypt. 20You shall fear the LORD your God; you shall serve him and cleave to him, and by his name you shall swear. 21He is your praise; he is your God, who has done for you these great and terrible things which your eyes have seen. 22Your fathers went down to Egypt seventy persons; and now the LORD your God has made you as the stars of heaven for multitude.

11 1'You shall therefore love the LORD your God, and keep his charge, his statutes, his ordinances, and his commandments always. 2And consider this day (since I am not speaking to your children who have not known or seen it), consider the discipline of the LORD your God, his greatness, his mighty hand and his outstretched arm, 3his signs and his deeds which he did in Egypt to Pharaoh the king of Egypt and to all his land; 4and what he did to the army of Egypt, to their horses and to their chariots; how he made the water of the Red Sea overflow them as they pursued after you, and how the LORD has destroyed them to this day; 5and what he did to you in the wilderness, until you came to this place; 6and what he did to Dathan and Abiram the sons of Eliab, son of Reuben; how the earth opened its mouth and swallowed them up, with their households, their tents, and every living thing that followed them, in the midst of all Israel; 7for your eyes have seen all the great work of the LORD which he did.

8 'You shall therefore keep all the commandment which I command you this day, that you may be strong, and go in and take possession of the land which you are going over to possess, ⁹and that you may live long in the land which the LORD swore to your fathers to give to them and to their descendants, a land flowing with milk and honey. ¹⁰For the land which you are entering to take possession of it is not like the land of Egypt, from which you have come, where you sowed your seed and watered it with your feet, like a garden of vegetables; ¹¹but the land which you are going over to possess is a land of hills and valleys, which drinks water by the rain from heaven, ¹²a land which the LORD your God cares for; the eyes of the LORD your God are always upon it, from the beginning of the year to the end of the year.

13 'And if you will obey my commandments which I command you this day, to love the LORD your God, and to serve him with all your heart and with all your soul, ¹⁴he will give the rain for your land in its season, the early rain and the later rain, that you may gather in your grain and your wine and your oil. ¹⁵And he will give grass in your fields for your cattle, and you shall eat and be full. ¹⁶Take heed lest your heart be deceived, and you turn aside and serve other gods and worship them, ¹⁷and the anger of the LORD be kindled against you, and he shut up the heavens, so that there be no rain, and the land yield no fruit, and you perish quickly off the good land which the LORD gives you.

18 'You shall therefore lay up these words of mine in your heart and in your soul; and you shall bind them as a sign upon your hand, and they shall be as frontlets between your eyes. ¹⁹And you shall teach them to your children, talking of them when you are sitting in your house, and when you are walking by the way, and when you lie down, and when you rise. ²⁰And you shall write them upon the door-posts of your house and upon your gates, ²¹that your days and the days of your children may be multiplied in the land which the LORD swore to your fathers to give them, as long as the heavens are above the earth. ²²For if you will be careful to do all this commandment which I command you to do, loving the LORD your God, walking in all his ways, and cleaving to him, ²³then the LORD will drive out all these nations before you, and you will dispossess nations greater and mightier than yourselves. ²⁴Every place on which the sole of your foot treads shall be yours; your territory shall be from the wilderness to Lebanon and from the river, the river Euphrates, to the western sea. ²⁵No man shall be able to stand against you; the LORD your God will lay the fear of you and the dread of you upon all the land that you shall tread, as he promised you.

26 'Behold, I set before you this day a blessing and a curse: ²⁷the blessing, if you obey the commandments of the LORD your God, which I command you this day, ²⁸and the curse, if you do not obey the commandments of the LORD your God, but turn aside from the way which I command you this day, to go after other gods which you have not known. ²⁹And when the LORD your God brings you into the land which you are entering to take possession of it, you shall set the blessing on Mount Gerizim and the curse on Mount Ebal. ³⁰Are they not beyond

the Jordan, west of the road, toward the going down of the sun, in the land of the Canaanites who live in the Arabah, over against Gilgal, beside the oak of Moreh? ³¹For you are to pass over the Jordan to go in to take possession of the land which the LORD your God gives you; and when you possess it and live in it, ³²you shall be careful to do all the statutes and the ordinances which I set before you this day.'

The text of Deut. 10.12–11.32 is very difficult to analyse; it is difficult also to discover the right points of division and the form-critical characteristics of the subsections. Considerations of style make it certain that this section has nothing to do with the narrative in the first person singular in Deut. 9.7–10.11. Nor can it be said that the sequence of the sermons in Deut. 6.10–9.6, which are clearly marked off from each other, is continued here. The best clue to the contents of this section is to grasp its formal structure. An examination of this reveals a whole series of fragments of the formal covenant pattern (see on this the Introduction, pp. 21f.). The section in 10.12–11.1 exemplifies the style of the 'declaration of basic principle' (11.18 does so as well). Deuteronomy 11.2–7 is a 'previous history'; 11.10–12 a 'description of the land' and 11.16–17, 22–25, 26–31 contain 'blessing and curse'.[1] We observe that the subdivisions of this pattern do not follow each other in their traditional order; they become more or less independent; moreover, they have appeared in a definite hortatory style. Yet we can hardly doubt their relationship to the formal pattern of the covenant. Of course, this provides no answer yet to the question how this hortatory recital of its separate parts came into being. Was it the custom to interpret to the laity this formal wording of the covenant section by section? What is quite particularly puzzling in this section is the continuous alternation of the mode of address between the second person singular and the plural.

[10.12–11.1] Not only the characteristic formula of transition, 'and now' (cf. for this Ex. 19.5; Josh. 24.14), but even more so the verbs describing the basic qualities of Israel's relationship to Yahweh are derived from the style of the 'declaration of principle'. Yahweh expects obedience. The expression 'to fear God', 'the fear of God' simply means obedience, the acceptance of his commandments (cf. Gen. 20.11; 22.12 etc.). He expects a response of love and whole-hearted surrender. Even though this formulation may be determined by a predominantly hortatory purpose, we should not fail to

[1] K. Baltzer, Das Bundesformular, pp. 45ff.

recognize the theological achievement lying behind these formularies. We have here an independent and novel attempt to define Israel's total relationship to Yahweh. Deuteronomy was, in fact, the first place where such far-reaching efforts were made to gain a theoretical understanding of the relationship to Yahweh. Earlier times were not aware of this need for such clearly defined concepts. The argument from Yahweh's rule over the whole world actually reminds us of the zeal of Deutero-Isaiah, who is fond of proving the trustworthiness of Yahweh by pointing to the creation of the world (Isa. 42.5; 44.24). Against such a background (the fact that the whole world belongs to Yahweh) the paradox of his choice of Israel's fathers is felt more acutely.

Perhaps the real substance of the declaration of basic principle is limited to Deut. 10.12–14; 11.1, with some further declarations and admonitions in 10.15–22. Amongst these the demand to circumcise the heart is noteworthy as an attempt to give fresh significance to old cultic customs by means of a more spiritual reinterpretation. We know very little about the real significance which the early Israelites attributed to circumcision. Yet perhaps we can infer from this passage or from Jer. 4.4 that circumcision was understood at least at times as an act of dedication and of cleansing. We may compare with the condensed statement that Yahweh is 'your praise' the similar one in Jer. 2.11 that Yahweh was Israel's 'glory'. In vv. 17, 18 particularly the speech passes into the style of a hymn.

[11.2–9] From Deut. 11.2 onwards the reader is invited to look back once more to the acts of God in history. This mode of expression is familiar to us from that part of the covenant-pattern called the 'previous history'. It is not quite clear what is meant by the introductory hint that it is not just the children of the present listeners but they themselves who are witnesses of the great acts of God. If we decide that the place where Moses made this speech was in the land of Moab beyond the Jordan, we meet with the difficulty that at that time the generation which had experienced the exodus from Egypt was no longer alive (Deut. 2.14f.; Num. 14.29ff.). Or were those who were being addressed still children at that time? The fact that the story of Dathan and Abiram is mentioned, whilst that of Korah, which is now closely interwoven with it, is not, is generally considered to be a proof that our Deuteronomic compiler knew only the earlier stratum in the narrative of Num. 16. But we are entitled to question the assumption that he could have had before him nothing but the tradition in Num. 16. The style and formulation of this historical account, too, make it clear that it is modelled on the hymn. This may also explain its somewhat unfortunate syntactical shape (the final clause of this long and detailed sentence is not reached until v. 7). It is characteristic of the rationalizing trend in Deuteronomy that Israel is 'disciplined' by the divine working in history, that the story of God's actions is regarded principally from its educational aspect.

[11.10–15] This section contains a description of the land. The sequence (a) 'previous history' (b) 'description of the land', is known also in ancient Near Eastern treaties and must have come from these into the pattern of the covenant. But this one differs from the descriptions of the land in Deut. 6.10f.; 8.7–10 in not following the traditional plan (country, cities, vineyards); instead it devotes itself to exuberant praise of the abundance of water in the land which can be cultivated without effort and which is portrayed to the hearers as though it were paradise itself. The preacher is giving a rather Utopian picture, far exceeding reality, of the promised land, since in abundance of water the hill country of Judea or Ephraim, the original area where the immigrants settled, can hardly be rated above the valley of the Nile. The twofold sentence in v. 12, 'a land which the Lord your God cares for, the eyes of the Lord your God are always upon it', might be thought to be modelled on the parallelism of some hymn-like poem. The early rain, usually in October, introduces the winter period of rainfall. Greater importance attaches to the latter rain in April, for it is the final rainfall and on it depends the whole successful growth of the seed already scattered in the winter.

[11.16–32] If we want to find our way about in the subject-matter of this section, we must hold fast to the fact that the threats in vv. 16f. recall strongly the cultic curse formulae in which it is traditional for the withholding of rain to play a great part (Deut. 28.12, 24; Lev. 26.4). The counterpart, the promise of blessing, follows in vv. 22ff. Verses 26ff., 'Behold, I set before you this day a blessing and a curse', will then have to be understood as a final summary. Blessing and curse are only just mentioned here, but no further description is given of their content, because that has, in fact, been done previously. These two parts, the curse in vv. 16f. and the blessing in vv. 22–25, must be considered to have belonged together originally. It is true that they are now separated from each other, as though by a foreign body, by the exhortation in vv. 18–21. Its original position here has already been questioned by earlier commentators, because it agrees almost word for word with the exhortation in 6.6–9. Undoubtedly the Deuteronomic preachers are very monotonous in their stock of ideas and their phraseology; but we cannot maintain that they repeat the wording of complete passages.

The instruction to 'set' the blessing on Mount Gerizim and the curse on Ebal reappears once more in a similar form in 27.11ff. We are told in Josh. 8.30ff. how these instructions were carried out. Although no hint is given of this unusual rite in the earlier sources, yet it is a very probable hypothesis that there has been preserved here information of a very primitive custom. Perhaps this is a description of a ceremonial which formed the climax of the sacral celebration at the central sanctuary of the tribal union before the era of the monarchy (cf. on this the commentary on 27.11ff.). The oracle oak or terebinth is mentioned also in Gen. 12.6; 35.4; Josh. 24.26; Judg. 9.6. The rest of the statements about localities in v. 30 are obscure, indeed difficult, in view of the fact that the Gilgal near Jericho must be meant, which is a rather long way from Ebal and Gerizim.

CHAPTER 12. 1–32

12 ¹"These are the statutes and ordinances which you shall be careful to do in the land which the LORD, the God of your fathers, has given you to possess, all the days that you live upon the earth. ²You shall surely destroy all the places where the nations whom you shall dispossess served their gods, upon the high mountains and upon the hills and under every green tree; ³you shall tear down their altars, and dash in pieces their pillars, and burn their Asherim with fire; you shall hew down the graven images of their gods, and destroy their name out of that place. ⁴You shall not do so to the LORD your God. ⁵But you shall seek the place which the LORD your God will choose out of all your tribes to put his name and make his habitation there; ⁶thither you shall go, and thither you shall bring your burnt offerings and your sacrifices, your tithes and the offering that you present, your votive offerings, your freewill offerings, and the firstlings of your herd and of your flock; ⁷and there you shall eat before the LORD your God, and you shall rejoice, you and your households, in all that you undertake, in which the LORD your God has blessed you. ⁸You shall not do according to all that we are doing here this day, every man doing whatever is right in his own eyes; ⁹for you have not as yet come to the rest and to the inheritance which the LORD your God gives you. ¹⁰But when you go over the Jordan, and live in the land which the LORD your God gives you to inherit, and when he gives you rest from all your enemies round about, so that you live in safety, ¹¹then to the place which the LORD your God will choose, to make his name dwell there, thither you shall bring all that I command you: your burnt offerings and your sacrifices, your tithes and the offering that you present, and all your votive offerings which you vow to the LORD. ¹²And you shall rejoice before the LORD your God, you and your sons and your daughters, your menservants and your maidservants, and the Levite that is within your towns, since he has no portion or inheritance with you. ¹³Take heed that you do not offer your burnt offerings at every place that you see; ¹⁴but at the place which the LORD will choose in one of your tribes, there you shall offer your burnt offerings, and there you shall do all that I am commanding you.

15 'However, you may slaughter and eat flesh within any of your

towns, as much as you desire, according to the blessing of the LORD your God which he has given you; the unclean and the clean may eat of it, as of the gazelle and as of the hart. [16]Only you shall not eat the blood; you shall pour it out upon the earth like water. [17]You may not eat within your towns the tithe of your grain or of your wine or of your oil, or the firstlings of your herd or of your flock, or any of your votive offerings which you vow, or your freewill offerings, or the offering that you present; [18]but you shall eat them before the LORD your God in the place which the LORD your God will choose, you and your son and your daughter, your manservant and your maidservant, and the Levite who is within your towns; and you shall rejoice before the LORD your God in all that you undertake. [19]Take heed that you do not forsake the Levite as long as you live in your land.

20 'When the LORD your God enlarges your territory, as he has promised you, and you say, "I will eat flesh", because you crave flesh, you may eat as much flesh as you desire. [21]If the place which the LORD your God will choose to put his name there is too far from you, then you may kill any of your herd or your flock, which the LORD has given you, as I have commanded you; and you may eat within your towns as much as you desire. [22]Just as the gazelle or the hart is eaten, so you may eat of it; the unclean and the clean alike may eat of it. [23]Only be sure that you do not eat the blood; for the blood is the life, and you shall not eat the life with the flesh. [24]You shall not eat it; you shall pour it out upon the earth like water. [25]You shall not eat it; that all may go well with you and with your children after you, when you do what is right in the sight of the LORD. [26]But the holy things which are due from you, and your votive offerings, you shall take, and you shall go to the place which the LORD will choose, [27]and offer your burnt offerings, the flesh and the blood, on the altar of the LORD your God; the blood of your sacrifices shall be poured out on the altar of the LORD your God, but the flesh you may eat. [28]Be careful to heed all these words which I command you, that it may go well with you and with your children after you for ever, when you do what is good and right in the sight of the LORD your God.

29 'When the LORD your God cuts off before you the nations whom you go in to dispossess, and you dispossess them and dwell in their land, [30]take heed that you be not ensnared to follow them, after they have been destroyed before you, and that you do not inquire about their gods, saying, "How did these nations serve their gods?—that I also may do likewise." [31]You shall not do so to the LORD your God; for every abominable thing which the LORD hates they have done for their gods; for they even burn their sons and their daughters in the fire to their gods.

32 'Everything that I command you you shall be careful to do; you shall not add to it or take from it.'

The ordinances for standardizing the cult and establishing only one sanctuary were and still are considered the most important and strikingly distinctive feature in all the new Deuteronomic arrangements for ordering Israel's life before its God. Hence the ordinances to centralize the cult at the place 'which Yahweh shall choose' have actually been called the basic Deuteronomic law. It was certainly evident to the lawgiver, as we shall see later on, that the centralization of the cult demanded by Deuteronomy would change profoundly the life of the country population in particular. But it has long been clear that it would be wrong to try to understand the whole of Deuteronomy with only this centralizing law in mind, almost as if it were its theological centre. On the contrary, scholars must set themselves the task of explaining the fact that, running parallel to a comparatively small number of 'centralizing laws', there are, after all, a large number of ordinances which neither mention the demand for centralization nor even seem to be at all aware of it. The ordinances which we must characterize as 'centralizing laws' in the narrower sense are: Deut. 12; 14.22–29; 15.19–23; 16; 17.8–13; 18.1–8; 19.1–13 (26.12–15). They belong closely together and are perhaps to be described as a special, somewhat later stratum of tradition in the book's complicated process of growth, unless we wish to separate them even more definitely from the main mass of earlier material and to assign them directly to a process of revision.

The legal part of Deuteronomy (12.2–26.15), beginning with the law of centralization, has an introduction which, apart from its hortatory form, recalls strongly the introduction to the Book of the Covenant (Ex. 21.1). The centralizing law appears in a triple form: vv. 2–7, 8–12, 13–19 (20–28). Each of these versions is built up logically on the statement that Israel be allowed to offer sacrifices solely in that place which Yahweh shall choose in one of the tribes 'to make his name dwell there.' (vv. 5, 11, 14). This statement, repeated three times with only small variations, can be called the real centralizing formula. It contains the standard declaration of the formula round which the hortatory expositions group themselves. It is therefore, so to speak, the legal text which is developed in somewhat different ways in the individual cases. It reminds us very much of the 'Law of the Altar' which precedes the Book of the Covenant (Ex. 20.24–26), except that the latter reflects much more primitive conditions. It is common to both sets of regulations that they see in the divine name the constituent element which makes a place to be a sanctuary.

Nevertheless, differences are visible here as well in so far as a much more carefully considered and discriminating conception of the divine name shows itself in the Deuteronomic wording. Even the law of the altar in the Book of the Covenant does not assume a personal presence of Yahweh, that is to say, his actual dwelling in the sanctuary. It speaks of Yahweh's 'coming', when he is invoked. But in Deuteronomy a more precise distinction is made between Yahweh and the sanctuary. The name dwells on earth in the sanctuary; Yahweh himself is in heaven (Deut. 26.15). Here we have a theologically very striking conception of the name, which is present at the shrine in almost material form, is regarded almost as a person, and acts as a mediator between Yahweh and his people. This idea must therefore be understood as a protest against popular conceptions of the actual presence of Yahweh at the sanctuary. It is, of course, open to question whether Deuteronomy is expressing by this means conceptions which had long been current in the Jerusalem temple, for Yahweh was imagined to be there in person (I Kings 8.12; II Kings 19.14; Isa. 8.18 etc.). Nathan's protest against the building of a temple and the notion that Yahweh might live in a building (II Sam. 7.5ff.) suggests the conjecture that Deuteronomy is reviving much earlier conceptions in this matter as well. In the period of the tribal union before the monarchy Israel already had something like a central shrine, or at any rate a system of cultic festivals at which the tribes assembled for common worship of Israel's God.

The phrase so frequently repeated in this connexion about the 'place which Yahweh will choose to put his name there' must be claimed as specifically Deuteronomic. The question very naturally arises whether its use by Deuteronomy implies a terminological link with an earlier conception. Yet research into the background of the history of the tradition of this phrase has so far yielded no reliable result.

The real intention of the three instructions in Deuteronomy has indeed in view something other than the old law of the altar in the Book of the Covenant. They actually seem to be its exact opposite, because they do not allow altars to be built freely wherever Yahweh 'causes his name to be remembered', but emphatically admit of only one altar in 'the place which Yahweh will choose out of all your tribes'. But however far-reaching a change may have been brought about in the public worship of the time by the practical consequences of this ordinance, yet it is not right to regard as its primary aspect and as an indication of an abrupt discontinuance of old usages. There is probably, after all, much that is traditional in this Deuteronomic rule which appears to be so revolutionary. This is evident in the resemblance of the form of the basic Deuteronomic law to the law of the altar in the Book of the Covenant. When compared with the latter, the formulation in Deuteronomy appears rather to be only a fresh wording.

When dealing with the legal regulations in Deuteronomy we shall often have to remind ourselves once more of the fact that in Israel's early days Yahweh's will was not available in the shape of a law complete in itself which had merely to be observed obediently. Yahweh's will was indeed announced in the old commandments, but how it was to be obeyed in the constantly changing circumstances of practical life was a matter which Israel had to work out afresh for itself in its own conscience again and again. Thus we shall have to understand the centralizing laws in Deuteronomy as a fresh interpretation, even if perhaps a harsh one, of the old cultic system, an interpretation which had become necessary owing on the one hand to abuses introduced in the meantime and on the other to quite new perceptions of Yahweh and his relationship to Israel. And this last consideration, namely a fresh theological basic conception of Israel's relationship to Yahweh, is probably the decisive factor.

Deuteronomy is essentially strongly didactic, so much so that it has not infrequently been reproached with a lack of a realistic sense of the world as it is. Hence it would be mistaken to seek to understand the demand to centralize the cult merely as a tactical measure in cultic politics. It is on the contrary a direct deduction from the basic conception underlying all these practical regulations, namely that of Yahweh's 'oneness', as it was already declared in Deut. 6.4 has the 'text' for all that follows. Israel's cult had become completely lacking in unity. The shrines cherished their local traditions, and the cult celebrated at what were in fact former Canaanite shrines was probably intended rather for Baal, the nature-god and weather-god, than for the God of Israel. The instructions to centralize the cult must have sprung from the conviction that the cult in the different country shrines could no longer be reincorporated into the ordinances of a pure faith in Yahweh.

In detail the three versions of the centralizing law go their several ways. But they are clearly constructed on a common plan. They start with the negative aspect and state what can under no circumstances be allowed. Then, with a transition marked by 'for' ([Heb. *kī*, RSV 'for' or 'but'] vv. 5, 9, 14) to substantiate what follows, the positive demand is unfolded. The negative arguments vary, but in the positive part the wording in each case is almost identical. But in neither part is it a question of 'laws' in the proper sense of the word, but explicitly of instructions to the laity. The speakers are not dealing (in strong contrast, for example, with the regulations for the cult in Lev. 1–7) with the special problems of ritual ceremonial when the various sacrifices are offered; on the contrary, they are endeavouring to make a large audience understand the new cultic arrangements. Hence they are concerned with one side of them, namely the fact that all sacrifices should be offered at the one sanctuary and the reason why this should be done, not with the manner of doing it. Once the fact is established, the duly qualified priests will no doubt attend to the manner in which the sacrifices are offered. Hence the enumerations of the various cultic offerings in vv. 6, 11, 14, 17 appear to be almost a perfunctory rhetorical gesture. The meaning is simply 'all of them'.

We now turn to the particular features of the three versions. We notice first of all that the last one alone (vv. 13–19) is composed in the second person singular and in consequence it must probably also be considered as the earliest. It is simpler as well, in so far as it begins at once with the demand for centralization, whilst in the other two versions this demand is set against a definite cultic practice which is contrasted with it.

[2–7] In the first version this is the non-Israelite cultic practice of the Canaanites. Here the antithesis is the most pronounced. It states that Israel not only must not follow the example of these cultic usages; on the contrary it must raze such places of worship with all their appurtenances to the ground. The reason for this aggressive attitude is to be found in the fact that the cults in question had been brought back to fresh life within the cultic domain of Yahweh himself (cf. on this Deut. 13.2ff.).

[8–12] In the second version the comparison is a quite different one, for it explains the new position historically. Its demand is: Not as hitherto! Here the contrast is one within Israel; or, more precisely, it is one concerned with salvation history. The custom in use up till now is due to the provisional nature of Israel's circumstances so far. But when Yahweh has fulfilled his promise and the people are settled in their land, then Israel will serve the one God at one altar. This state of fulfilment is paraphrased by the two expressions of 'inheritance' and 'rest'. The latter especially, although it is not often alluded to in Deuteronomy, is thoroughly characteristic of its conceptions of the saving benefits which God will confer on his people. It is the rest that comes after prolonged wanderings. In the conception of Deuteronomy this rest is undoubtedly a condition existing completely within history; it is the rest 'from all thine enemies round about' (Deut. 25.19), a rest which guarantees untroubled enjoyment of all the natural blessings bestowed by the land. But nevertheless at the same time it is certainly, according to Deuteronomy's conception, a condition in which Israel will belong altogether to its God and be wholly in his safe keeping. We recall that Deuteronomy has spoken of this land of Canaan almost as if it were a paradise (Deut. 8.7–9; 11.10–12).

[13–19] It is a peculiarity of the third version that it explicitly draws the conclusion which the others appear to assume tacitly, namely that slaughtering for secular use is permitted. The explanations with regard to this in vv. 15f. seem to assume that up till then every slaughtering was understood as a ritual act. Although it can hardly be imagined that one of the sanctuaries was visited each time for this purpose, yet this at any rate is clear, that Deuteronomy deprives this action of any sacral significance. The flesh is placed on a par with that of wild animals; the ritual regarding the blood must indeed be observed (vv. 16, 23f.; cf. on this Gen. 9.4), but this pouring out of the blood is definitely denied the character of a sacrifice (it is to be like water). Thereby an important sphere of the patriarchal life was set free to become a secular matter.

This last version can be seen even by the unpractised eye to be considerably amplified. Perhaps the early material is to be found in vv. 13–19. Amongst the additions, the expectation that the political area of Israel will be enlarged is particularly striking (cf. Deut. 19.8). This passage has usually been understood in connexion with King Josiah's planned policy of expansion (II Kings 23.15, 19). In that case it is probably a question of a secondary adaptation of an earlier text to Judean conditions. It is also quite possible that there is envisaged here in quite general terms the ideal increase of territory which David gave to the kingdom of Israel (I Kings 8.65), especially the former Canaanite plain in the west in which there were no sanctuaries of Yahweh. If the origin of Deuteronomy is thought to be in the Northern Kingdom, an extension towards the south might also be supposed (Deut. 33.7). Or should the enlargement expected by

Deuteronomy be brought into connexion with the seizure of territory carried out by Tiglath-pileser (II Kings 15.29)?

[20–32] This rather complicated unit of the regulations connected with centralization ends with a renewed sermon-like warning against any kind of imitation of Canaanite cultic usages. On the phrase 'You shall not add to it or take from it' see above on Deut. 4.2. Here on the lips of the preacher it has lost its specific significance (protection of the literary material) and is merely a rhetorical means of appealing for careful obedience.

The Deuteronomic law concerning the cult is so striking and is supported theologically in such a singular manner that we cannot help asking where a cult-theology with such a programme arose, and who fostered it. But the question is still wide open. It was indeed thought formerly that only Jerusalem could be intended by 'the place which Yahweh will choose'. But this was probably too hasty. Since Jerusalem is not named anywhere in Deuteronomy, the commentator must reserve judgment. The fact cannot indeed be disputed that later, during the course of Josiah's reform, the law was applied to the sanctuary at Jerusalem, but this proves nothing at all about the origin of the requirement. It was known, too, in the later period of the monarchy that after the entry of the tribes Yahweh had 'chosen' first Shechem and then Shiloh. In a Deuteronomistic passage (Josh. 8.30ff.) it is mentioned that Joshua built an altar near Shechem, 'as it is written in the book of the law of Moses', and in Jer. 7.12 (again in the phraseology of Deuteronomy) Shiloh is called the place where Yahweh 'caused his name to dwell'. All this shows that the interpretation of the centralizing formula was by no means restricted to Jerusalem. If it arose there in the circle of the priests (which must, of course, also be considered as one possibility amongst others), then the so-called centralizing laws (see above, pp. 16f.) must be held to have been added as a revision to the book which, on the balance of probability, originated in the Northern Kingdom. But the hypothesis is more likely that at least the centralizing formula in Deut. 12 does nevertheless in the last resort go back to one of the shrines in the kingdom of Israel (perhaps Shechem or Bethel).[1]

---

[1] An attempt to discover such connexions, in which much must indeed remain hypothetical, is to be found in F. Dumermuth, 'Zur dt. Kulttheologie und ihren Voraussetzungen', *ZAW* 70, 1958, pp. 59ff.

CHAPTER 13.1-18

13 ¹'If a prophet arises among you, or a dreamer of dreams, and gives you a sign or a wonder, ²and the sign or wonder which he tells you comes to pass, and if he says, "Let us go after other gods", which you have not known, "and let us serve them", ³you shall not listen to the words of that prophet or to that dreamer of dreams; for the LORD your God is testing you, to know whether you love the LORD your God with all your heart and with all your soul. ⁴You shall walk after the LORD your God and fear him, and keep his commandments and obey his voice, and you shall serve him and cleave to him. ⁵But that prophet or that dreamer of dreams shall be put to death, because he has taught rebellion against the LORD your God, who brought you out of the land of Egypt and redeemed you out of the house of bondage, to make you leave the way in which the LORD your God commanded you to walk. So you shall purge the evil from the midst of you.

6 'If your brother, the son of your mother, or your son, or your daughter, or the wife of your bosom, or your friend who is as your own soul, entices you secretly, saying, "Let us go and serve other gods", which neither you nor your fathers have known, ⁷some of the gods of the peoples that are round about you, whether near you or far off from you, from the one end of the earth to the other, ⁸you shall not yield to him or listen to him, nor shall your eye pity him, nor shall you spare him, nor shall you conceal him; ⁹but you shall kill him; your hand shall be first against him to put him to death, and afterwards the hand of all the people. ¹⁰You shall stone him to death with stones, because he sought to draw you away from the LORD your God, who brought you out of the land of Egypt, out of the house of bondage. ¹¹And all Israel shall hear, and fear, and never again do any such wickedness as this among you.

12 'If you hear in one of your cities, which the LORD your God gives you to dwell there, ¹³that certain base fellows have gone out among you and have drawn away the inhabitants of the city, saying, "Let us go and serve other gods", which you have not known, ¹⁴then you shall inquire and make search and ask diligently; and behold, if it be true and certain that such an abominable thing has been done among you, ¹⁵you shall

surely put the inhabitants of that city to the sword, destroying it utterly, all who are in it and its cattle, with the edge of the sword. ¹⁶You shall gather all its spoil into the midst of its open square, and burn the city and all its spoil with fire, as a whole burnt offering to the LORD your God; it shall be a heap for ever, it shall not be built again. ¹⁷None of the devoted things shall cleave to your hand; that the LORD may turn from the fierceness of his anger, and show you mercy, and have compassion on you, and multiply you, as he swore to your fathers, ¹⁸if you obey the voice of the LORD your God, keeping all his commandments which I command you this day, and doing what is right in the sight of the LORD your God.'

The chapter contains three clearly defined units in which the preacher attacks enticement and apostasy to idol-worship. What is to be done when the challenge, 'we will serve other gods', is heard in Israel (13.2, 6, 13)?

[1-5] The first unit deals with the possibility that the initiative proceeds from a 'prophet' or a 'dreamer'. We do not know how these two men are to be distinguished from each other as regards their professional functions. What is evident is merely that these are persons whose words have an authoritative influence by virtue of a special commission. The situation is made completely problematical by the possibility that the prophet might even be able to attest the authority conferred upon him by means of a 'sign' which he contrives. In Israel it was also customary for men of God to prove the credibility of their words by pointing to some sort of miraculous happening. Such signs were events of a conspicuous nature, occasionally unmistakably miraculous; but sometimes the miracle was confined to the fact that the man of God could predict the sign by clairvoyance (I Sam. 10.1ff.; I Kings 13.3; II King 19.29 etc.). Such a confirmation of the prophet's instructions, which could be perceived by the senses and had been visibly brought about by the deity, must, of course, banish all doubt about the authority of the speaker.

But the Deuteronomic preacher is speaking in a period which was already burdened with confusing experiences (cf. also Ex. 7.22; 8.3). It is just in this respect that he wants to come to people's help. He declares that they need not necessarily be impressed even by messages confirmed by signs. In particular they need not be impressed when these messages call in question the fact that Israel belongs indissolubly to Yahweh. In an obvious expansion, which passes into the second person plural, a later writer has expressed his opinion about the natural question as to how such signs should be judged. Did they come from Yahweh at all? Yes, they did; for behind such phenomena, too, there stands Yahweh, that is to say, he is using a deliberate divine method of teaching. In ways like this he devises a test of Israel's loyalty. (Micaiah ben Imlah gave a quite different interpretation of the counsel of false prophets, namely, that it was a means to delude Israel, and to bring the nation under judgment [I Kings 22.22f.]). The interesting point here is that faith in the fact that Israel belongs to Yahweh is set above all else; not even a sign coming from the divine world is able to shake this assurance. It is not easy to say what kind of prophets the preacher in Deuteronomy has in mind. Did Canaanite prophets (I Kings 18.19) pass over in this way to the offensive against the faith of Yahweh? Samaria had no sanctuary of Yahweh, but a temple of Baal (II Kings 10.23). Here such an awakening of Canaanite self-assurance might no doubt be imagined. Or is it a question of conditions in the former Northern Kingdom in the period after 722, when the faith of Yahweh found itself driven back on the defensive in what was now an Assyrian province?

[6–11] The second section starts by assuming that the summons to apostasy was heard in the inner circle of the family. What is interesting about this is the way in which here the faith of Yahweh, which in the early days had been just a matter of the public cult and particularly of the men assembled by levy, has now brought its tensions into the sphere of the family. It is here a matter for personal decision— even for the women—and must stand the test in the face of quite personal temptations. It is such an important matter that in certain circumstances it might break up the unity of the family.

[12–18] The third section treats of the most serious case: when the movement for aspotasy grips a whole city. In the Northern Kingdom such a thing was quite possible. In the great cities that were formerly Canaanite, such as Megiddo, Taanach, Beth-shean, had the faith of Yahweh ever really established itself at all? Here the old ancestral cult of Baal could have awakened to a fresh self-assurance and have brought the believers in Yahweh, too, under its spell. In such a case the whole of Israel is summoned to a campaign against it. It is still in every way the sacral form of the holy war which Israel is to undertake if this happens. Every living thing in the place is to be put under the ban, the place itself is to be destroyed and all booty burned 'as a whole burnt offering for Yahweh'. Such a rising by the whole union of the tribes against an insubordinate member of the great cultic community had already taken place in ancient times, as is shown by the story of the war of the amphictyony against Benjamin in Judg. 20. We may doubt whether the Israel of the late period of the kings could still be induced to undertake a campaign of this kind in order to preserve the purity of its worship of God. As a conclusion to such a campaign, considered, as we have said, as a sacral one, a curse which forbids for all time the rebuilding of the ruins is invoked on the site (cf. Josh. 6.26).

The inexorable severity with which apostasy from the God of Israel is to be punished is common to the three passages. But it is important to observe that Deuteronomy in this matter, too, revives an old sacral organization of the tribal union, which had perhaps in the interval fallen into oblivion. Already in the Book of the Covenant the principle is codified: 'He that sacrificeth unto any god, save unto Yahweh only, shall be utterly destroyed' (Ex. 22.20). This exclusive attitude towards all alien cults is part of the most essential character of the faith of Yahweh and stretches right back to its origins. It is true that the Deuteronomic exposition gives us the impression that at that time it already needed some display of rhetoric in order to achieve amongst the broad mass of the people the proper appreciation of such harsh demands. We can understand that the language becomes specially forcible in cases where the question of being for or against Yahweh had to be settled within the intimate sphere of the family. The interests of Yahweh must be set above all human and family considerations.

CHAPTER 14.1-29

14 ¹"You are the sons of the LORD your God; you shall not cut yourselves or make any baldness on your foreheads for the dead. ²For you are a people holy to the LORD your God, and the LORD has chosen you to be a people for his own possession, out of all the peoples that are on the face of the earth.

3 'You shall not eat any abominable thing. ⁴These are the animals you may eat: the ox, the sheep, the goat, ⁵the hart, the gazelle, the roebuck, the wild goat, the ibex, the antelope, and the mountain-sheep. ⁶Every animal that parts the hoof and has the hoof cloven in two, and chews the cud, among the animals, you may eat. ⁷Yet of those that chew the cud or have the hoof cloven you shall not eat these: the camel, the hare, and the rock badger, because they chew the cud but do not part the hoof, are unclean for you. ⁸And the swine, because it parts the hoof but does not chew the cud, is unclean for you. Their flesh you shall not eat, and their carcasses you shall not touch.

9 'Of all that are in the waters you may eat these: whatever has fins and scales you may eat. ¹⁰And whatever does not have fins and scales you shall not eat; it is unclean for you.

11 'You may eat all clean birds. ¹²But these are the ones which you shall not eat: the eagle, the vulture, the osprey, ¹³the buzzard, the kite, after their kinds; ¹⁴every raven after its kind; ¹⁵the ostrich, the nighthawk, the sea gull, the hawk, after their kinds; ¹⁶the little owl and the great owl, the water hen ¹⁷and the pelican, the carrion vulture and the cormorant, ¹⁸the stork, the heron, after their kinds; the hoopoe and the bat. ¹⁹And all winged insects are unclean for you; they shall not be eaten. ²⁰All clean winged things you may eat.

21 'You shall not eat anything that dies of itself; you may give it to the alien who is within your towns, that he may eat it, or you may sell it to a foreigner; for you are a people holy to the LORD your God. 'You shall not boil a kid in its mother's milk.

22 'You shall tithe all the yield of your seed, which comes forth from the field year by year. ²³And before the LORD your God, in the place which he will choose, to make his name dwell there, you shall eat the tithe of your grain, of your wine, and of your oil, and the firstlings of

your herd and flock; that you may learn to fear the LORD your God
always. ²⁴And if the way is too long for you, so that you are not able to
bring the tithe, when the LORD your God blesses you, because the place
is too far from you, which the LORD your God chooses, to set his name
there, ²⁵then you shall turn it into money, and bind up the money in
your hand, and go to the place which the LORD your God chooses,
²⁶and spend the money for whatever you desire, oxen, or sheep, or wine
or strong drink, whatever your appetite craves; and you shall eat there
before the LORD your God and rejoice, you and your household. ²⁷And
you shall not forsake the Levite who is within your towns, for he has no
portion or inheritance with you.

28 'At the end of every three years you shall bring forth all the tithe
of your produce in the same year, and lay it up within your towns;
²⁹and the Levite, because he has no portion or inheritance with you,
and the sojourner, the fatherless, and the widow, who are within your
towns, shall come and eat and be filled; that the LORD your God may
bless you in all the work of your hands that you do.'

The material brought together in this chapter is somewhat heterogeneous in form. If we have divided it correctly, at least three
rather large separate units have been placed side by side, and each
of these again reveals a not uncomplicated construction. As regards
content, the subject-matter of vv. 1–2 and 3–21a is closely connected,
in so far as both sections deal with the regulation of ritual questions,
namely with the demarcation between clean and unclean. The
reader of today must from the outset form a clear idea in his mind
on two points when framing an opinion on subjects of this kind. He
must not suspect them of being 'external matters' which obstruct
genuine piety rather than serve it. Such religious observances are
deeply rooted in a conception of wholeness, according to which external things take place within as well, and what is within expresses
itself in concrete externals. Secondly he must as far as possible refrain from asking the questions which spring so readily to our lips
about the 'meaning' of the symbolism and of the observances. Observances keep themselves astonishingly unaltered, whilst the spiritual
associations to which at any given time they owe their significance
are subject to frequent change. We may allow ourselves to doubt
whether the Israelite during the period of the monarchy knew precisely why, when someone died, he shaved a bare patch on his fore-
head. But he could know that it was bound up with cultic ideas re-
pugnant to the worship of Yahweh. It is in this way, that is to say, as
cultic affirmations, that we must in the main understand the following

regulations. According to v. 23 the tithing of farm produce is intended to teach Israel the fear of Yahweh!

[1-2] This section contains an ordinance disguised as an admonition and phrased apodictically against the cult of the dead. To call the Israelites 'the sons of Yahweh' is unique in Deuteronomy and in the whole Old Testament as well (cf. possibly Ex. 4.22; Hos. 11.1). Did early Israel in the language of the cult invoke Yahweh as father? Perhaps it is only a question of a rhetorical phrase with no particular sacral tradition behind it (cf. 8.5). The reason given in v. 2 is a different matter. It is at once natural to conjecture that the expression 'a holy people' reaches back to the period of the tribal union, hence to that of the judges. The concept 'holy' does not denote a particular human quality, but chiefly the idea of being singled out for Yahweh and the idea of inviolability derived from this (Ex. 19.6; Lev. 19.2; Jer. 2.3). Here in v. 2 and particularly in v. 21 the idea of the holiness of the people is still largely determined by primitive ritual. This appears in the form of refraining from certain ritual practices. The spokesmen in Israel for faith in Yahweh attacked with great harshness all forms of the cult of the dead, indeed all traces and vestiges connected with it. Death and the grave confronted primitive man with something divine, numinous, particularly impressive and demanding a cult. Hence there arose here a *status confessionis*. Israel deprived the dead and the grave of every sacral quality. This was a great achievement!

[3-21] This section also starts from a cultic maxim framed apodictically. This time it stands at the beginning: 'You shall not eat any abominable thing.' The corresponding Hebrew word (*tōʿēbā*) is frequent in the Old Testament and denotes originally something disqualified from cultic use (Deut. 17.1; 22.5; 23.18; 25.16; but also Gen. 43.32); thus from the standpoint of Israel something which displeases Yahweh and defiles Israel (Lev 18.22; 20.13 etc.). The apodictic maxim is followed by an explanatory list of unclean animals which with its heading, 'These are the animals . . .', must be considered to be a unit by itself. It uses the characteristic style of Torah teaching in the imperative which constantly interrupts the enumeration ('you may eat', 'you may not eat', etc.). The mammals come first, then the aquatic animals, then the birds. Thus the order differs from that in Gen. 1. Lists like this were not improvised by the Deuteronomic writer out of his head. On the contrary he employed catalogues such as were no doubt drawn up by the priests

at the sanctuaries. The catalogue in Lev. 11.1ff. is rather fuller, but agrees with our text so closely that both texts seem to go back to one and the same list.[1] Strange to say, the hare is considered in both places to be a ruminant. But, in not a few other cases, it is no longer possible for us to give a zoologically exact translation of the Hebrew animal names.

As regards the distinction between clean and unclean, we can say virtually nothing more about the reasons which led to an animal being disqualified. We merely know in the case of the swine, i.e. the wild boar, that it was considered as a sacred animal in the Syrian and Phoenician cults.[2] Since in early times the slaughter of animals was never a completely secular affair (and these cultic classifications certainly reach back into the earliest times), the sacral disqualification was an inevitable consequence of the religion of Yahweh. Nevertheless here, too, it may be doubted whether the Israelite in the period of the monarchy, who was bound to observe these ordinances, was still aware of their connexions with the history of the cult. What is definite is the fact that Deuteronomy, too, still found a meaning for the observance of these ordinances in the fact that Israel belonged to Yahweh, a connexion which could never be broken (v. 21). The individual Israelite had to give his assent to this separation of Israel by Yahweh from all the other cults by means of certain abstentions as a profession of his fath. Since the duty of obedience is brought into connexion with Yahweh's claim to cultic exclusiveness in so one-sided a manner, it is quite consistent that unclean flesh can be left to strangers or foreigners who were not bound in the same way to observe these ordinances. The rule which recurs several times in the Old Testament not to boil a kid in its mother's milk (Ex. 23.19; 34.26) seems intended to ward off a milk-spell, as has been discovered from an Ugaritic text.

[22–29] This section contains one of the laws of centralization, that is, an ordinance which springs explicitly out of the demand to centralize the cult (see above, p. 16). It regulates the payment of the tithes at the sanctuary. The custom of tithing the yield of the peasant's land was certainly very old (Gen. 28.22; Lev. 27.30f.; Amos 4.4). As it involved a kind of sacrifice, the delivery of the produce had to be transferred to the one sanctuary. Hence a fresh rule dealing with this custom was made for the benefit of those who lived

---

[1] For further details see K. Koch, *Die Priesterschrift von Ex. 25–Lev. 16*, 1959, pp. 74ff.

[2] M. Noth, *Gesammelte Studien zum Alten Testament*, 1957, pp. 78ff.

out in the country and might perhaps have had to transport their tithes a long way. By this rule they received permission to sell their tithe where they lived and to use the proceeds to buy at the sanctuary what they needed for the sacrificial feast. From the standpoint of old conceptions of a sacrifice this is an astonishing rationalization of cultic usage! (Cf. also Lev. 27.30ff.) It is no doubt accepted as a matter of course that payments to the sanctuary had to be deducted from the tithe and that it was not consumed completely by those offering it. An inconsistency arises also because v. 22 speaks only of payments of vegetable produce, but in v. 23, which is a kind of instruction how to carry out the regulation, the first-born of animals are mentioned as well. Finally the relationship of the cultic tithe proper to the tax paid every three years for the poor at home is by no means clear (vv. 28f.). The most obvious meaning seems to be that the tithe of each third year may be consumed in one's own community. The last regulation is intended to prevent the impoverishment of the country priests who had lost their livelihood through the centralization (see also v. 27).

CHAPTER 15.1–23

15 ¹'At the end of every seven years you shall grant a release. ²And this is the manner of the release: every creditor shall release what he has lent to his neighbour*; he shall not exact it of his neighbour, his brother, because the LORD's release has been proclaimed. ³Of a foreigner you may exact it; but whatever of yours is with your brother your hand shall release. ⁴But there will be no poor among you (for the LORD will bless you in the land which the LORD your God gives you for an inheritance to possess), ⁵if only you will obey the voice of the LORD your God, being careful to do all this commandment which I command you this day. ⁶For the LORD your God will bless you, as he promised you, and you shall lend to many nations, but you shall not borrow; and you shall rule over many nations, but they shall not rule over you.

7 'If there is among you a poor man, one of your brethren, in any of your towns within your land which the LORD your God gives you, you shall not harden your heart or shut your hand against your poor brother, ⁸but you shall open your hand to him, and lend him sufficient for his need, whatever it may be. ⁹Take heed lest there be a base thought in your heart, and you say, "The seventh year, the year of release is near", and your eye be hostile to your poor brother, and you give him nothing, and he cry to the LORD against you, and it be sin in you. ¹⁰You shall give to him freely, and your heart shall not be grudging when you give to him; because for this the LORD your God will bless you in all your work and in all that you undertake. ¹¹For the poor will never cease out of the land; therefore I command you, You shall open wide your hand to your brother, to the needy and to the poor, in the land.

12 'If your brother, a Hebrew man, or a Hebrew woman, is sold to you, he shall serve you six years, and in the seventh year you shall let him go free from you. ¹³And when you let him go free from you, you shall not let him go empty-handed; ¹⁴you shall furnish him liberally out of your flock, out of your threshing floor, and out of your wine press; as

* The translation given is only conjectural. The Hebrew word used, 'promissory note'(?), is not clear. Does it mean a security placed at the disposal of the creditor, or a sum on which the debtor has obtained a loan?

104

the Lord your God has blessed you, you shall give to him. 15You shall remember that you were a slave in the land of Egypt, and the Lord your God redeemed you; therefore I command you this today. 16But if he says to you, "I will not go out from you", because he loves you and your household, since he fares well with you, 17then you shall take an awl, and thrust it through his ear into the door, and he shall be your bondman for ever. And to your bondwoman you shall do likewise. 18It shall not seem hard to you, when you let him go free from you; for at half the cost of a hired servant he has served you six years. So the Lord your God will bless you in all that you do.

19 'All the firstling males that are born of your herd and flock you shall consecrate to the Lord your God; you shall do no work with the firstling of your herd, nor shear the firstling of your flock. 20You shall eat it, you and your household, before the Lord your God year by year at the place which the Lord will choose. 21But if it has any blemish, if it is lame or blind, or has any serious blemish whatever, you shall not sacrifice it to the Lord your God. 22You shall eat it within your towns; the unclean and the clean alike may eat it, as though it were a gazelle or a hart. 23Only you shall not eat its blood; you shall pour it out on the ground like water.'

[1–11] At the beginning of the section concerning the sabbatical year there stands a legal maxim formulated apodictically, on which the whole of this section (vv. 1–11) is based, and round which it has crystallized. The maxim is then developed and interpreted in different directions. By the 'release' (*šemiṭṭā*), actually 'letting go', early Israel understood the practice of leaving the land fallow, which took place at the end of every cycle of six years.[1] This custom was determined not primarily by social, still less by economic considerations, but was a definitely sacral arrangement. Even in the comparatively late regulations of Deuteronomy this ancient conception has not changed at all; it is a 'Yahweh's release' (v. 2b). In the Law of Holiness this fallow period is defined as a time of rest, which the land shall keep 'to Yahweh' (Lev. 25.3f.). Here we clearly have to do with the manifestation of a primitive state of affairs, and more particularly of the original claim of God to the cultivated land (Lev. 25.23). This sacral arrangement corresponded to a patriarchal peasant economy.

But the social and economic conditions of Israel have changed. We need not suppose that the money economy did not appear in Israel until later, for the existence side by side of a money economy

[1] Cf. Ex. 23. 10f., and on this M. Noth, *Exodus* pp. 189f.

and one based on barter and exchange of goods reaches back in Palestine into very early times. But a change in the social and economic structure within Israel during the period of the monarchy, the increasing development of *latifundia*, and also the burden of state taxes were a growing threat to the economic freedom of the rural peasantry. Often enough the peasant, in order to tide over certain crises, was obliged to borrow 'capital'. Then when a year of release arrived, it was he alone who had to bear the burden of this sacral ordinance, whilst the financial side of the economy experienced no interruption.

It is interesting to see that Israel in the significant v. 2 adapted the old law to these altered circumstances, and to note how it did so; by v. 2 the 'release' is extended to debts. Verse 2 is therefore to be understood as an 'legal interpretation', as Horst suggests; the rule which it accordingly lays down originated historically in a different period from that of the ancient apodictic legal maxim that preceded it. The important question, whether the debt should thereby be cancelled or merely deferred receives, strange to say, no answer. The logic of v. 9 probably favours a complete discharge of the debt. The word 'to exact' (*nāgas*) is to be understood as a legal proceeding against the debtor on the ground of his personal liability (cf. II Kings 23.35). The foreigner is not included in the sacral ordinance (see above on Deut. 14.21).

What follows after the old precept and its legal interpretation, that is, vv. 3–11, is preaching. This passage differs from the apodictic command because of its wordy prolixity, and differs from the legal interpretation because of its lively interest in the personal aspect, and its lack of specifically legal considerations. This sermon is a summons to meet the poor at all times with an open hand and an open heart. It is just the appeal to the heart which is characteristic. The interest of the lawgiver was satisfied when he had made the ordinance obligatory. But the preacher was concerned that the man at whom the law was aimed should also lay it upon his conscience and realize that it was not the law which drove him to take up an anti-social attitude towards the poor (v. 9). This preacher has realistic ideas about poverty; he knows that Israel will always have to deal with it (v. 11). This conception seems to have provoked a contrary opinion, namely, that complete obedience will be answered by a complete divine blessing, and hence by the end of all poverty (vv. 4–6). In both conceptions, but more clearly in the second one, there is expressed the negative and quite unascetic estimate of poverty characteristic of the earlier Israel. It is an evil out of which nothing of value can be extracted. The promise in v. 6 raises the question whether as early as that time economic transactions between the nations already included loans.

[12–18] In the law concerning slaves, which comes next, the preacher again bases himself upon an old legal ordinance, this time a conditional one. This law already occurs in an essentially older form in the Book of the Covenant (Ex. 21.1–11).[1] The wording which lies before the Deuteronomic preacher has undergone a characteristic change when compared with its earlier form. Here it no longer has to do with the purchase of a man who is not free, or in any case of one who is not of the same blood, but of an Israelite who once was free and has sold himself into slavery. The legal rule is completely different in so far as it also allows for a woman enslaving herself, and this must assume that in the meantime the woman has become able to own landed property and thus to sell herself into slavery for debt also (cf. II Kings 8.3, or the legal circumstances in the book of Ruth). Accordingly she, like the man, could decide independently to accept permanent slavery. The early law had prescribed for this case a procedure at a sanctuary (Ex. 21.6); but in Deuteronomy, owing to the centralization of all cultic matters, this transaction must lose its sacral character. It now symbolizes the attachment of the bondman to the house of his master. All this has also changed the concept of 'Hebrew' which was taken over from the old legal system. It did not, in fact, denote those who belonged to a particular nation, but, according to the evidence of many ancient Near Eastern documents, people who belonged to a particular social grade in their nation. Hence from the sociological point of view it denotes a fluctuating element of the population and so from the legal and economic point of view those in a lower class (the class next above them is that of the 'freedman').[2] But in Deuteronomy the expression is no longer used with this particular meaning. According to 15.12, whoever entered into a contract of service as a Hebrew was, in fact, already entitled to the full rights of a member of the covenant-people. Thereby a beginning had been made in the process by which the concept of Hebrew could then in later texts become the name of a man's nationality (Gen. 14.13; Jonah 1.9). The contribution of the Deuteronomic preacher to this

[1] See on this M. Noth, *op. cit.*, pp. 177–9.
[2] Cf. M. Noth, *op. cit.*, pp. 177f.

legal regulation of slavery for debt consists, as in the previous case concerning the release from debt, in making the whole affair more
personal. He lays the question of obedience in a most intimate
manner on the hearer's conscience. He is concerned about the attitude, and so the thoughts, of the man to whom the law applies (v. 15),
and also with not making its observance a burden (v. 18). The
Hebrew word *mišne* in v. 18 should not be translated by 'a half'; it
probably indicates a technical legal word meaning 'equivalent to'.[1]

[19–23] The section concerning the offering of the firstlings is constructed quite similarly to the two previous ones. It opens with an
apodictic maxim which in a completely general form states simply the
demand (v. 19a). Probably the old legal maxim should be limited
to the words, 'All firstling males you shall consecrate to Yahweh your
God.' All the rest is a partly legal, partly homiletic accretion. What is
consecrated to Yahweh, i.e. what is singled out for him to be his
peculiar possession, was naturally withdrawn from all use for economic
purposes. It was allowed to be offered only at the annual pilgrimage
to the one sanctuary and to be consumed at a sacrificial meal. On the
other hand, it ought not to occur to anyone that he might devote to
Yahweh an animal the economic value of which was impaired (cf.
Mal. 1.7f.). An animal with any kind of blemish may not be offered
as a firstling; the lawgiver sets it free for secular slaughter and secular
consumption (see on 12.20 for secular slaughtering and the prohibition of consuming the blood).

[1] M. Tsevat, 'Alalakhiana', *Hebrew Union College Annual* 29, 1958, pp. 125f. On
this law cf. also the *Lipit Ishtar Law Code* 14 (*ANET*, p. 160).

CHAPTERS 16.1–17.1

16 [1]'Observe the the month of Abib, and keep the passover to the LORD your God; for in the month of Abib the LORD your God brought you out of Egypt by night. [2]And you shall offer the passover sacrifice to the LORD your God, from the flock or the herd, at the place which the LORD will choose, to make his name dwell there. [3]You shall eat no leavened bread with it; seven days you shall eat it with unleavened bread, the bread of affliction—for you came out of the land of Egypt in hurried flight—that all the days of your life you may remember the day when you came out of the land of Egypt. [4]No leaven shall be seen with you in all your territory for seven days; nor shall any of the flesh which you sacrifice on the evening of the first day remain all night until morning. [5]You may not offer the passover sacrifice within any of your towns which the LORD your God gives you; [6]but at the place which the LORD your God will choose, to make his name dwell in it, there you shall offer the passover sacrifice, in the evening at the going down of the sun, at the time you came out of Egypt. [7]And you shall boil it and eat it at the place which the LORD your God will choose; and in the morning you shall turn and go to your tents. [8]For six days you shall eat unleavened bread; and on the seventh day there shall be a solemn assembly to the LORD your God; you shall do no work on it.

9 'You shall count seven weeks; begin to count the seven weeks from the time you first put the sickle to the standing grain. [10]Then you shall keep the feast of weeks to the LORD your God with the tribute of a freewill offering from your hand, which you shall give as the LORD your God blesses you; [11]and you shall rejoice before the LORD your God, you and your son and your daughter, your manservant and your maidservant, the Levite who is within your towns, the sojourner, the fatherless, and the widow who are among you, at the place which the LORD your God will choose, to make his name dwell there. [12]You shall remember that you were a slave in Egypt; and you shall be careful to observe these statutes.

13 'You shall keep the feast of booths seven days, when you make your ingathering from your threshing floor and your wine press; [14]you shall rejoice in your feast, you and your son and your daughter, your

manservant and your maidservant, the Levite, the sojourner, the father-less, and the widow who are within your towns. ¹⁵For seven days you shall keep the feast to the LORD your God at the place which the LORD will choose; because the LORD your God will bless you in all your pro-duce and in all the work of your hands, so that you will be altogether joyful.

16 'Three times a year all your males shall appear before the LORD your God at the place which he will choose: at the feast of unleavened bread, at the feast of weeks, and the feast of booths. They shall not appear before the LORD empty-handed; ¹⁷every man shall give as he is able, according to the blessing of the LORD your God which he has given you.

18 'You shall appoint judges and officers in all your towns which the LORD your God gives you, according to your tribes; and they shall judge the people with righteous judgment. ¹⁹You shall not pervert justice; you shall not show partiality; and you shall not take a bribe, for a bribe blinds the eyes of the wise and subverts the cause of the righte-ous. ²⁰Justice, and only justice, you shall follow, that you may live and inherit the land which the LORD your God gives you.

21 'You shall not plant any tree as an Asherah beside the altar of the LORD your God which you shall make. ²²And you shall not set up a pillar, which the LORD your God hates.

17 ¹'You shall not sacrifice to the LORD your God an ox or a sheep in which is a blemish, any defect whatever; for that is an abomination to the LORD your God.'

[16.1–8] Deuteronomy 16 deals with the feasts of Israel. The most striking characteristic of all cultic life is undoubtedly its loyalty to the old ways and its careful preservation of what has been handed down. Yet naturally in the course of centuries cultic customs, too, change. Since there are many differences in local traditions, it is felt to be necessary to make these customs known, to unify them and to carry changes into effect. In Deuteronomy in particular this determination to unify, as we have already seen, expresses itself in a clear theological programme based on definite principles. So we must expect from the start that Deuteronomy, especially when making rules for the feasts, will not abide by what is traditional. We shall come across positively revolutionary interventions. Nevertheless, even a very resolute re-formation of cultic usages must reckon with what is in existence and attempt to link it up with the new. As we read the Deuteronomic regulations concerning the feasts, we must bear in mind both a passionate determination to make things new, and also at the same time a tender care to retain what is traditional. However, a text like this one does not simply reflect the state of affairs at a particular time. Both the early ordinances preserved in it above all the interpolations and additions provide a whole segment of the cultic history of early Israel with its progressive and its retrograde trends. This fact makes it important to read Deuteronomy from the perspective of history. The 'calendars of the festivals' in Ex. 23.14ff. and 34.18ff., which are older from the literary point of view, must be brought in for comparison throughout.

The earliest item of the whole series here, too, is the legal maxim, phrased apodictically and placed first as a heading. In Hebrew it is formulated in exactly the same wording as the commandment concerning the sabbath in the Decalogue, and it is obviously near to it both historically and in its theme. The use of the Canaanite name of the month Abib (=month of the green ears—about April) also indicates the age of the regulation, for in the period of the later monarchy it was customary to number the months according to the 'spring-calendar' (the Hebrew word *ḥōdeš* in v. 1 ought possibly to be translated not by 'month' but by 'new moon'). The historical reason given as an explanation is already an interpretative addition to the old commandment; it is, in fact, in the style of the historical reason given for the commandment about the sabbath in 5.15. This connecting of the feast of passover with the episode of the Exodus reaches back to the earliest days of Israel. But perhaps passover was a still earlier rite of nomadic shepherds for the protection of their flocks and was brought only secondarily by Israel into relation with the event in salvation history.

In v. 2 the great Deuteronomic innovations already make their appearance. In order to understand their significance it is necessary to know that three traditional annual feasts, namely: Mazzoth, being the feast of unleavened bread; the feast of weeks, being the feast of the wheat harvest; and the feast of booths, being the feast of the vintage and the beginning of the new year (cf. Ex. 23.16), were pilgrimage feasts. Passover on the contrary was formerly celebrated not at the sanctuary but by the family- or kin-groups (Ex. 12.21 J; 12.1ff. P). At this point the new Deuteronomic system made itself felt namely by making passover a pilgrimage feast which can be celebrated only at the sanctuary. It is a consistent plan, since Deuteronomy is trying to unify Israel's life and worship and especially to reduce the various local cultic events to some few feasts for the whole of Israel. On the other hand, this rule denotes one of the most fundamental changes on which the reforming zeal of the Deuteronomic circles had decided, and it is not surprising that they did not succeed in enforcing this radical act completely. The new Deuteronomic arrangements were, in fact, by no means restricted to the external change of the place at which the passover was henceforth to be celebrated. Once the passover was transferred from the home to the sanctuary, the whole ceremony had to be altered. It had to be adapted to the sacral activities of a sanctuary, i.e. in this case to the ritual of sacrifices. This had also been the idea of the reforming lawgiver. He wanted passover to be understood as one of the ceremonies at which sacrifices were offered and this took place at the sanctuary. This is evident from the use of the technical term 'sacrifice', which was not customary hitherto at the passover. The passover was 'killed'. This is particularly clear from the description of the animals named for the purpose (sheep and oxen). These are the animals suitable for sacrifice which from time immemorial were offered in the cult at the sanctuary. Thus oxen also could now be 'sacrificed' at the passover! For the rest (omitting the section vv. 3aβ, 4, 8), Deuteronomy still has the passover celebrated at night. It is striking that the meat is not to be roasted as hitherto (Ex. 12.8), but boiled (v. 7), which probably corresponds to the custom at the sanctuaries where the meat to be eaten by the worshipping congregation was boiled in large cauldrons (I Sam. 2.12ff.).

There was yet another spring feast, the feast of unleavened bread (Mazzoth). Unlike passover, it had from olden times been a pilgrimage feast, and in consequence it is also named first in the list of the great pilgrimage feasts in the Book of the Covenant (Ex. 23.14f.). It was one of the agricultural feasts which was celebrated in Canaan also, before Israel's arrival, at the time of the barley harvest. Then Israel, which had in the meantime taken possession of the land, gradually adopted the feast and thereupon soon connected it for its part with the saving event of the exodus from Egypt.[1] But in our account this feast of unleavened bread is mentioned only in a later addition which cannot be called a particularly happy one (vv. 3aβ, 4, 8). It is now to be supposed that the feast of unleavened bread lasting seven days follows directly on the passover. But the old ordinance, according to which the passover congregation is to return home straight away the next morning, stands as an inconsistency beside the later combination of the feasts of passover and of un-

[1] Ex. 23.15; 12.15ff.; 13.3ff., and on this M. Noth, *Exodus*, p. 97.

leavened bread. If Deuteronomy did not originally make provision for the feast of unleavened bread, this can hardly have been unintentional. Was the feast too heavily burdened with Canaanite traditions? In any case the history of the text of 16.1–8 shows that the feast of unleavened bread will not, after all, allow itself to be thrust aside. Even if the original Deuteronomy still recognized passover alone as the spring feast, yet at a slightly later stage the feast of unleavened bread, neglected by Deuteronomy, had nevertheless come into use again. Since the passover had in the interval become a pilgrimage feast, that could only lead to the two originally independent feasts standing side by side, the one succeeding the other. This combination, in fact, is seen in the later legislation concerning feasts (Lev. 23.5f.; Ex. 12.1ff., 15ff.). Thus we can see that further historical development tended to bring about a compromise. Amongst the radical innovations of Deuteronomy the transformation of passover into a pilgrimage feast was the only one which lasted. On the other hand, it was never fitted permanently into the ritual of sacrifices. Passover remained a celebration in the home and the family. In Jesus' time the pilgrims assembling in Jerusalem did indeed slaughter their passover lambs in the temple area, but the meal was then eaten in the houses.

[16.9–17] There are much simpler rules about the feast of weeks and the feast of booths. The first marks the end of the corn harvest, the other the end of the vintage. Strange to say, neither of the two feasts is given any reason connected with salvation history, such as we have in Lev. 23.43, where dwelling in 'booths' is intended to be a reminder of the period of wandering in the desert. In the calendar of feasts in the Book of the Covenant the feast of weeks is called the 'feast of harvest' (Ex. 23.16). The Deuteronomic regulations give no hint of the supreme significance which the feast of booths had at every period of the religious history of Israel, so much so that it was occasionally called simply *the* pilgrimage feast (I Kings 8.2, 65; 12.32; Neh. 8.14). It is difficult to explain the recapitulation in v. 16 which places the feast of unleavened bread (and not, as might in fact be expected, the passover feast) at the head of the three pilgrimage festivals. Is the sentence an addition, and thus a later summary, which now calls the spring festival briefly the feast of unleavened bread? But it is just as likely to be a pre-Deuteronomic survey of the pilgrimage feasts, which restored the correct position after the feasts of passover and of unleavened bread had meanwhile been combined. Deuteronomy shows a strangely one-sided interest in the passover. At all events the summary in v. 16 is contradictory.

We observe already at this point that the succession up till now of large themes treated in broad flowing phrases is increasingly interrupted by shorter passages, until in ch. 22–25 lists of smaller and smaller sacral and legal traditions alone remain. Yet it is possible to detect in 16.18–18.22 that for the treatment of the great public offices an arrangement was planned; namely, judge in 16.18ff.; king in 17.14ff.; priest in 18.1ff.; prophet in 18.9ff.

[16.18–20] Verse 18 is somewhat difficult to understand correctly. Originally the administration of justice in Israel was by no means the duty of a professional specialized bench of judges. It was the task of the body of the elders in the towns and villages, through whose mouth the whole community, in fact, dispensed justice. We know nothing about the elders being specially nominated and authorized for their office. Thus the real difficulty in v. 18 consists on the one hand in the demand to appoint 'judges', on the other in the juxtaposition of 'judges' and 'officers'. The latter were, according to all that we know, officials of the State, and hence their position and function as well as their authority was essentially different from that of the elders, whose authority rested on the ancient tribal constitution. The 'officers' (šōṭᵉrîm) on the contrary were royal officials, whose sphere, so far as we can see, lay chiefly in the affairs of the army. It is therefore more natural to regard as royal officials the judges who were to be appointed (Deut. 1.16; 17.9; 19.17f.). Perhaps a memory of such a reorganization in the administration of justice has been preserved in II Chron. 19.5–11.[1] The rise of such a body of officials shows a trend for the machinery of administration to come under the control of the monarchy, a trend which can be perceived in other spheres of life as well. But it seems as if this trend did not get beyond certain early stages. Even the Israel of the period of the monarchy never achieved a complete constitution as a state. The last part of the sentence in v. 18 demanding just judgment cannot apply equally to both offices, since the officers can hardly have carried out the functions of judges. Hence it probably applies only to the first of the two offices. To sum up, no earlier legal system can be detected behind v. 18, as can so often be done elsewhere.

The three following rules, where it is a question of apodictic

---

[1] On the question of royal judges see R. Knierim, 'Ex. 18 und die Neuordnung der mosaischen Gerechtsbarkeit', *ZAW* 73, 1961, pp. 146ff.

commands, are quite different. They are expressed in a rudimentary and concise style which leads us to assume an early date:

You shall not pervert justice.
You shall not show partiality.
You shall not take a bribe.

Obviously we have here a kind of 'model for judges', a series of commandments which is addressed to the elders judging in the gate, similar to the series preserved in the Book of the Covenant (Ex. 23.1-3, 6-9).[1] The reason given for the prohibition against taking a bribe ('for . . .') is a good example of using experience to elucidate an old legal maxim. This explanation can be classified as a wisdom saying and the original parallelism can still be clearly recognized. On the other hand, v. 20 is again an example of the homiletic guise in which the old earlier material in Deuteronomy is so often presented.

[16.21-17.1] The next ordinances in this section resemble the passage in vv. 19, 20. Here, too, we find a similar ancient series. Its theme is certainly quite different, namely a cultic one, for it aims at keeping unseemly objects away from the altar of Yahweh. *Asherim* are cultic wooden posts which penetrated into the cult of Yahweh from the Canaanite fertility cult, but which in conservative circles were regarded as impermissible. The case was the same with the stone pillars, not infrequently in the form of a *phallus*. Stripped of later interpretative additions the series may have appeared as:

You shall not plant an Asherah beside the altar of Yahweh.
You shall not set up a pillar.
You shall not sacrifice to Yahweh an ox or a sheep with a blemish.

We may state here with more assurance that the tradition must have come from the pre-Deuteronomic period. The prohibition of erecting *Asherim* and *Masseboth* beside the altar of Yahweh certainly, presupposes a number of sanctuaries and not the centralization of the cult. These commandments, too, expressed in a very concise form, were expanded gradually by interpretative additions and by the language of exhortation.

[1] Cf. M. Noth, *Exodus*, pp. 188f.

CHAPTER 17.2-20

17 2'If there is found among you, within any of your towns which the Lord your God gives you, a man or woman who does what is evil in the sight of the Lord your God, in transgressing his covenant, ³and has gone and served other gods and worshipped them, or the sun or the moon or any of the host of heaven, which I have forbidden, ⁴and it is told you and you hear of it; then you shall inquire diligently, and if it is true and certain that such an abominable thing has been done in Israel, ⁵then you shall bring forth to your gates that man or woman who has done this evil thing, and you shall stone that man or woman to death with stones. ⁶On the evidence of two witnesses or of three witnesses he that is to die shall be put to death; a person shall not be put to death on the evidence of one witness. ⁷The hand of the witnesses shall be first against him to put him to death, and afterward the hand of all the people. So you shall purge the evil from the midst of you.

8 'If any case arises requiring decision between one kind of homicide and another, one kind of legal right and another, or one kind of assault and another, any case within your towns which is too difficult for you, then you shall arise and go up to the place which the Lord your God will choose, ⁹and coming to the Levitical priests, and to the judge who is in office in those days, you shall consult them, and they shall declare to you the decision. ¹⁰Then you shall do according to what they declare to you from that place which the Lord will choose; and you shall be careful to do according to all that they direct you; ¹¹according to the instructions which they give you, and according to the decision which they pronounce to you, you shall do; you shall not turn aside from the verdict which they declare to you, either to the right hand or to the left. ¹²The man who acts presumptuously, by not obeying the priest who stands to minister there before the Lord your God, or the judge, that man shall die; so you shall purge the evil from Israel. ¹³And all the people shall hear, and fear, and not act presumptuously again.

14 'When you come to the land which the Lord your God gives you, and you possess it and dwell in it, and then say, "I will set a king over me, like all the nations that are round about me"; ¹⁵you may indeed set as king over you him whom the Lord your God will choose. One from

among your brethren you shall set as king over you; you may not put a foreigner over you, who is not your brother. ¹⁶Only he must not multiply horses for himself, or cause the people to return to Egypt in order to multiply horses, since the LORD has said to you, "You shall never return that way again." ¹⁷And he shall not multiply wives for himself, lest his heart turn away; nor shall he greatly multiply for himself silver and gold.

18 'And when he sits on the throne of his kingdom, he shall write for himself in a book a copy of this law, from that which is in charge of the Levitical priests; ¹⁹and it shall be with him, and he shall read in it all the days of his life, that he may learn to fear the LORD his God, by keeping all the words of this law and these statutes, and doing them; ²⁰that his heart may not be lifted up above his brethren, and that he may not turn aside from the commandment, either to the right hand or to the left; so that he may continue long in his kingdom, he and his children, in Israel.'

[2–7] The 'if' at the beginning of this section is not that of a genuine casuistic statute, but that of the Deuteronomic preacher who uses the same style throughout the whole section. Hence the offence is a general one and is denoted by an expression taken from the language of theology rather than from that of the law, namely, 'transgressing his covenant' (v. 2). The mention of the Assyrian worship of the heavenly bodies in v. 3b (cf. on this II Kings 23.5, 11) seems, in fact, to be a later addition as is clear from the awkward connexion and the break in the style (God now speaks in the first person). If we are looking for an earlier sacral statute on which this whole ordinance rests, we might think of such an early maxim as Ex. 22.20 or of the first commandment in the Decalogue. We do not know whether the demand for the evidence of two witnesses for the prosecution should be regarded as an innovation introduced into the judicial proceedings in use hitherto. Certainly the care to be exercised in such cases is strongly emphasized by Deuteronomy (cf. v. 4). If the witnesses are to initiate the carrying out of the sentence, they expose themselves in the case of false evidence to the serious danger of blood revenge. In form and content the whole ordinance approaches very closely to those in Deut. 13. On the two witnesses cf. Deut. 19.15.

[8–13] The ordinance concerning the possibility of settling a particularly difficult legal case at 'the place which Yahweh will choose' (cf. on this also Deut. 1.17), belongs to the group of laws connected with centralization (see above p. 16). The ordinance is a permissive one, and, in cases where the legal decision is too difficult for a local community, it provides the possibility of transferring the decision to the highest tribunal at the place of the central sanctuary. The list of cases which might perhaps be dealt with in this way merely permits the observation that capital crimes in particular are concerned. But only the bench of judges, and not the accused, can make use of this possibility. Hence it is not a question of appeal proceedings instituted by the accused. Unfortunately the information about the final court of appeal is somewhat vague. This alone is certain, that the 'judge' and the 'Levitical priests' were not named together. Only one of the two offices can have been taken into consideration in the original ordinance, probably that of the judge. If he was not one of those judges appointed by the king mentioned in 16.18, we might think of the office of the 'judge of Israel' (it does not mean the king) whose existence is confirmed for us at any rate by the prophet Micah (Micah 5.1).[1] Possibly this office was superseded later by the Levitical priests. The text does not enable us to discover how this method of administering justice differs from the one practised throughout the country. Since it took place at the sanctuary, it can be assumed that seeking the guidance and accepting the verdict of God played a great part in it (cf. on this particularly Num. 5.11ff.). But in that case the so-called 'prayers of the accused' (Pss. 7; 26; 35; I Kings 8.31f.) must be brought into connexion with this procedure. In addition to the direct questioning of God, the mere fact of much wider experience and knowledge of precedents will have enabled these officials to administer justice with superior authority. In any case they claimed for their sentences a very high, even a divine mandate. Failure to obey the sentence was regarded as a crime deserving the death penalty.

[14–20] It is astonishing to find a law concerning the king in a theological scheme so thoroughly intent on a revival of the old ordinances of the tribal union before the monarchy. In fact, none of the legal compilations in the Old Testament contain anything of this kind, and that is easy to understand, because they hand down the old legal traditions of the early period. The office of the king appeared comparatively late in Israel's history, at a time when the great cultic, legal and military institutions had long since established themselves. In fact, these soon came into conflict with the kingship (I Sam. 15; II Sam. 24). But the kingship gained the upper hand, and at the time of Deuteronomy the life of Israel could no longer be imagined

[1] M. Noth, 'Das Amt des Richters Israels', *Festschrift für A. Bertholet*, 1950, pp. 404ff.

without it. It is interesting to observe how Deuteronomy succeeded in handling this large new-comer. The 'law concerning the king', more than almost any other section of the book, is typical both of the political aspirations of Deuteronomy and of its limitations. We can see at once that kingship is conceived, almost reluctantly, as a concession to historical reality. As a matter of fact, this law concerning the king comes very far short of describing correctly the full powers, varied and extensive as they were, of the one who wore the crown. Deuteronomy is concerned only 'to prevent kingship from disturbing the organization of the people's life as set forth in Deuteronomy'.[1] Possibly vv. 18–19, the only ones which assign to the king a definite task, are a later addition. In them Deuteronomy is thought of as a literary document (see above, Introduction, pp. 29f.). Moreover, v. 20 is better understood as the direct continuation of v. 17.

No clear answer can be given to the question which constitutional form of kingship can be glimpsed behind this new system, whether it was that of Judah or of Northern Israel, especially in view of this trend to diminish, to confine, indeed almost to distort. The idea that the creation of kingship resulted merely from the demand of the people and not from the initiative of Yahweh is contrary both to the ideas of Judah and to those of Northern Israel. But it resembles those of Hosea (8.4) and the accounts in I Sam. 8.1ff.; 10.17ff. Yet the law concerning the king does contain some features (cf. the phrase 'whom the Lord your God will choose' in v. 15) which suggest its connexion with conditions experienced in the Northern Kingdom by the kingship there, which had a charismatic basis.[2] The words 'he and his children', limping behind in a somewhat clumsy style in v. 20b, would then have to be understood as a later *interpretatio judaica*.

The prohibition in v. 16 against procuring horses for a corps of military chariots seems to have something to do with an exchange transaction, namely the supply of Hebrew soldiers in return for Egyptian horses, of which the king had been guilty (cf. I Kings 10.28; it is in this way that garrisons of mercenaries, like that in Elephantine, may have come into being in Egypt). Deuteronomy's theory of salvation history regards such behaviour as an offence against Yahweh's guidance in history and against an explicit saying of Yahweh, admittedly not known to us elsewhere (but cf. Deut. 28.68). Hence, in order to emphasize the fact that enterprises like

---

[1] A. Alt, 'Die Heimat des Deuteronomiums', *Kleine Schriften* II², 1959, p. 264.
[2] K. Galling, 'Das Königsgesetz im Deuteronomium', *TLZ* 1951, cols. 133ff.

this are forbidden, something approaching the use of a proof-text is adduced, although, as usually occurs in such cases, the divine word cited is applicable only in certain respects to the matter in question. Hence the one-sidedness of this law concerning the king consists in the fact that Deuteronomy sees in kingship not an office which Yahweh could use for the welfare of his people, but only an institution in which the holder must live in a sphere of extreme peril because he is tempted by his harem or his wealth either to turn away from Yahweh or to 'lift up his heart above his brethren'. Intimate knowledge and daily study of Deuteronomy, of which he must always have a copy at hand, can alone preserve him from this behaviour. Hence merely a shadowy existence is allowed here to kingship in Israel.

We must recall the enormous scale of the functions and prerogatives extolled in the royal psalms (Pss. 2; 20f.; 45; 72; 110), in which the king sits as the great proxy at the right hand of Yahweh. Hence it is necessary to call to mind what Deuteronomy does not say about the king in order to understand its own position aright. On the one hand, Deuteronomy feels it to be impossible to avoid mention of this institution altogether; after all, it had a history in Israel, and, in fact, a history endorsed by Yahweh. It knows that Yahweh can 'choose' (v. 15) even kings to be instruments for his control of history. On the other hand, the first and real initiative when founding the kingship comes from the people. In view of the popular desire to have a king like other nations the law concerning the king almost gives us the impression of being merely an 'optional arrangement'.[1] It cannot be seen clearly how this initiative of the people is related to the divine act of choosing, which is nevertheless also taken for granted here. At any rate this act can no longer be understood, as it certainly was long ago, as the manifestation of a special divine purpose of salvation.

[1] A. Alt, 'Das Königtum in den Reichen Israel und Juda', *Kleine Schriften* II[2], 1959, p. 116.

CHAPTER 18.1-22

18 ¹"The Levitical priests, that is, all the tribe of Levi, shall have no portion or inheritance with Israel; they shall eat the offerings by fire to the LORD, and his rightful dues. ²They shall have no inheritance among their brethren; the LORD is their inheritance, as he promised them. ³And this shall be the priests' due from the people, from those offering a sacrifice, whether it be ox or sheep: they shall give to the priest the shoulder and the two cheeks and the stomach. ⁴The first fruits of your grain, of your wine and of your oil, and the first of the fleece of your sheep, you shall give him. ⁵For the LORD your God has chosen him out of all your tribes, to stand and minister in the name of the LORD, him and his sons for ever.

6 'And if a Levite comes from any of your towns out of all Israel, where he lives—and he may come when he desires—to the place which the LORD will choose, ⁷then he may minister in the name of the LORD his God, like all his fellow-Levites who stand to minister there before the LORD. ⁸They shall have equal portions to eat, besides what he receives from the sale of his patrimony.

9 'When you come into the land which the LORD your God gives you, you shall not learn to follow the abominable practices of those nations. ¹⁰There shall not be found among you any one who burns his son or his daughter as an offering, any one who practises divination, a soothsayer, or an augur, or a sorcerer, ¹¹or a charmer, or a medium, or a wizard, or a necromancer. ¹²For whoever does these things is an abomination to the LORD; and because of these abominable practices the LORD your God is driving them out before you. ¹³You shall be blameless before the LORD your God. ¹⁴For these nations, which you are about to dispossess, give heed to soothsayers and to diviners; but as for you, the LORD your God has not allowed you so to do.

15 'The LORD your God will raise up for you a prophet like me from among you, from your brethren—him you shall heed—¹⁶just as you desired of the LORD your God at Horeb on the day of the assembly, when you said, "Let me not hear again the voice of the LORD my God, or see this great fire any more, lest I die." ¹⁷And the LORD said to me, "They have rightly said all that they have spoken. ¹⁸I will raise up for

them a prophet like you from among their brethren; and I will put my words in his mouth, and he shall speak to them all that I command him. ¹⁹And whoever will not give heed to my words which he shall speak in my name, I myself will require it of him. ²⁰But the prophet who presumes to speak a word in my name which I have not commanded him to speak, or who speaks in the name of other gods, that same prophet shall die." ²¹And if you say in your heart, "How may we know the word which the LORD has not spoken?"—²²when a prophet speaks in the name of the LORD, if the word does not come to pass or come true, that is a word which the LORD has not spoken; the prophet has spoken it presumptuously, you need not be afraid of him.'

[1–8] As we might expect, in the law concerning the priests the well-known Deuteronomic conception of Levi as the priestly tribe comes to the fore as its basic theme. But we must ask ourselves (just as we did with regard to the law concerning the king) whether Deuteronomy is here reflecting an historical fact well known and commonly recognized in Israel, or whether it is using this law to raise claims more in accordance with its programme, which in the earlier period had never been generally accepted as valid. Undoubtedly this law of the priests, too, contains pre-Deuteronomic elements. Thus perhaps the very matter-of-fact regulations about maintenance in v. 3 belong to the earliest stratum, whilst vv. 4f., being in the hortatory style, show themselves to be specifically Deuteronomic. Further, the fact that the Levites own no landed property is rooted in early events of which the sociological aspect is no longer clear to us. The case might be somewhat similar with regard to the maxim which sounds like a slogan in a religious programme, 'Yahweh is their inheritance' (cf. Num. 18.20). On the other hand, the second part (vv. 6–8) naturally assumes the demand for centralization. This 'permissive' ordinance should probably not be brought into connexion with the forcible measures in II Kings 23.8. Besides, there is no evidence that the Levites living in the towns were all priests of the high places. The translation and understanding of v. 8 are disputed.

[9–22] The comprehensive law concerning the prophets is quite clearly arranged: it deals first in vv. 9–14 with mantic practices, which were not permissible, then positively with the office of a prophet itself, actually founded at Sinai (vv. 15–18), and finally with disobedience to the prophet's word and with possible corruption of the prophet's office itself (vv. 19–22). It is more than obvious that these statements are to be dated at the earliest in the period of the monarchy. Cultic practices, and especially religious questionings, which in this form were unknown in Israel's early period (the cult of Moloch, for instance), are here taken for granted. We no longer know what techniques and purposes lay behind the individual practices in vv. 10–11. In the list completeness seems to be attempted, though we must probably not assume that all these practices could be sharply distinguished from each other. They are merely mentioned here because of the one, and, in the last resort, the decisive fact that everyone who meddles with such things breaks faith with Yahweh, the God of Israel. The simplicity and clarity of this view is undoubtedly only the outcome of a long debate which swayed this way and that, and presupposes a slow clarification of what is compatible with the cult of Yahweh and what is completely incompatible with it, what is 'an abomination to Yahweh'. Yahweh demands that Israel 'shall be blameless before the Lord'. The expression is very typical of the religious thought of Israel which received its standards far less from ideas than from certain conditions of fellowship. It is not moral and religious 'perfection' which is demanded of Israel, but rather an undivided commitment, without any reinsurance by consulting strange gods, spirits of the dead, etc., to the conditions of fellowship with Yahweh.

For—here the ordinance becomes positive—Yahweh has made known to Israel a quite different possibility of communicating with him, namely the office of the prophet. In that Deuteronomy (perhaps rather too summarily) sees in the practices named here attempts to ascertain the will of the deity, it reaches the antithesis, splendid in its simplicity, between any mantic technique on the one hand and the prophetic office on the other. This antithesis, too, though it is so simple, is the outcome of lengthy meditation on Israel's part about the peculiar quality of the prophetic revelation. It is now possible to sweep aside, as with a wave of the hand, the motley arsenal of mantic and occult practices, all the attempts to obtain a share of the divine powers or of divine knowledge. A quite different possibility has been disclosed to Israel, namely the Word of its prophet. In recent exegesis this promise has been understood to mean that by means of a prophet Israel may be assured at all times of the most intimate association with its God. But we must ask whether the promise in Deuteronomy is really concerned with such a wide vision into the flight of time, and not rather with one single fulfilment, that is to say, with the coming of an 'eschatological' prophetic mediator. In any

case the prophet 'like Moses' means for Deuteronomy an example of
the one outstanding office by means of which Israel comes into quite
direct contact with God. Deuteronomy outlines the function of this
prophet only so far as to say that he will be for Israel the mouth of
God. But we must not think here of the pattern of the great prophets
of judgment, but of the way in which Moses himself discharged the
duties of his office in accordance with the Deuteronomic conception:
interceding, suffering as the representative, actually dying (Deut.
4.21f.; 9.18ff., 25ff.), and therefore this portrait of a prophet is in
harmony with that of the suffering servant of God in Deutero-
Isaiah.

But how did the preacher in Deuteronomy come to expect anything so audacious? Can he appeal in this matter to a promise of
Yahweh? In fact, the supreme significance of this office, and also
undoubtedly the novelty of the conception of it, obliges him to produce a detailed and convincing proof out of the tradition. We see
here an extremely interesting example of the way in which the sacred
tradition was treated in those days. The Deuteronomist could not
appeal to an explicit divine promise of such a prophetic office. But
he was in a position to support his assertion by means of the exegesis
of an old tradition. For this purpose he adduces a kind of scriptural
proof by interpreting the earlier tradition of the event at Sinai as
follows. On that occasion Israel had begged to be spared the necessity
of hearing the divine voice directly. Moses was to listen to it and then
give Israel an account of it. Yahweh granted this request and thus
the prophetic office of mediator came into being (cf. Deut. 5.24ff.;
Ex. 20.19ff.). Since Deuteronomy takes such elaborate trouble to
prove the authority of this prophetic office, it is natural to ask whether
it did not have in view a quite definite institution, and so one which was
already in existence (an announcer of the law or a mediator of the
covenant?). Our text permits no reliable inference. If the promise
did not point to a succession of prophets, but to the coming of one
final mediator, a new Moses, then there would be less evidence for
inferring the existence of such an office.[1]

But the times for which Deuteronomy was speaking had already
had a number of unhappy experiences of the prophetic office; it was
known that prophets did not always have the right to claim an
authorization by Yahweh. Hence in this final section the law concerning the prophets threatens with death any prophet who speaks

[1] H. J. Kraus, *Worship in Israel*, ET 1966, pp. 106ff.

in the name of Yahweh anything not commanded him, and particularly one who presumes to speak in the name of other gods. Deuteronomy believes it can provide its hearers with an infallible criterion for distinguishing between true and false prophecy: the word spoken merely presumptuously does not come true. However in setting up criterion the preacher is probably making things too easy for himself. If a serious matter arose, could the question of the genuine authority of the prophet be left in suspense until it had at last appeared that his message had come true? Jeremiah, too, was endeavouring to discover a universally valid and objective criterion for what is true and false (Jer. 28.8f.).

CHAPTER 19.1-21

19 [1]'When the LORD your God cuts off the nations whose land the LORD your God gives you, and you dispossess them and dwell in their cities and in their houses, [2]you shall set apart three cities for you in the land which the LORD your God gives you to possess. [3]You shall prepare the roads, and divide into three parts the area of the land which the LORD your God gives you as a possession, so that any manslayer can flee to them.

[4] 'This is the provision for the manslayer, who by fleeing there may save his life. If any one kills his neighbour unintentionally without having been at enmity with him in time past—[5]as when a man goes into the forest with his neighbour to cut wood, and his hand swings the axe to cut down a tree, and the head slips from the handle and strikes his neighbour so that he dies—he may flee to one of these cities and save his life; [6]lest the avenger of blood in hot anger pursue the manslayer and overtake him, because the way is long, and wound him mortally, though the man did not deserve to die, since he was not at enmity with his neighbour in the time past. [7]Therefore I command you, You shall set apart three cities. [8]And if the LORD your God enlarges your border, as he has sworn to your fathers, and gives you all the land which he promised to give to your fathers— [9]provided you are careful to keep all this commandment, which I command you this day, by loving the LORD your God and by walking ever in his ways—then you shall add three other cities to these three, [10]lest innocent blood be shed in your land which the LORD your God gives you for an inheritance, and so the guilt of bloodshed be upon you.

[11] 'But if any man hates his neighbour, and lies in wait for him, and attacks him, and wounds him mortally so that he dies, and the man flees into one of these cities, [12]then the elders of his city shall send and fetch him from there, and hand him over to the avenger of blood, so that he may die. [13]Your eye shall not pity him, but you shall purge the guilt of innocent blood from Israel, so that it may be well with you.

[14] 'In the inheritance which you will hold in the land that the LORD your God gives you to possess, you shall not remove your neighbour's landmark, which the men of old have set.

15 'A single witness shall not prevail against a man for any crime or for any wrong in connection with any offence that he has committed; only on the evidence of two witnesses, or of three witnesses, shall a charge be sustained. 16If a malicious witness rises against any man to accuse him of wrongdoing, 17then both parties to the dispute shall appear before the LORD, before the priests and the judges who are in office in those days; 18the judges shall inquire diligently, and if the witness is a false witness and has accused his brother falsely, 19then you shall do to him as he had meant to do to his brother; so you shall purge the evil from the midst of you. 20And the rest shall hear, and fear, and shall never again commit any such evil among you. 21Your eye shall not pity; it shall be life for life, eye for eye, tooth for tooth, hand for hand, foot for foot.'

[1–13] The law about the cities of refuge is arranged as follows. Verses 1–3 contain the basic ordinances. After the entry, the land is to be divided into three legal districts, and three cities of refuge are to be set apart to which a manslayer can flee (for the interpretation of *rāṣaḥ* see on Deut. 5.17). The meaning of the passage about the roads in v. 3a is not clear. Steuernagel translates the first verb by 'measure off' instead of by 'prepare'. In vv. 4–7 there follows the legal interpretation introduced in the same way as in 15.2. In principle it is possible for a man to claim asylum only if he had become guilty of a person's death unintentionally and carelessly, as, for instance, when the head of a man's axe slips from the handle and gives another man a mortal blow. Verses 8–9, like Deut. 12.20, contain an additional ordinance according to which, when the expected enlargement of the territory takes place, the number of cities is to be doubled (see above, pp. 93f.). The whole section ends in v. 10 with a general hortatory warning against all shedding of innocent blood, in which possibly an early apodictic prohibition has been preserved ('Thou shalt not shed innocent blood in your land'). There then follows, somewhat separated from the main subject by this general sermon-like appeal, a special ordinance in legal form to deal with the case of an unlawful claim on the right of asylum: if a deliberate manslayer has sought asylum in the city of refuge, he must be fetched by the elders of his native city and handed over to the avenger of blood. This special ordinance, too, ends in v. 13 with a general exhortation in the manner of a sermon.

The institution of the right of asylum serves above all to limit the rights of blood-revenge, which in itself has absolute authority; that is,

whenever one of a family is killed the next of kin know that they will be
called upon to exact vengeance. Our lawgiver too takes for granted
that the avenger of blood 'in hot anger' cannot be expected to distinguish between murder and unintentional killing. At the same time
blood-revenge is not by any means a custom which the lawgiver
wishes to abolish. Under normal circumstances, however, this institution tends to be replaced by the growing power of the State. However, this development, which can be observed widely in judicial
history, did not take place in Israel. So far as we can see, kingship and
the power of the State have no effective influence on legal practice,
certainly in the countryside. Hence, in cases of murder in Israel, blood-
revenge remained a quite legitimate institution in itself and is still completely regarded as such by our comparatively late law (v. 12). We may
perceive on the part of the religion of Yahweh a certain resistance to
letting such severe disturbances in man's social life be settled outside
the sphere of personal responsibility. Thus, for example, Israel was
strictly forbidden to limit the legal right of blood-revenge by the payment of a ransom, i.e. monetary compensation (Num. 35.31f., but also
Ex. 21.23).

But difficulties arise over the question of fitting this law into its
correct place in the history of early Israelite law. In view of our increasing knowledge of the system of asylum in the ancient Near East
and of its various possibilities, we ought not to allow ourselves to
reconstruct a picture of the corresponding conditions in Israel out of
the relatively scanty statements in the Old Testament alone. In Israel
the practice was more general than the few legal ordinances enable
us to recognize (Ex. 21.13f.; Num. 35.9–28; Deut. 4.41f.; Josh.
20.1–6, 9). Up till now our law concerning asylum has been understood as a necessary outcome of the centralization of the cult. In the
course of abolishing the local sanctuaries the system of asylum has to
be regulated anew. But it is open to question whether the establishment of cities of refuge was an innovation first required by Deuteronomy. For what happened to those who sought protection at the
altar (cf. I Kings 1.50f.; 2.28ff.)? It is difficult to imagine that they
all remained for the rest of their lives in the confined area of the
sacred precincts. Perhaps Deuteronomy's innovation consists merely
in the elimination of the procedure of *hiketeia*, that is, the invocation
of divine protection in the sacral place, so directing the man entitled
to asylum to make his way at once to the city of refuge. But was
asylum up to the time of Deuteronomy to be found on principle and

consistently only at the altar, and did a complete secularization of the system of asylum set in suddenly at this point? A searching examination of the right to asylum must probably in any case have taken place, for the distinction between murder and manslaughter was long established in Israel, and made a procedure of this kind necessary (Ex. 21.13). On the whole subject, compare the regulations in Num. 35 which originated in the Priestly Document.

[14–21] From the point of view of the history of the tradition this section is rather heterogeneous. Its earliest components are certainly the two apodictic commandments in vv. 14, 15, 'You shall not remove your neighbour's landmark' and 'A single witness shall not prevail against a man for any crime.' (The prohibition against removing a landmark has a parallel in the Shechem Dodecalogue in Deut. 27.17.) Both commandments are now expanded, the first merely by one of those rhetorical flourishes so frequent in Deuteronomy, the second by a detailed legal interpretation. This latter contains several strata, and already takes account of the recent institution of a body of judges established by the State (see on Deut. 16.18). Since the early Israelite legal procedure laid the burden of proof largely on the accused man, the influence of the witnesses could have a very dangerous effect on the verdict. In order to guard against this, an ordinance which is probably already pre-Deuteronomistic lays it down that only evidence corroborated by at least two persons shall be accepted against the accused. A false witness shall suffer the punishment which would have been inflicted on the accused. An abbreviated form of the *lex talionis* or law of retaliation is brought in as the reason for this strict rule. The law occurs again in Ex. 21.23–25; Lev. 24.19f. This ancient and weighty legal maxim occupies merely a modest position here, being cited as part of a sermon-like addendum. The *lex talionis* (except for its first term) was perhaps even in the early days no longer obeyed in its literal sense. It was no doubt originally intended to hold the balance in the relations of human society by means of a negative procedure of compensation.[1]

---

[1] D. Daube, *Studies in Biblical Law*, 1947, p. 128. On the *lex talionis* cf. also M. Noth on Ex. 21.23–25, *Exodus*, p. 182.

CHAPTER 20.1–20

20 ¹'When you go forth to war against your enemies, and see horses and chariots and an army larger than your own, you shall not be afraid of them; for the LORD your God is with you, who brought you up out of the land of Egypt. ²And when you draw near to the battle, the priest shall come forward and speak to the people, ³and shall say to them, "Hear, O Israel, you draw near this day to battle against your enemies: let not your heart faint; do not fear, or tremble, or be in dread of them; ⁴for the LORD your God is he that goes with you, to fight for you against your enemies, to give you the victory." ⁵Then the officers shall speak to the people saying, "What man is there that has built a new house and has not dedicated it? Let him go back to his house, lest he die in the battle and another man dedicate it. ⁶And what man is there that has planted a vineyard and has not enjoyed its fruit? Let him go back to his house, lest he die in the battle and another man enjoy its fruit. ⁷And what man is there that has betrothed a wife and has not taken her? Let him go back to his house, lest he die in the battle and another man take her." ⁸And the officers shall speak further to the people, and say, "What man is there that is fearful and fainthearted? Let him go back to his house, lest the heart of his fellows melt as his heart." ⁹And when the officers have made an end of speaking to the people, then commanders shall be appointed at the head of the people.

10 'When you draw near to a city to fight against it, offer terms of peace to it. ¹¹And if its answer to you is peace and it opens to you, then all the people who are found in it shall do forced labour for you and shall serve you. ¹²But if it makes no peace with you, but makes war against you, then you shall besiege it; ¹³and when the LORD your God gives it into your hand you shall put all its males to the sword, ¹⁴but the women and the little ones, the cattle, and everything else in the city, all its spoil, you shall take as booty for yourselves; and you shall enjoy the spoil of your enemies, which the LORD your God has given you. ¹⁵Thus you shall do to all the cities which are very far from you, which are not cities of the nations here. ¹⁶But in the cities of these peoples that the LORD your God gives you for an inheritance, you shall save alive nothing that breathes, ¹⁷but you shall utterly destroy them,

the Hittites and the Amorites, the Canaanites and the Perizzites, the Hivites and the Jebusites, as the LORD your God has commanded; 18that they may not teach you to do according to all their abominable practices which they have done in the service of their gods, and so to sin against the LORD your God.

19 'When you besiege a city for a long time, making war against it in order to take it, you shall not destroy its trees by wielding an axe against them; for you may eat of them, but. you shall not cut them down. Are the trees in the field men that they should be besieged by you? 20Only the trees which you know are not trees for food you may destroy and cut down that you may build siegeworks against the city that makes war with you, until it falls.'

[1–9] The section concerning the war speeches (vv. 1–9), too, is not a 'law' as regards its type, but is itself also clothed in the form of a war sermon. It is distinguished from the familiar examples of this type in 7.1ff.; 9.1ff. merely by the fact that it includes unaltered an earlier legal ordinance concerning the dismissal of men unsuitable for military service. It presents itself even to the unpractised eye as a body of tradition composed of several strata which can only slowly have acquired the form which we have before us today. It begins with a very general exhortation not to fear in war even the superior power of enemies. Especially during the period of the first hostile encounters with the Israelites, the Canaanites were the stronger owing to their technical proficiency in battle, that is, in their use of war chariots (Josh. 11.4; 17.16; Judg. 1.19; 4.3; I Kings 20.23ff.). From this time forward the alternative of trust either in Yahweh or in war chariots ('horses and chariots') had become a central concern of the religion of Yahweh. For the prophets, too, all trust in chariots is plainly a symptom of lack of faith (Isa. 30.16; 31.1ff.; Hos. 14.3).

The next section concerning the war speech of the priest does not fit into the context, for the second person plural is used (instead of the singular as in v. 1), and it must probably be considered as the latest stratum of the tradition. However, this literary judgment still does not give us the right to regard the subject-matter itself as a late innovation. It could, of course, also be that the Deuteronomist, who is known to be much addicted to restorations, is reviving an arrangement which is, in fact, as regards its details earlier than the function of the officers elaborated in vv. 5–8. The speech of the priest is a summary, reduced to its most concise form, of those war sermons whose proper shape and content we know from Deut. 7.16ff.; 9.1ff.; 31.3ff.

With astonishing abruptness the law passes over in v. 5 to the speech which the officers are to make to the army. With this we move into the stratum which is earlier from the literary point of view, but which cannot be however very early, since these 'officers' were royal officials, whose function in the military sphere was concerned with the conscription of those liable for service in the army (see above on 16.18). Hence the earliest stratum of the law does not reach farther back than the period of the monarchy. The speech of the officers deals with cases which lead to release from military service: the building of a new house, the first produce from a vineyard and a betrothal. In each of these cases the reason given for a release starts with a 'lest', which is based on the idea that these men have a right to property and its produce which ought not to be curtailed by a possible death in action. But this decidedly humane reason (cf. also on this Deut. 24.5) can be understood only as a very 'modern' interpretation of the ordinance which proceeded originally from quite different suppositions. According to very ancient and widespread beliefs, a bridegroom, and, in fact, anyone who had anything to inaugurate, was threatened to an unusual extent by demons. Hence these men were eliminated originally in the interests of magical and ritual purity, and so for the protection of the levy and its effectiveness.[1] But now in the speech of the officers, this archaic custom, which is really no longer in the least understood, makes its appearance permeated and illuminated by a quite unarchaic and humane mentality.

The fourth problem of the officers is of a quite different kind and, since the speakers are reintroduced here again unnecessarily,v. 8 can easily be recognized as a later accretion. This sentence brings us up once more against the specifically Deuteronomic concern that fear would be lack of faith. Discouragement, regarded as lack of faith, is not only a personal affair for the man who has been assailed by it; it threatens the whole army. All this shows that the regulation about the war speeches in its early stratum in vv. 5–7, 9 may go back to the pre-Deuteronomic period of the monarchy. Verse 8 is an addition which harmonizes with Deuteronomic ideas. The passage about the priest's speech is still later, but it probably refers back to a much earlier sacral institution.

[10–20] The two following laws concerning war, in vv. 10–18 and 19–20, presuppose conditions regarding politics and strategy such

[1] F. Schwally, *Semitische Kriegsaltertümer*, 1901, pp. 75ff.; a somewhat different view in J. Pedersen, *Israel III–IV*, 1940, pp. 8ff.

as are inconceivable before the period of the monarchy. Even if the general levy of the tribal union in the period of the judges had ever actually decided on a regular siege, yet it would certainly never have done so 'very far' away from its own territory (contrast however the episodes in II Kings 3.25f.; or in II Sam. 12.26ff.). Moreover, we have reason to suppose that the amphictyonic levy mainly took the field for defence only. Wars far outside its own territory were first caused by political conflicts of a much more far-reaching nature which arose when Israel itself had become an active factor on the great political scene. Finally we cannot well imagine the ancient levy of the tribes to have had experience of such a complicated siege technique as is taken for granted in v. 20.

The differences in the ordinances concerning the treatment of the besieged cities again shows something of the theoretical nature of Deuteronomy which is easily inclined to be doctrinaire. If such differences in carrying out the ancient commands about the ban occurred here and there in practice, the decision was certainly not made on account of the risk of religious contagion (cf. with this Deut. 21.10ff.). But with Deuteronomy this stands in the foreground, for it was unable to understand Israel's conflict with the Canaanite enclaves in any other way than as a religious and cultic conflict (cf. with this the war sermons in 7.1ff., 16ff.; 9.1ff.). The reason given in v. 18 for the difference in treatment passes into the plural form of address and is perhaps a later amplification. It only expresses what already lay behind the regulations themselves. The fact that Deuteronomy contains in the context of its laws concerning war a rule to protect fruit-growing is probably unique in the history of the growth of a humane outlook in ancient times. Deuteronomy is really concerned to restrain the vandalism of war and not with considerations of utility. The ordinance that no fruit trees are to be used for the necessary siege-works (II Chron. 26.15), of course, takes for granted a wide choice of standing timber, which was not likely to exist everywhere.

CHAPTER 21.1-23

21 ¹'If in the land which the LORD your God gives you to possess, any one is found slain, lying in the open country, and it is not known who killed him, ²then your elders and your judges shall come forth, and they shall measure the distance to the cities which are around him that is slain; ³and the elders of the city which is nearest to the slain man shall take a heifer which has never been worked and which has not pulled in the yoke. ⁴And the elders of that city shall bring the heifer down to a valley with running water, which is neither ploughed nor sown, and shall break the heifer's neck there in the valley. ⁵And the priests, the sons of Levi shall come forward, for the LORD your God has chosen them to minister to him and to bless in the name of the LORD, and by their word every dispute and every assault shall be settled. ⁶And all the elders of that city nearest to the slain man shall wash their hands over the heifer whose neck was broken in the valley; ⁷and they shall testify, "Our hands did not shed this blood, neither did our eyes see it shed. ⁸Forgive, O LORD, thy people Israel, whom thou hast redeemed, and set not the guilt of innocent blood in the midst of thy people Israel; but let the guilt of blood be forgiven them." ⁹So you shall purge the guilt of innocent blood from your midst, when you do what is right in the sight of the LORD.

10 'When you go forth to war against your enemies, and the LORD your God gives them into your hands, and you take them captive, ¹¹and see among the captives a beautiful woman, and you have desire for her and would take her for yourself as wife, ¹²then you shall bring her home to your house, and she shall shave her head and pare her nails. ¹³And she shall put off her captive's garb, and shall remain in your house and bewail her father and her mother a full month; after that you may go in to her, and be her husband, and she shall be your wife. ¹⁴Then, if you have no delight in her, you shall let her go where she will; but you shall not sell her for money, you shall not treat her as a slave, since you have humiliated her.

15 'If a man has two wives, the one loved and the other disliked, and they have borne him children, both the loved and the disliked, and if the first-born son is hers that is disliked, ¹⁶then on the day when he

134

assigns his possessions as an inheritance to his sons, he may not treat the son of the loved as the first-born in preference to the son of the disliked, who is the first-born, [17]but he shall acknowledge the first-born, the son of the disliked, by giving him a double portion of all that he has, for he is the first issue of his strength; the right of the first-born is his.

18 'If a man has a stubborn and rebellious son, who will not obey the voice of his father or the voice of his mother, and, though they chastise him, will not give heed to them, [19]then his father and his mother shall take hold of him and bring him out to the elders of his city at the gate of the place where he lives, [20]and they shall say to the elders of his city, "This our son is stubborn and rebellious, he will not obey our voice; he is a glutton and a drunkard." [21]Then all the men of the city shall stone him to death with stones; so you shall purge the evil from your midst; and all Israel shall hear, and fear.

22 'And if a man has committed a crime punishable by death and he is put to death, and you hang him on a tree, [23]his body shall not remain all night upon the tree, but you shall bury him the same day, for a hanged man is accursed by God; you shall not defile your land which the LORD your God gives you for an inheritance.'

[1–9] The instructions regarding the ritual to be observed in the event of a murder by an unknown hand are among the most interesting material included in Deuteronomy. In the present form of the section ancient customs are woven together with recent institutions and the mature conceptions of a comparatively late period to form one whole, a perfect example of the process. The commentators have always been eager to work out the earliest meaning which can be conjectured for the procedure. The reader of today must above all understand the problem which arose when such a crime was discovered. Thus, just as sexual offences, too, resulted in the land being polluted (see below on Deut. 24.4; Jer. 3.3f.), so a murder involved the community in blood-guilt, and the ideas of the ancients were very realistic about the consequences of such a crime, namely that an actual curse threatened the capacity of the community to worship. If the murderer could be caught, the calamity which had been set in motion could be averted from the community by his death. But what was the position if the murderer remained unknown? Could the community ever at all rid itself of the blood-guilt, now pressing heavily upon it, and of its sinister consequences? In such an unusually serious case ancient Israel knew of a ritual of which the strange details become to some degree intelligible only against the background of antiquity's terror of unexpiated blood-guilt.

Those who performed the sacral operation were originally the elders of the city which lay nearest to the site of the murder. The appearance of 'the priests, the sons of Levi' occurs quite abruptly in v. 5. This passage, as it is easy to recognize, is a not particularly skilful addition. The interpolator was clearly not in a position to assign to the priests a distinct function of their own in the conduct of the operation; they remain on the scene rather like supernumeraries. The mention of the (national) judges also no doubt arises out of the needs of a much later age. The ritual to be performed cannot, in fact, itself be compared in any way with the well-known methods of sacrifice customary in Israel. On the contrary, it differs from them in all details so definitely that we must ask whether we are here concerned with a sacrifice at all. The animal is not even to be killed at a place of worship, but at a place which is the exact opposite, namely a waste plot of land, which has never yet been cultivated. The method of killing, too, breaking the neck, is not that used in sacrificing; the manipulation of the blood, which there is so important, can accordingly also not take place here. The waste plot where the killing has to be carried out, and also the regulation that the animal in question must not be profaned by being used for other purposes beforehand, supports the conjecture that originally it was not a matter of a sacrifice at all. It was, on the contrary, a magical procedure for getting rid of sin, possibly to be compared with the sending away of the scapegoat into a desert place, where according to later Jewish accounts it would plunge to its death (Lev. 16.22). The washing of the hands, which we must picture to ourselves as originally intended to be a real and not a symbolic action, and the elders' confession of innocence in v. 7 might still have belonged to the old pre-Yahwistic ritual, but the whole procedure has been given a new interpretation by the prayer to Yahweh in v. 8. Now it is no longer a magical procedure, efficacious in itself, which diverts the calamity towards an uncultivated area, but it is God who in his mercy purges the guilt. This passage tells decisively against the widespread opinion that it is Yahweh who receives the expiation; on the contrary, he is the real agent in the operation of expiation, for he averts the curse caused by the murder. It is Israel who is the recipient of the expiation. Verse 9 (a concluding formula often found in Deuteronomy; cf. 13.5; 17.7; 19.13 etc.) can only mean, when connected appropriately with what precedes it: 'This is what you must do and how you must pray; then Yahweh will take the blood-guilt away from you.' Understood in this way, that is, as related to Yahweh, the whole ritual has, after all, to be understood as the offering of a sacrifice.

[10–14] The ordinance concerning the marriage of an Israelite with a war captive is in its form a homogeneous whole. It contains no breaks in style, pointing to the revision of older material. Since it is introduced by the same form of words as in Deut. 20.1, it must be placed as regards its origin beside the Deuteronomic law concerning war. As we have it, it is arranged together with two other laws which also deal with questions of family law. This ordinance, too, rests on a humane motive. Even a woman taken captive in war may not be misued; the relationship with her must become a legal one. If it is dissolved, the woman's social status, which has been given her in the meantime, must not be impaired.[1]

As little as possible should be asked about the mourning customs which are taken for granted here. If once in primitive times the purpose of the rites had been to make the survivor unrecognizable by the spirit of the departed one through disfigurement (though other interpretations are possible), the Deuteronomist no longer understood them in this sense and evidently considered them an inoffensive usage. Nor can we explain any longer why the customs mentioned in Deut. 14.1 are judged more severely. But the whole regulation is important because it shows how little even in such an advanced period the family was considered to be the real mainstay of the religion of Yahweh. It is still far from the thoughts of the lawgiver that the household could be infected by a foreign religion through a woman with a background of quite different cultic loyalties. The mainstays of the religion of Yahweh in this period, too, were the men and the great public institutions, and not, as we like to imagine, the houses and the families. Only in the period immediately after the Exile does a change seem to have taken place in this matter. It was only then that the danger to religion from the foreign woman attracted attention (Ezra 9f.; Neh. 10.30; 13.23).

[15–17] The law of succession of the first-born differs from the preceding ordinance in that it is not composed in the second person singular, but in the impersonal legal style throughout. As a result no trace of the specifically Deuteronomic method of framing laws can be recognized in it. In accordance with this law of inheritance only the sons are heirs. The discussion of the complication

[1] On the difficult expression *hit'ammēr* in vv. 14f. see A. Alt, *VT* 2, 1952, pp. 153ff.

arising from the lack of male descendants (cf. Num. 27.1–11) could be omitted here, because the law only intends to guard against an arbitrary action which might occur if there are two sons born to different mothers. The strong preference shown to the first-born when the inheritance is divided seems to have been an old custom in Israel (Gen. 27; 48.14). Yet the Deuteronomic rule differs from earlier usages in that it makes the concept of the first-born, in the biological sense, an absolute one and guarantees it against any arbitrary attempt to make it a relative one. (On the double portion of the inheritance for the first-born, cf. II Kings 2.9.)

[18–21] The rule about the action to be taken against a rebellious son is also composed, like the previous one, in the neutral conditional style. Only at the very end in v. 21aβ does it pass into the hortatory style of the second person singular. When set against the only comparable piece of legal history which we possess, namely, the sentence of death passed by Judah upon his daughter-in-law in Gen. 38.24, our law represents a much later stage of development. The head of the family has no jurisdiction of his own over the adult members of his family; he must hand the case over to those who administer justice, namely, the elders of his city. Nor is it unimportant that the mother has to appear as a competent plaintiff. Evidently the lawgiver insists on both parents acting in agreement when they decide upon this final step. (Yahweh's indictment in Isa. 1.2 is to be understood with this legal possibility available to the father in mind. Yahweh has decided upon this final action and accuses his own son in open court.)

[22–23] The regulation about the body of a man who has been hanged, one of those in the second person singular, starts from the very ancient conception that the land must be protected against ritual pollution (see above on Deut. 21.1ff.). From this point of view the customary degrading exhibition of the corpse should be limited in time. The maxim in v. 23 explaining the reason for the ordinance uses as an argument a conception which must have been generally widespread, namely, that the corpse of a hanged man is a threat to the cultic purity of the land, and thus might interfere with its yield. On the hanging up of a corpse after execution cf. Josh. 8.29; 10.26f.; II Sam. 4.12; 21.8f. The maxim about being cast out into the domain of the curse appears again, used by Paul in Gal. 3.13, as a weighty argument in a christological discussion.

CHAPTER 22.1-30

22 ¹'You shall not see your brother's ox or his sheep go astray, and withhold your help from them; you shall take them back to your brother. ²And if he is not near you, or if you do not know him, you shall bring it home to your house, and it shall be with you until your brother seeks it; then you shall restore it to him. ³And so you shall do with his ass; so you shall do with his garment; so you shall do with any lost thing of your brother's, which he loses and you find; you may not withhold your help. ⁴You shall not see your brother's ass or his ox fallen down by the way, and withhold your help from them; you shall help him to lift them up again.

5 'A woman shall not wear anything that pertains to a man, nor shall a man put on a woman's garment; for whoever does these things is an abomination to the LORD your God.

6 'If you chance to come upon a bird's nest, in any tree or on the ground, with young ones or eggs and the mother sitting upon the young or upon the eggs, you shall not take the mother with the young; ⁷you shall let the mother go, but the young you may take to yourself; that it may go well with you, and that you may live long.

8 'When you build a new house, you shall make a parapet for your roof, that you may not bring the guilt of blood upon your house, if any one fall from it.

9 'You shall not sow your vineyard with two kinds of seed, lest the whole yield be forfeited to the sanctuary, the crop which you have sown and the yield of the vineyard. ¹⁰You shall not plough with an ox and an ass together. ¹¹You shall not wear a mingled stuff, wool and linen together.

12 'You shall make yourself tassels on the four corners of your cloak with which you cover yourself.

13 'If any man takes a wife, and goes in to her, and then spurns her, ¹⁴and charges her with shameful conduct, and brings an evil name upon her, saying, "I took this woman, and when I came near her, I did not find in her the tokens of virginity", ¹⁵then the father of the young woman and her mother shall take and bring out the tokens of her virginity to the elders of the city in the gate; ¹⁶and the father of the

young woman shall say to the elders, "I gave my daughter to this man to wife, and he spurns her; [17]and lo, he has made shameful charges against her, saying, 'I did not find in your daughter the tokens of virginity.' And yet these are the tokens of my daughter's virginity." And they shall spread the garment before the elders of the city. [18]Then the elders of that city shall take the man and whip him; [19]and they shall fine him a hundred shekels of silver, and give them to the father of the young woman, because he has brought an evil name upon a virgin of Israel; and she shall be his wife; he may not put her away all his days. [20]But if the thing is true, that the tokens of virginity were not found in the young woman, [21]then they shall bring out the young woman to the door of her father's house, and the men of her city shall stone her to death with stones, because she has wrought folly in Israel by playing the harlot in her father's house; so you shall purge the evil from the midst of you.

22 'If a man is found lying with the wife of another man, both of them shall die, the man who lay with the woman, and the woman; so you shall purge the evil from Israel.

23 'If there is a betrothed virgin, and a man meets her in the city and lies with her, [24]then you shall bring them both out to the gate of that city, and you shall stone them to death with stones, the young woman because she did not cry for help though she was in the city, and the man because he violated his neighbour's wife; so you shall purge the evil from the midst of you.

25 'But if in the open country a man meets a young woman who is betrothed, and the man seizes her and lies with her, then only the man who lay with her shall die. [26]But to the young woman you shall do nothing; in the young woman there is no offence punishable by death, for this case is like that of a man attacking and murdering his neighbour; [27]because he came upon her in the open country, and though the betrothed young woman cried for help there was no one to rescue her.

28 'If a man meets a virgin who is not betrothed, and seizes her and lies with her, and they are found, [29]then the man who lay with her shall give to the father of the young woman fifty shekels of silver, and she shall be his wife, because he has violated her; he may not put her away all his days.

30 'A man shall not take his father's wife, nor shall he uncover her who is his father's.'

[1-4] The ordinance about the care of domestic animals which have strayed is already found in the Book of the Covenant in Ex. 23.4f., where however it applies even to the cattle of 'thine enemy'. But this difference is not to be explained by the fact that the stricter demand, which is harder to fulfil, was modified in course of time in favour of a more convenient conception, according to which such

services are only to be rendered to one's 'brother'. In the Book of the Covenant the ordinance appears within a group of laws all dealing with behaviour in cases of legal proceedings. Hence the meaning of the ordinance in that book is no doubt that even the fact of a conflict in a lawsuit does not exonerate a man from the general duty of rendering help.[1] In Deuteronomy on the other hand this ordinance has been reduced to the most general terms. It applies to every fellow-countryman.

[5–12] In the ordinance about clothing in v. 5 something more is involved than mere observance of what is seemly, or obedience to a rule prescribed by nature. The reason offered makes use of a very weighty argument ('an abomination to Yahweh'), which suggests some cultic offence. The formula 'an abomination to Yahweh' denotes cultic taboos which endanger the purity of the religion of Yahweh. We learn from later sources (Lucian of Samosata) that in the worship of Astarte such masquerading took place.

By contrast, the ordinance about behaviour towards birds sitting on a nest can probably be attributed only to humane motives and hardly to considerations of utility. A different reason is assigned for the rule about making a parapet for the flat roof of the house; here it is a matter of blood-guilt which would rest on the house, and would indeed endanger the capacity for worship of the community. The ordinance against mingling dissimilar things in vv. 9–11 prohibits age-old magic customs which it is hard to suppose were still a real danger to the faith of Yahweh at the period of Deuteronomy (but cf. Lev. 19.19). Perhaps the law was handed on without the old significance of the prohibited customs being known. Contrary to our legislator's habit, the ordinance about wearing tassels on the cloak lacks any explanation. One is supplied in Num. 15.37–41. Evidently here, too, it has to do originally with a magical apotropaic custom; but as it was possible to reinterpret it so completely in an educational sense (as a warning and reminder to observe the commandments), it has been retained; indeed, the law demanded that it should be obeyed.

[13–21] There follows next a whole group of ordinances dealing with family law. The first one in vv. 13–21 is remarkably clearly set out and is clothed in the objectively judicial language of conditional law. Only at the end of each of the two parts of the law the lawgiver departs from the style of objective statements and allows himself to

[1] See M. Noth, *ad loc.*, *Exodus*, p. 189.

add a reason explaining the judgment (vv. 19, 21). A change of style does not occur until right at the end in the hortatory closing formula in the last part of v. 21b (it appears again in v. 22b). The arrangement of the section is as follows: First, the legal case: a man brings against the woman whom he has taken as his wife the accusation that he did not find her to be a virgin; this is evidently an unjust accusation for the purpose of being able to divorce her. Secondly, the procedure: the legal defence of a woman who has fallen into disrepute in this way must be undertaken by her father (and according to v. 15a by her mother as well). He must bring his complaint before the elders, who are the persons duly authorized to administer justice in that place. As evidence they shall produce the garment, used to cover the bed (Ex. 22.25f.), with the bloodstains resulting from the first co-habitation (according to Arabic sources the parents of the bride used to preserve this garment). By this means the man is convicted and there follows, thirdly, the decision. It is very remarkable and certainly a sign of advanced administration of justice that the slanderer receives a double punishment, a corporal one and in addition a fine (the hypothesis that the verb *yissēr* in v. 18 only means to 'censure', to 'reprimand' is unlikely). Moreover, the man loses the right ever again to send his wife away by divorcing her. The reason given for the punishment, 'because he has brought an evil name upon a virgin of Israel', still has something of the proud self-respect of the earlier Israel (cf. on this II Sam. 13.12).

Verses 20f. regulate the other possibility in the case: namely, that the man's accusation was based on the truth. In this event the woman must be stoned in front of her parents' house. Here also the reason given is the fame of 'Israel' (and this means here, as always in Deuteronomy, the sacral tribal union, not the kingdom of Israel), in the area of which a crime has been committed. The expression *nebala* is often translated by 'folly'; but it denotes a primary breach of a sacral law, especially of laws dealing with sexual matters (Gen. 34.7; Judg. 19.23; 20.6–10; II Sam. 13.12).

[22–29] Unchastity with a married woman is punished by the death of the two parties concerned, similarly unchastity with a betrothed woman. However, in the latter case the place where the offence is committed makes a difference. If it took place in the open country the lawgiver takes for granted that the girl was raped against her will; her appeal to the legal protection of the community (*ṣāʿaq*) was merely not heard. Our customary translation 'betrothed' is, in fact, not quite correct, because it concerns a girl in whose case all the legal business preceding the marriage, in particular the payment of the *mōhar*, has been completed, and thereby all the impediments to the marriage have been removed. The lawgiver expresses a different opinion about the rape of a girl who is not betrothed (vv. 28f.). In this case the man is forced to pay the customary bride-price (*mōhar*) and to marry the girl; he is not allowed ever to send her away.

At the end of this group of homogeneous legal maxims, all framed in the conditional style, there is an apodictic command with a very different origin (v. 30). It resembles the group of very ancient commands in Lev. 18.6ff., and also in Deut. 27.20. In these passages we are dealing with ordinances which regulate a definite sociological form of community life, namely the living together in the framework of the 'extended family'. Hence they are ordinances which from their nature reach back into times very early in the period before the existence of the State.[1]

[1] K. Elliger, 'Das Gesetz Leviticus 18', *ZAW* 67, 1955, pp. 1ff.

CHAPTER 23.1-25

23 'He whose testicles are crushed or whose male member is cut off shall not enter the assembly of the LORD.

2 'No bastard shall enter the assembly of the LORD; even to the tenth generation none of his descendants shall enter the assembly of the LORD.

3 'No Ammonite or Moabite shall enter the assembly of the LORD; even to the tenth generation none belonging to them shall enter the assembly of the LORD for ever; 4because they did not meet you with bread and with water on the way, when you came forth out of Egypt, and because they hired against you Balaam the son of Beor from Pethor of Mesopotamia, to curse you. 5Nevertheless the LORD your God would not hearken to Balaam; but the LORD your God turned the curse into a blessing for you, because the LORD your God loved you. 6You shall not seek their peace or their prosperity all your days for ever.

7 'You shall not abhor an Edomite, for he is your brother; you shall not abhor an Egyptian, because you were a sojourner in his land. 8The children of the third generation that are born to them may enter the assembly of the LORD.

9 'When you go forth against your enemies and are in camp, then you shall keep yourself from every evil thing.

10 'If there is among you any man who is not clean by reason of what chances to him by night, then he shall go outside the camp, he shall not come within the camp; 11but when evening comes on, he shall bathe himself in water, and when the sun is down, he may come within the camp.

12 'You shall have a place outside the camp and you shall go out to it; 13and you shall have a stick with your weapons; and when you sit down outside, you shall dig a hole with it, and turn back and cover up your excrement. 14Because the LORD your God walks in the midst of your camp, to save you and to give up your enemies before you, therefore your camp must be holy, that he may not see anything indecent among you, and turn away from you.

15 'You shall not give up to his master a slave who has escaped from his master to you; 16he shall dwell with you, in your midst, in the place

144

which he shall choose within one of your towns, where it pleases him best; you shall not oppress him.

17 'There shall be no cult prostitute of the daughters of Israel, neither shall there be a cult prostitute of the sons of Israel. 18You shall not bring the hire of a harlot, or the wages of a dog, into the house of the LORD your God in payment for any vow; for both of these are an abomination to the LORD your God.

19 'You shall not lend upon interest to your brother, interest on money, interest on victuals, interest on anything that is lent for interest. 20To a foreigner you may lend upon interest, but to your brother you shall not lend upon interest; that the LORD your God may bless you in all that you undertake in the land which you are entering to take possession of it.

21 'When you make a vow to the LORD your God, you shall not be slack to pay it; for the LORD your God will surely require it of you, and it would be sin in you. 22But if you refrain from vowing, it shall be no sin in you. 23You shall be careful to perform what has passed your lips, for you have voluntarily vowed to the LORD your God what you have promised with your mouth.

24 'When you go into your neighbour's vineyard, you may eat your fill of grapes, as many as you wish, but you shall not put any in your vessel. 25When you go into your neighbour's standing grain, you may pluck the ears with your hand, but you shall not put a sickle to your neighbour's standing grain.'

[1–8] In the law concerning the assembly in vv. 1–8 a splendid piece of ancient Yahwistic legal matter has been preserved for us.[1] It consists of a series in five parts in apodictic style; it is thus a text which must be considered first as a definite unit. It can easily be seen that it is now interspersed with a variety of interpretative expansions. Thus the somewhat long-winded reason based on an episode of salvation history in vv. 4–5 is couched in a style quite different from the vigorous prohibitions (for this reason cf. Num. 20.14ff.). Nevertheless, it is not easy to reconstruct the series in its original form. Did the passage about the tenth (third) generation in vv. 2, 3 and 8 belong to it? The prohibition in v. 6 is probably an expansion, since it uses the second person singular. Ancient series of commandments like these were originally framed in a uniform style, but here three items in it begin with 'no . . . shall enter', whilst two start with 'Thou shalt not abhor'. Hence it is natural to assume that the present series must be regarded as having been composed out of even earlier components.

[1] K. Galling, 'Das Gemeindegesetz in Dt. 23', Festschrift für A. Bertholet, 1950, pp. 176ff.

The Hebrew word which can be translated as 'assembly' (*qāhāl*)
denotes the cultic levy (the Norse *Thing*) of the free men, whether for
purposes of war or for the annual feasts, that is to say, for events at
which the sacral union of the tribes appeared in full array. We may
think here of events such as are narrated in Judg. 20.1, 18; I Sam.
1.3; 11.6ff. Of course, only the worshippers of Yahweh took part in
this levy. Yet at the fringes, so to speak, the question might arise
whether members of other nations, especially those who had perhaps
lived for generations as aliens in Israel, might be allowed to join in
the levy. At that time membership could, in fact, only involve taking
a full share in all the concerns of the cultic assembly. So it is astonishing in view of the harsh exclusiveness of the religion of Yahweh
towards other cults that the series did not insist on a wholesale rejection. But this exclusiveness was perhaps harsher in theory than in
practice. It is difficult to discover the reason for the preferential
treatment of the Edomites and the Egyptians. It is unlikely to be
found in certain positive political connexions of these nations with
Israel. Here the determining factor was probably really of cultic
origin which was comparatively independent of the fluctuating good-
will or ill-will in political relations. Moreover, in our text we must
distinguish between arguments concerned originally entirely with cult
and ritual and later arguments based on salvation history. The
Hebrew equivalent for our 'ahbor' (*tᵉaʿēb*) means here 'to treat as unclean from the point of view of the cult' (cf. Deut. 7.26).

The exclusion of mutilated men in v. 1 also indicates that the
criteria for admission and exclusion were originally entirely concerned
with cult and ritual (cf. on this Lev. 21.16ff.). We do not know what is
meant precisely by a bastard (*mamzēr*). The later Jewish exegesis con-
nects it with cases such as those of which an account is given in Neh.
13.23 (a prophetic instruction in a completely opposite sense, dating
from a period which had outgrown the old sacral ordinances, occurs
in Isa. 56.3ff.). So we have here an ordinance concerning the assembly which has not been fashioned by one period alone. In its early
shape it certainly reaches back to the time before there was a state in
Israel.

[9–14] The law of the camp takes us into a quite similar mental
atmosphere, in so far as these rules, too, are determined by the cultic
and ritual assumptions of early holy wars. Israel knew that in these
it was standing especially close and unprotected in Yahweh's field of
operation. Therefore everything that was displeasing to Yahweh must

bc eliminated with more than usual care, that is to say, the camp must be 'holy'. The concept of holiness does not mean, as can be well perceived here, a particular enhancement of human moral qualities. It takes Yahweh's favour towards his people for granted and means at first simply the condition of being set apart for Yahweh and for his plans in history. The demand made on Israel was thus merely the observance of some few ritual customs. By means of these it kept itself aloof from the sphere of unclean things, to which in particular all excretions of the body belonged (cf. Lev. 15; Num. 5.1–4). The reason given as an explanation in v. 14, 'because Yahweh walks in the midst of your camp', sounds a little as though it were addressed to people who had to be made aware of this aspect of the matter for the first time. But if it was necessary to make the cultic customs intelligible to such an extent, the time had already passed away when their validity was taken for granted. Consequently we are probably dealing here rather with an old ordinance which has been revived. The style of the whole section supports this. It is not composed in the terms of the genuinely old sacral ordinances, but in that conditional sermon-style which is so characteristic of many 'laws' in Deuteronomy.

[15–16] There are many reasons for thinking that the runaway slave who is to be given the right to dwell in Israel is considered as a man coming from a foreign country. Otherwise the legal aspect of the affair could not be so easily ignored, for the slave was, in fact, a valuable possession of his master. The phrase 'in your midst' in v. 16 also supports the supposition that Israel as a whole is addressed here. Such fugitives may at times have become a real national nuisance (I Sam. 25.10) because, combined with other groups, they formed a fluctuating and by no means harmless class at the bottom of society (I Sam. 22.2). Non-Israelite legal codes also had to concern themselves with this problem. It is regulated by them in the same way by means of agreements between states (e.g. by Alalak). Of course, in the case of slaves it could not be a question of a formal application for asylum. There was all the greater need of an appeal to regulate such cases in a humane spirit. The rule is intended above all to prevent anyone from exploiting the precarious position of the slave and from reducing him again to slavery (for that is, in fact, the exact meaning in law of the verb *yānā*; cf. Ex. 22.21; Lev. 19.33).

[17–18] This section has to do with a religious phenomenon alien to Western man, but all the more dangerous to early Israel, namely sacral prostitution, which was firmly embedded in the fertility cult

(Ishtar-Astarte) of the whole ancient East from Cyprus to Babylon. Women especially offered themselves to sanctuaries in consequence of a vow (Herodotus I, 199). In addition cult prostitutes of both sexes were available at the sanctuaries, which acquired money by this means. Yet the expression 'the wages of a dog' is probably not to be understood in a derogatory sense, as has usually been thought. Outside Israel, too, 'dog' is used to indicate a cult individual dedicated to a deity.[1] Deuteronomy is particularly harsh in attacking these Canaanite cultic practices, which had penetrated into Israel as well during the period of the monarchy (I Kings 14.24; II Kings 23.7).

[19–20] The prohibition against taking interest from a fellow-countryman (cf. Lev. 25.35ff.), actually known amongst other nations too, arose from the consciousness of a blood-brotherhood which was still alive amongst early people. The enormous height of the rates of interest in those days (between twenty and fifty per cent) must also be remembered. Since Israel even as late as the time of Deuteronomy was almost exclusively a nation of peasants, it was really only foreigners who acted as traders and merchants (cf. Neh. 10.31; 13.15ff.). Occasionally the word 'Canaanite' means simply trader (Zech. 14.21; Prov. 31.24). The lawgiver raises no objection against taking interest from these foreigners.

[21–26] If we may assume that the subject-matter in vv. 15–20 goes back to early commandments, the passage about the vow appears somewhat odd beside it, since it concerns a matter which could certainly never become the subject of legal regulation. It is more likely to be a piece of advice from the sphere of proverbial wisdom, where, in fact, we find a similar admonition (Eccles 5.4ff.). But then the Deuteronomic preachers did not treat only of legal matters. Perhaps the case of the rule concerning 'pilfering food' is similar; it is probably intended to express a humane custom rather than a legal rule in the narrower sense of the word.

---

[1] D. Winton Thomas, 'Kelebh, "Dog": its Origin and Some Usages of it in the Old Testament', *VT* 10, 1960, pp. 424ff.

CHAPTER 24.1-22

24 ¹ 'When a man takes a wife and marries her, if then she finds no favour in his eyes because he has found some indecency in her, and he writes her a bill of divorce and puts it in her hand and sends her out of his house, and she departs out of his house, ²and if she goes and becomes another man's wife, ³and the latter husband dislikes her and writes her a bill of divorce and puts it in her hand and sends her out of his house, or if the latter husband dies, who took her to be his wife, ⁴then her former husband, who sent her away, may not take her again to be his wife, after she has been defiled; for that is an abomination before the LORD, and you shall not bring guilt upon the land which the LORD your God gives you for an inheritance.

5 'When a man is newly married, he shall not go out with the army or be charged with any business; he shall be free at home one year, to be happy with his wife whom he has taken.

6 'No man shall take a mill or an upper millstone in pledge; for he would be taking a life in pledge.

7 'If a man is found stealing one of his brethren, the people of Israel, and if he treats him as a slave or sells him, then that thief shall die; so you shall purge the evil from the midst of you.

8 'Take heed, in an attack of leprosy, to be very careful to do accord-to all that the Levitical priests shall direct you; as I commanded them, so you shall be careful to do. ⁹Remember what the LORD your God did to Miriam on the way as you came forth out of Egypt.

10 'When you make your neighbour a loan of any sort, you shall not go into his house to fetch his pledge. ¹¹You shall stand outside, and the man to whom you make the loan shall bring the pledge out to you. ¹²And if he is a poor man, you shall not sleep in his pledge; ¹³when the sun goes down, you shall restore to him the pledge that he may sleep in his cloak and bless you; and it shall be righteousness to you before the LORD your God.

14 'You shall not oppress a hired servant who is poor and needy, whether he is one of your brethren or one of the sojourners who are in your land within your towns;¹⁵you shall give him his hire on the day he earns it, before the sun goes down (for he is poor, and sets his heart

upon it); lest he cry against you to the LORD, and it be sin in you.
16 'The fathers shall not be put to death for the children, nor shall
the children be put to death for the fathers; every man shall be put to
death for his own sin.

17 'You shall not pervert the justice due to the sojourner or to the
fatherless, or take a widow's garment in pledge; 18but you shall remember that you were a slave in Egypt and the LORD your God redeemed
you from there; therefore I command you to do this.

19 'When you reap your harvest in your field, and have forgotten a
sheaf in the field, you shall not go back to get it; it shall be for the sojourner, the fatherless, and the widow; that the LORD your God may
bless you in all the work of your hands. 20When you beat your olive
trees, you shall not go over the boughs again; it shall be for the sojourner, the fatherless, and the widow. 21When you gather the grapes
of your vineyard, you shall not glean it afterward; it shall be for the
sojourner, the fatherless, and the widow. 22You shall remember that you
were a slave in the land of Egypt; therefore I command you to do this.'

[1–4] The law does not deal with divorce in general, but with the
impossibility of remarrying a woman who has been separated from
her husband once already. The legal case is thus a very special one.
Hence the lawgiver, in spite of the utmost economy of language,
requires a whole series of protases in order to describe its preliminary
history (for this style of composition cf. Ex. 21.1–6). The apodosis
with the binding legal decision only appears at v. 4. The meaning of
'indecent', 'objectionable' (cf. 23.14) must have been clear in the
time of Deuteronomy; otherwise the matter would certainly have
been defined more exactly. By Jesus' time it was being debated in the
rabbinical schools whether in such cases a lapse on the part of the
woman is in mind or whether she possessed some repellent quality.
The law refrains from giving a real reason for the negative decision.
It contents itself with the very archaic comment that to remarry this
woman would be 'an abomination before the Lord'. Thus the legal
decision rests on very ancient cultic conceptions (see above on 22.5).
The same applies also to the additional reason given in v. 4b. In the
Old Testament we often meet the realistic conception that unchastity
defiles the land (Lev. 18.25, 28; 19.29; Num. 5.3; Hos. 4.3; Jer.
3.2, 9). This ordinance troubled Jeremiah when considering Yahweh's relationship to Israel (Jer. 3.1ff.). Hosea 3 is possibly dealing
with an actual suspension of this law. In Hosea's view what is impossible for the law is, in fact, done by God.[1]

[1] H. W. Wolff, *Hosea* (Biblischer Kommentar), 1956, *ad loc.*

[5–13] On the release of a newly married man from military service cf. 20.7 The prohibition against taking a mill or a millstone in pledge might well be an isolated apodictic instruction. As a rule the women ground and baked bread for one day at a time. A pledge of this kind would deprive a poor man of the necessities of life. On the other hand, the regulation about pledges in vv. 10–13, composed now in the style of a sermon, seems to have been originally at one time a piece of case-law. The legal and economic conditions are extremely simple ones, such as can be supposed to exist only in settlements of small farmers. The meaning of this instruction, by being turned into an exhortation, has been twisted from a humanitarian rule into a theological one. The gratitude of the man who has been treated with consideration will bring blessing on the man who was considerate to him. On the question of imputing righteousness see above on 6.25.

On the commandment in v. 7 which is composed in the conditional style and deals with stealing a man, see above on 5.19. In the section about leprosy in vv. 8–9 the passage about the Levitical priests must be judged to be a secondary addition, not only because it passes into the second person plural, but particularly because it changes abruptly into the form of direct speech by God which is quite alien to Deuteronomy. In Israel the priests were responsible both for the diagnosis and also for the treatment of severe illnesses, since such a serious threat to life affected directly a man's relationship to God. The expression 'act of God' (*nega‘*) is evidently an ancient priestly technical term. Cf. on this and on sacral medicine Lev. 13–14. As happens so frequently, Deuteronomy underlines the urgency of its exhortation by referring to an example taken from the old salvation history (Num. 12.9ff.). Here we cannot, of course, take it implicitly for granted that our passage must have been acquainted merely with this version of the tradition.

[14–18] The apodictic command not to curtail (*‘āšaq* is a technical term for unlawful behaviour, cf. I Sam. 12.3f.; Ezek. 18.18; Micah 2.2) the rights of the hired servant resembles the rule about taking pledges in vv. 10–13, for it brings the originally humanitarian motive into the sphere of religion by commanding that the poor man must not be obliged to appeal to God against his oppressor. Evidently the commandments in v. 14a and v. 17 also belong together on account of their related subject-matter. We can reconstruct out of them the fragment of a sequence of commandments:

v. 14 You shall not oppress a hired servant.
v. 17 You shall not pervert the justice due to the sojourner.
You shall not take a widow's garment in pledge.

The regulation that fathers shall not be put to death for their children, nor children for their fathers, seems to contain a rather revolutionary innovation in the administration of justice in early Israel. For in earlier days executions are reported which were carried out according to the law of corporate liability, so that the whole family was involved in the calamity which befell the guilty person (Josh. 7.24f.; II Sam. 3.29; 21.1ff.). However, it is related of King Amaziah that, contrary to the prevailing custom, he let himself be guided by this regulation when executing his father's murderers (II Kings 14.6). But it has become doubtful whether so revolutionary a change in the legal practice of ancient Israel may be read into this account found within the scheme of the Deuteronomistic historical work. A thorough study of early legal history, including that outside Israel, has shown that the conception of a general development from collective to individual liability is incorrect. The principle of personal responsibility was by no means unknown in the earlier times. The whole Book of the Covenant knows nothing of such corporate liability within the family. Therefore we must reckon with the possibility that our Deuteronomic regulation is after all much earlier than was formerly assumed.

[19–22] In this section very ancient rules about the harvest are put together; they forbid gleaning when gathering the crop in the cornfields, olive orchards or vineyards. The memory of the originally sacral background (leaving something for the deity or the spirits of the fields?) has certainly disappeared here. The rules now appeal exclusively to the social and humane attitude of the owner towards the economically weak.

25 ¹'If there is a dispute between men, and they come into court, and the judges decide between them, acquitting the innocent and condemning the guilty, ²then if the guilty man deserves to be beaten, the judge shall cause him to lie down and be beaten in his presence with a number of stripes in proportion to his offence. ³Forty stripes may be given him, but not more; lest, if one should go on to beat him with more stripes than these, your brother be degraded in your sight.

4 'You shall not muzzle an ox when it treads out the grain.

5 'If brothers dwell together, and one of them dies and has no son, the wife of the dead shall not be married outside the family to a stranger; her husband's brother shall go in to her, and take her as his wife, and perform the duty of a husband's brother to her. ⁶And the first son whom she bears shall succeed to the name of his brother who is dead, that his name may not be blotted out of Israel. ⁷And if the man does not wish to take his brother's wife, then his brother's wife shall go up to the gate to the elders, and say, "My husband's brother refuses to perpetuate his brother's name in Israel; he will not perform the duty of a husband's brother to me." ⁸Then the elders of his city shall call him, and speak to him: and if he persists, saying, "I do not wish to take her", ⁹then his brother's wife shall go up to him in the presence of the elders, and pulls his sandal off his foot, and spit in his face; and she shall answer and say, "So shall it be done to the man who does not build up his brother's house." ¹⁰And the name of his house shall be called in Israel, The house of him that had his sandal pulled off.

11 'When men fight with one another, and the wife of the one draws near to rescue her husband from the hand of him who is beating him, and puts out her hand and seizes him by the private parts, ¹²then you shall cut off her hand; your eye shall have no pity.

13 'You shall not have in your bag two kinds of weights, a large and a small. ¹⁴You shall not have in your house two kinds of measures, a large and a small. ¹⁵A full and just weight you shall have, a full and just measure you shall have; that your days may be prolonged in the land which the LORD your God gives you. ¹⁶For all who do such things, all who act dishonestly, are an abomination to the LORD your God.

153

17 'Remember what Amalek did to you on the way as you came out of Egypt, [18]how he attacked you on the way, when you were faint and weary, and cut off at your rear all who lagged behind you; and he did not fear God. [19]Therefore when the LORD your God has given you rest from all your enemies round about, in the land which the LORD your God gives you for an inheritance to possess, you shall blot out the remembrance of Amalek from under heaven; you shall not forget.'

[1-3] The regulation concerning the observance of due limits when inflicting a beating as a punishment approaches the matter from the outside in a curiously roundabout manner. It starts from the dispute which has arisen, moves on to the appeal to the court and its procedure and concludes with the condemnation. The beating imposed is to be measured in proportion to the seriousness of the offence, yet it shall not exceed a definite number of strokes. The lawgiver does not really let himself be guided here by theological considerations, but rather by the concept of human dignity which may not be offended. What kind of office must we suppose the 'judge' to hold who is mentioned in v. 2? See above on 16.18. The prohibition against muzzling the ox when it draws the threshing-sledge over the heaped grain springs, like the rules in Duet. 22.4, 6, from an animal-loving attitude. We should be inclined to look for its original setting in the ancient tribal ethos. (See on this the Introduction, p. 18.)

[5-10] This regulation deals with the case of a man's refusal to marry his brother's widow. Its form is again an exellent example of those accurately expressed and circumspect conditional legal maxims by means of which disputes within the local community (v. 8a) were settled. The custom by which the marriage of a man who dies before he has produced a male descendent must be continued by one of his brothers is known to us in the legal system of other nations also. The purpose of this custom was 'to raise up' the name of the dead man (Ruth 4.5, 10) and to 'build up his house' (v. 9). Yet economic motives, such as keeping the family property together, may also have been the controlling factor. This legal arrangement seems to assume, at any rate as regards Israel, the existence of the 'extended family', that is to say, the living together of all the sons and daughters-in-law under the jurisdiction of the paternal head of the family, in circumstances such as are presupposed in the story of Tamar in Gen. 38. Our law, too, assumes that the brothers are living together (v. 5). Indeed, it really gives the impression that it is considered valid only

if this can be taken for granted. But the legal case described here probably assumes that the supreme head of the family is no longer alive, or that in the course of the dissolution of the extended family he has already surrendered his authority to make legal decisions. So his place is simply taken by the legal regulation. A further difference appears in contrast to Gen. 38, which can be interpreted as a sign of a certain decay of the ancient custom. It consists in the fact that according to the Deuteronomic conception the custom assumes a certain degree of choice. We do not know whether the humiliating ceremony in v. 9 had special legal consequences as well. But we must exercise care when making a comparison with the working out of the levirate ordinance in Ruth 4, because, in the case described in that book, Ruth's brothers-in-law are no longer available. Moreover, the situation there is made more complicated by its combination with the duty of redemption (Lev. 25.25).

[11–12] The regulation in these verses must go back to a particular legal case, and people have certainly been justified in enquiring why the decision based on such a peculiar case had to be raised to a law of general validity. The punishment of corporal mutilation is frequently mentioned in the Code of Hammurabi, but is not provided for elsewhere in Israel's legislation.

[13–16] This section consists of two apodictic prohibitions, which in vv. 15–16 are inculcated once more by exhortation. The regulation (cf. Lev. 19.35f.) is to be explained by the lack of official standards of weights and measures (Amos 8.5).

[17–19] The section about the Amalekites cannot have belonged to the preceding collection of legal regulations which are presented in a more or less hortatory manner. But we must reflect that this legal part of Deuteronomy comes to an end with ch. 25, since from Deut. 26 onwards there follow rituals and liturgical texts. Thus the addition of an appendix becomes easier to understand. Strange to say, the encounter with the Amalekites is described in greater detail and in a manner less creditable to Israel than in Ex. 17.8–16, which is probably an earlier account. Were yet other traditions still current in certain circles in the period of Deuteronomy? And, above all, what could be the contemporary significance of demanding this duty at a time when this notorious Bedouin tribe was hardly likely to be any longer in existence? Evidently we have here a regulation expounded in a theoretical way on the basis of the traditions of salvation history.

CHAPTER 26.1-19

26 ¹'When you come into the land which the LORD your God gives you for an inheritance, and have taken possession of it, and live in it, ²you shall take some of the first of all the fruit of the ground, which you harvest from your land that the LORD your God gives you, and you shall put it in a basket, and you shall go to the place which the LORD your God will choose, to make his name to dwell there. ³And you shall go to the priest who is in office at that time, and say to him, "I declare this day to the LORD your God that I have come into the land which the LORD swore to our fathers to give us." ⁴Then the priest shall take the basket from your hand, and set it down before the altar of the LORD your God.

5 'And you shall make response before the LORD your God, "A wandering Aramean was my father; and he went down into Egypt and sojourned there, few in number; and there he became a nation, great, mighty, and populous. ⁶And the Egyptians treated us harshly, and afflicted us, and laid upon us hard bondage. ⁷Then we cried to the LORD the God of our fathers, and the LORD heard our voice, and saw our affliction, our toil, and our oppression; ⁸and the LORD brought us out of Egypt with a mighty hand and an outstretched arm, with great terror, with signs and wonders; ⁹and he brought us into this place and gave us this land, a land flowing with milk and honey. ¹⁰And behold, now I bring the first of the fruit of the ground, which thou, O LORD, hast given me." And you shall set it down before the LORD your God, and worship before the LORD your God; ¹¹and you shall rejoice in all the good which the LORD your God has given to you and to your house, you, and the Levite, and the sojourner who is among you.

12 'When you have finished paying all the tithe of your produce in the third year, which is the year of tithing, giving it to the Levite, the sojourner, the fatherless, and the widow, that they may eat within your towns and be filled, ¹³then you shall say before the LORD your God, "I have removed the sacred portion out of my house, and moreover I have given it to the Levite, the sojourner, the fatherless, and the widow, according to all thy commandment which thou hast commanded me; I have not transgressed any of thy commandments, neither have I for-

gotten them; [14]I have not eaten of the tithe while I was mourning, or removed any of it while I was unclean, or offered any of it to the dead; I have obeyed the voice of the LORD my God, I have done according to all that thou hast commanded me. [15]Look down from thy holy habitation, from heaven, and bless the people Israel and the ground which thou hast given us, as thou didst swear to our fathers, a land flowing with milk and honey."

16 'This day the LORD your God commands you to do these statutes and ordinances; you shall therefore be careful to do them with all your heart and with all your soul. [17]You have made the LORD declare this day that he will be your God,* and that you will walk in his ways, and keep his statutes and his commandments and his ordinances, and will obey his voice; [18]and the LORD has declared this day concerning you that you are a people for his own possession, as he has promised you, and that you are to keep all his commandments, [19]that he will set you high above all nations that he has made, in praise and in fame and in honour, and that you shall be a people holy to the LORD your God, as he has spoken.'

[1–11] The ordinance about bringing in the first fruits and about the liturgical ceremonial to be used when offering them is also clothed in that hortatory style typical of Deuteronomy, which sees the entry into the promised land as being still in the future. However, the whole account is so manifestly uneven that a secondary working over of earlier material suggests itself *a priori* as a hypothesis. According to the existing text, the man presenting the offering must twice make a solemn declaration, of which the prescribed contents are then imparted *verbatim* in direct speech (the first in v. 3, the second in vv. 5ff.). Both declarations are addressed directly to God. The discrepancy regarding the presentation ceremonial (according to v. 4 the basket is handed to the priest right at the beginning of the ceremony, according to v. 10b not until the end) makes it perfectly clear that here an earlier cultic tradition has been revised by the Deuteronomist, thus producing certain inconsistencies in the text. This earlier material will be found particularly in vv. 5–11. It is less easy to decide whether this revision (like that in 20.1–9) must be imagined as a literary process, thus indicating a literary interpolation. In fact, the obstacles disappear when vv. 3–4 alone are regarded as a later addition. But it would also be not impossible to consider

* This follows von Rad's translation, which here differs from the RSV. Translator.

the whole text as homogeneous from the literary point of view, and to explain the inconsistencies as a pre-literary combination of earlier traditional material. The first fruits have already been mentioned in Deut. 18.4 as being given to the priests. There is no contradiction between that ordinance and the one here. Unfortunately Deuteronomy supplies no information with which to answer the question whether, in addition to the annual delivery of first fruits, an annual payment of a tithe was also required out of the same produce (Deut. 12.17f.; 14.22; 26.12). Deuteronomy is, after all, not the work of a lawgiver, but a collection of cultic and legal materials which are in part very heterogeneous and which have scarcely been brought into agreement with each other.

The most important item of the whole ceremonial is the declaration to be made by the offerer, of which two forms are given, as we have said. The first appears merely as the epitome of the second. Neither of them can be described as prayers. The name of the one to whom they are addressed is lacking and God is spoken of in the third person. Moreover, requests and praises are both absent. Instead the speaker rehearses the chain of the acts of salvation from Jacob onwards (for, in fact, it is he who is meant by the 'Aramean' [Gen. 24.4ff.; 31.24]) up to the entry into Canaan. The historical period compressed in this outline of the events corresponds to that of our great source documents of the Pentateuch, except that it confines itself to noting the most essential and basic facts. The possibility of considering it on that account as a subsequent abbreviation of those fuller outlines cannot be ruled out in itself. However, we come across several of such short historical summaries in quite different literary contexts as well. Hence the conclusion is more natural that there has been preserved in these summaries of salvation history the earlier and more original form of an historical outline which we possess in a much more fully developed form in the sources of the Pentateuch. Of course, we are speaking here of the form, of the type, of this recital of history which refrains from any interpretation. The form of the pattern, given us in vv. 5–10, its literary arrangement, cannot be considered to be very early in all its details. The familiar phraseology of Deuteronomy has an unmistakable share in it. We may also ask whether the scheme of the psalm of individual thanksgiving (distress—appeal—deliverance) was from the beginning typical of the layout of the historical material (yet cf. Josh. 24.2ff.; I Sam. 12.7ff.). Yet the assonance with which the declaration begins (*'arammī 'ōbēd 'ābī*) gives the impression of being very ancient. The verb used here occurs principally when describing the straying of gregarious animals which have lost their way, and this meaning can undoubtedly be retained in view of Gen. 20.13, in which the wanderings of the patriarchs are also described by this word. If this introductory formula were not so brief, it might possibly enable us to obtain a picture of the patriarchal period differing considerably from that in our Pentateuchal sources.

It is noteworthy that in the enumeration of the events what happened at Sinai is missing. The text passes from the distress in Egypt, described with an unusual wealth of words, and from the rescue out of bondage, directly to the entry into Canaan. Now all the similar and comparable summaries also make no mention of the Sinai event which, particularly in Deuteronomy, surpassed in importance all other events in Israel's early history (cf. on Deut. 6.20ff.). Hence it is hardly possible to avoid the conclusion that what happened at Sinai did not belong to the events recorded by the tradition in those summaries. Of course, this does not tell us anything at all about the age and trustworthiness of the Sinai tradition. We deduce only just this, that it did not belong to the basic stock of the historical facts recorded in those summaries. It must have been a complex of distinct religious traditions and as such have had its own history and its own special setting.

In v. 9 the recital of the historical events comes to an end. With v. 10 the speech becomes quite personal, for the speaker now puts himself into the situation of which he has just recounted the historical background. The fruits he has to offer come from 'the ground which thou, O Lord, hast given me'. With these words the speaker has taken his place in the story of salvation and, in a splendid foreshortening of time, has acknowledged himself to be a direct recipient of the act of salvation which was the gift of the promised land. The fact that in a thanksgiving for the fruits of the earth it is not the creation nor the blessings of the first article of the creed which are recalled, but solely God's historical deeds of deliverance, conforms to the particular concentration, in the early religion of Yahweh, on the saving acts experienced by Israel.

[12–15] The regulation concerning the payment of the tithe in the third year is a curious hybrid composition from the standpoint of the history of the tradition. When it deals with the payment of the tithe, which is not to be taken to the central sanctuary but is to be used for the benefit of the needy members of the local community (cf. 14.28f.), we find ourselves within the sphere of those comparatively late rules which became necessary owing to the centralization of the cult. Verse 13 forms the transition to a solemn profession which is to be recited on this occasion (here, too, there is no question of a prayer) and at this point the puzzles begin. It is true that the first part of the profession is composed quite in the Deuteronomic spirit, since it refers to the charitable nature of the payment made. But what is meant by the instruction that this statement is to be recited 'before Yahweh', that is, in what is after all a cultic situation? On this particular occasion the worshipper has not made a pilgrimage to the central sanctuary. The question is answered when we read the continuation of the profession (from v. 14 on) for at v. 14 there begins a series of affirmations which originated in a quite different mental and spiritual atmosphere.

I have not eaten of the tithe while I was mourning;
I have not removed any of it while I was unclean;
I have not offered any of it to the dead.

These are parts of a liturgical series of solemn professions which have also been called a manual for confession.[1] But the man who is speaking in this way is certainly not making a confession, but is professing his loyalty. After this there no doubt followed in some form or other an absolution by the priest, since the whole character of these precepts assume the worshipper to be present at a sanctuary.

The thought-world in which these three statements move is that of archaic sacral concepts, completely different from the rational and humanitarian thought-world of Deuternonomy. These ancient ritual ordinances and concepts certainly lie to some extent outside the religious sphere of interest of the Deuteronomic sermons. The bread of mourners pollutes (Hos. 9.4); if a mourner ate of the tithe, that would defile the sacredness of the whole tithe. The same applies if anyone in a state of bodily uncleanness has eaten of it (Hag. 2.13) and all the more if he has put any of it into a grave as 'food for the dead'. Thus these precepts are based on the very ancient idea of the material effect of the unclean on the clean (Lev. 22.3ff.; the opposite process, the effect of the sacred on the unclean, is rejected in Hag. 2.12). The main concern of these precepts is therefore to make sure of the undefiled ritual cleanness of the tithe offering. All this can surely only be understood as indicating that the solemn profession was recited origin-

---

[1] K. Galling, 'Der Beichtspiegel', *ZAW* 47, 1929, pp. 125ff.

ally when conveying the gift to Yahweh and not to the poor of the locality. But the Deuteronomic preacher wanted to retain this regulation for the altered state of affairs as well, and he was able to do this because the offering of unclean food to the poor was not allowed either. Thus the old ritual has been transferred to a secular situation, and this solution must be considered as a somewhat confused compromise. In this case what does 'before Yahweh' mean? In v. 15 we have again the words of the Deuteronomic reviser of the early cultic ordinance to whom we had to ascribe the introductory sayings in v. 14 as well. Since something quite new in both form and content starts in v. 17, it is natural to understand v. 16 as a hortatory conclusion of the whole part which began with ch. 12.

[17-19] This section differs from all the preceding units by not containing any individual regulation needing to be brought up to date, nor yet a sermon. Its form looks like the draft of a contract in which each of two parties makes its declaration, that is, each causes the other to bind itself by means of a declaration. The causative formulation, according to which each partner of the contract causes the other to make his declaration is very remarkable. Does this not assume that a third person is thought to be present who mediates between the parties? Now, if we reflect that the speaker who cites these two declarations is Moses, who formulates the declarations made by both sides as though from a third position, it is easy to see Moses here in the role of a 'covenant mediator', a role in the execution of covenants which has only recently been recognized.[1] The actual contract formula, when the somewhat wordy declarations woven round it are stripped off, runs as follows: Yahweh has declared that he wishes to be Israel's God; Israel has declared that it wishes to be Yahweh's people. This formula occurs often in the Old Testament and is known to us as the 'formula of the Sinai Covenant' (Ex. 6.7; Jer. 31.33; Ezek. 36.28 etc.). The special name for Israel, a peculiar people, occurs also in the earlier Sinai tradition in Ex. 19.5.

So far—that is, when we consider the basic declarations on which the whole rests—the covenant appears to be strictly bilateral, since each partner binds himself by his proclamation. Yet it is noticeable that in the explanatory homiletic additions the theological emphases have shifted considerably. For by these hortatory supplements the equilibrium of the bilateral nature of the covenant has been upset,

---

[1] Cf. on this Josh. 24.25; II Kings 23.3, and H. W. Wolff, 'Jahwe als Bundesvermittler', *VT* 6, 1956, pp. 316ff.

in so far as both declarations, not only that of Israel but also that of Yahweh, speak of obligations which must be fulfilled by Israel alone. Hence the covenant is interpreted here (this is by no means the case throughout the Old Testament) with all its contents unilaterally from the point of view of the obedience rendered by Israel. The phrase 'in praise and in fame and in honour' seems to have been a regular formula. We can gather from Jer. 13.11; 33.9 that Israel is become a glory for Yahweh. The hypothesis that vv. 17–19 is to be regarded as the formula of the covenant concluded by King Josiah with the people after the discovery of Deuteronomy (II Kings 23.1–3) has often been brought forward.

CHAPTER 27.1–26

27 ¹Now Moses and the elders of Israel commanded the people, saying, 'Keep all the commandment which I command you this day. ²And on the day you pass over the Jordan to the land which the LORD your God gives you, you shall set up large stones, and plaster them with plaster; ³and you shall write upon them all the words of this law, when you pass over to enter the land which the LORD your God gives you, a land flowing with milk and honey, as the LORD, the God of your fathers, has promised you. ⁴And when you have passed over the Jordan, you shall set up these stones, concerning which I command you this day, on Mount Ebal, and you shall plaster them with plaster. ⁵And there you shall build an altar to the LORD your God, an altar of stones; you shall lift up no iron tool upon them. ⁶You shall build an altar to the LORD your God of unhewn stones; and you shall offer burnt offerings on it to the LORD your God; ⁷and you shall sacrifice peace offerings, and shall eat there; and you shall rejoice before the LORD your God. ⁸And you shall write upon the stones all the words of this law very plainly.'

9 And Moses and the Levitical priests said to all Israel, 'Keep silence and hear, O Israel: this day you have become the people of the LORD your God. ¹⁰You shall therefore obey the voice of the LORD your God, keeping his commandments and his statutes, which I command you this day.'

11 And Moses charged the people the same day, saying, ¹²'When you have passed over the Jordan, these shall stand upon Mount Gerizim to bless the people: Simeon, Levi, Judah, Issachar, Joseph, and Benjamin. ¹³And these shall stand upon Mount Ebal for the curse: Reuben, Gad, Asher, Zebulun, Dan, and Naphtali. ¹⁴And the Levites shall declare to all the men of Israel with a loud voice:

15 ' "Cursed be the man who makes a graven or molten image, an abomination to the LORD, a thing made by the hands of a craftsman, and sets it up in secret." And all the people shall answer and say "Amen."

16 ' "Cursed be he who dishonours his father or his mother." And all the people shall say, "Amen."

17 ' "Cursed be he who removes his neighbour's landmark." And all the people shall say, "Amen."

18 ' "Cursed be who who misleads a blind man on the road." And all the people shall say, "Amen."

19 ' "Cursed be he who perverts the justice due to the sojourner, the fatherless, and the widow." And all the people shall say, "Amen."

20 ' "Cursed be he who lies with his father's wife, because he has uncovered her who is his father's." And all the people shall say, "Amen."

21 ' "Cursed be he who lies with any kind of beast." And all the people shall say, "Amen."

22 ' "Cursed be he who lies with his sister, whether the daughter of his father or the daughter of his mother." And all the people shall say, "Amen."

23 ' "Cursed be he who lies with his mother-in-law." And all the people shall say, "Amen."

24 ' "Cursed be he who slays his neighbour in secret." And all the people shall say, "Amen."

25 ' "Cursed be he who takes a bribe to slay an innocent person." And all the people shall say, "Amen."

26 ' "Cursed be he who does not confirm the words of this law by doing them." And all the people shall say, "Amen." '

[1–8] Chapter 27 begins with a summons by Moses, after the crossing of the Jordan, to write down on stones on Mount Gerizim 'all the words of this law', and furthermore to build an altar there. Verses 9–10 stand rather by themselves; they state that Israel has today become the people of Yahweh, and must keep the commandments. Lastly, vv. 11–26 also seem to be a relatively independent body of tradition. They contain the instruction to draw up the tribes in two liturgical choirs and then to have the 'Dodecalogue of Shechem' recited by the Levites. These three units confront the commentators with almost insoluble difficulties, especially as regards their mutual relationship. Let us picture the situation. From ch. 6 onwards Deuteronomy had been presented as a single hortatory speech to Israel. Since Moses was the speaker, there was no necessity, in fact it was not even possible to introduce him as the subject in the third person. But here this occurs three times (vv. 1, 9, 11), in each of which a narrator speaks of Moses in the past tense. The last place in which Moses had been spoken of in the third person and in the past tense was 5.1. In fact, Moses is not mentioned in Deuteronomy at all except in introductory headings or in secondary additions.[1]

Now, 27.1–8, 11–26 differ also in content from all the rest of

[1] Within Deut. 4.44–30.20 Moses is mentioned only in 4.44–46; 5.1; 27.1, 9, 11; 28.69 and 29.1f.

Deuteronomy, in which general rules for life valid for all time were promulgated. These passages are concerned with cultic instructions, one in each passage; when they have been carried out there is no more to be done. Moreover, what is the relationship of the altar on Gerizim to the place 'in one of the tribes where Yahweh will let his name dwell', of which the situation in Israel was, as we know, left mysteriously open? It is quite unlikely that Deuteronomy at last revealed its secret here, that is, when telling of the order to build an altar on Mount Gerizim. For we know from the history of the cult at least this much about that sacred place, that during the period of the monarchy no particularly far-reaching significance was attached to it. But it must be assumed from the outset that Deuteronomy considered its central place of worship to be one of the great and famous sanctuaries.

Did it, then, after all permit yet another altar in addition to the place where Yahweh will let his name dwell? There is strong support for the suggestion that at any rate in vv. 1–8 and 11–26 we have a tradition which was originally pre-Deuteronomic, and which possibly originated very early in Shechem. It is now, in vv. 1–8 (though this is not very easy to understand), clothed completely in the language of the Deuteronomic phraseology. Moreover, vv. 1–8 are not themselves a homogeneous section. Because of the doublets a materially shorter parallel version has long since been noticed in vv. 2–3a. Since it orders the stones to be set up immediately after the passage of the Jordan (strictly speaking, on the day of the passage), it seems as if originally the sanctuary of Gilgal (cf. Josh. 4) was in mind. We now naturally think of Deuteronomy as the law which is to be written on the stones. Yet originally surely a much shorter text was presupposed (cf. Ex. 24.4; Josh. 24.26). On the command not to use an iron tool on the stones for the altar, see Ex. 20.25.

[9–10] Verse 9 differs from v. 1, in which 'Moses and the elders' were speaking, by beginning with an address by Moses and the Levitical priests. These two verses have no kind of connexion at all with what precedes them, for they are concerned not with later tasks but with the present; it is now that Israel has become the people of Yahweh. Therefore we must reckon seriously with the possibility that we have before us here the direct continuation of the section about the contract in 26.17–19. Both parties have made their declarations; by these the covenant has been concluded; Israel is now Yahweh's people (the reintroduction here of Moses as the speaker was no doubt necessitated by 26.19, at the end of which Yahweh's words were cited). The passage, in fact, clearly has a liturgical stamp and seems to indicate a definite point in the course of a ritual. The proclamation of a cultic silence at the climax of a ceremony occurs also in Neh. 8.11; Zeph. 1.7; Zech. 2.13. The solemn statement that Israel has become Yahweh's people must have been followed in 28.1ff. by the concluding announcement of blessings and curses. The relationship between the covenant and obedience is formulated with exemplary clarity in vv. 9–10 from the standpoint of biblical theology. These verses show that the covenant was established when Israel had as yet no possibility of demonstrating its obedience; that the covenant was Yahweh's free gift, which would not only become effective on the assumption that adequate obedience would be rendered by Israel. This obedience was not made a condition preceding the covenant, but results from it. Quite in the spirit of Deuteronomy, obedience springs from the motive of gratitude (cf. 8.1ff., 9.1ff.).

[11–14] The section concerning the cultic ceremony between Mount Ebal and Mount Gerizim is not all of a piece. There are evidently two quite distinct ceremonies which are here ordered to be performed. In the first, the twelve tribes are to take up their position in two semi-choruses of six tribes each on the slopes of Mount Ebal and Mount Gerizim opposite each other and are to reply to each other, evidently with alternate words of blessing and curse. It may be asked whether this ceremony is identical with the one mentioned in Deut. 11.29. While in Deut. 27.12f. the people receive the blessing, in Deut. 11.29 the blessing and the curse are to be laid upon the two mountains, which is surely not the same thing. In the latter case (and also in Josh 8.33) we can really only imagine the ceremony to have been arranged so that the two semi-choruses stood back to back and had to shout blessings and curses at the mountains.[1] In the second ceremony the Levites, who in the first had no particular function apart from the other tribes, are here the real reciters of the liturgy. For they pronounce 'with a loud voice' the sentences of the Dode-calogue of Shechem, whilst the remaining tribes reply merely with 'Amen'. We must therefore allow for the possibility that behind both instructions there stand memories of two different cultic celebrations which took place in the early days at Shechem. When they were com-bined the first one was admittedly very much abridged in favour of the second, for we are told nothing more about the words of the

[1] Cf. on this S. Bülow, *Zeitschrift des Deutschen Palästina-Vereins*, 1957, pp. 102f.

blessings and curses themselves. We receive an actual account of the course of the liturgy only in the case of the second ceremony.

[15-26] The Dodecalogue of Shechem is the most ancient series of prohibitions preserved for us in the Old Testament and one of the most important documents enabling us to perceive something of the spirit and liturgical form of the early faith of Yahweh. As in the case of the decalogue, we must assume here, too, that the individual items of the series were originally given a quite uniform shape. This primitive, very concise style is still beautifully preserved in the group in vv. 16-19, while other maxims, especially the prohibition of images in v. 15, have been amplified by later interpretations. The last item in v. 26 does not deal, like all the preceding ones, with a quite definite transgression against the will of God expressed in legal form, but speaks somewhat vaguely about a neglect of all 'the words of this law'. Moreover, it departs from the strictly maintained positive formulation (instead of: 'cursed be he who . . .', we read here, 'cursed be he who does not . . .'). All these points suggest that it must be considered a later hortatory addition.

The word for 'cursed' (' ārūr) denotes a curse coming from God. Ancient peoples considered such a curse to be a real destructive power which fastened itself upon the person concerned, so real, indeed, that it could even establish itself in his house and its timbers (Zech. 5.4). The 'Amen' with which the congregation makes its response to each of the individual precepts can be translated by 'certainly'. But, particularly in connexion with curses, this 'Amen' involves much more than merely a personal confirmation or agreement; it is a vital part of a sacral legal ceremony which had an intrinsic significance for the validity of the whole. For this 'Amen' involves an affirmation of this expression of Yahweh's will. The cultic community accepts the situation produced by the curses which have been proclaimed (on this 'Amen' to a curse cf. Num. 5.22; Neh. 5.13; Jer. 11.5). Indeed, the congregation does not only acknowledge its agreement with Yahweh's wrath against the law-breaker; it also places itself at his disposal to give effect to it by dissociating itself from such law-breakers. As bearers of the curse these are thrust out of the cultic community; as proscribed men they can no longer abide anywhere; their fate is a terrible one. Thus the curse actually becomes effective only through the community's word of acceptance.

First in the series here is the prohibition of images. It has lost more of its original shape by explanatory additions than all the rest.

For in Hebrew the *'ārūr* ought to be followed by a participial construction. The statement that to make an image is an abomination to the Lord, is intended to account for the prohibition. This reason still deals in cultic categories; but the reference to 'the hands of a craftsman' appeals to sound common sense. However, this argument, that it is absurd for weak human beings to portray God, dates from a comparatively late period (cf. Isa. 44.9ff.; Jer. 10.1ff.; Ps. 115. 4–7).[1] It is not stated whether the prohibition refers to actual images of Yahweh or to representations of Yahweh in the image of a foreign deity. In our opinion the first possibility is more likely. The conception of prohibited images as representations of foreign deities has established itself in the Decalogue only by way of a careful reinterpretation (for the prohibition of images cf. also the explanation on Deut. 5.8).

The Hebrew verb *qālā* (Hiphil) in v. 16 does not really mean 'to curse', but 'to regard and to treat as despicable, as accursed', cf. Ex. 21.17; Lev. 20.9.[2] On v. 17, cf. Deut. 19.14. On v. 18 cf. Lev. 19.14. On v. 19 cf. Ex. 22.20–23; 23.3. On vv. 20, 22 cf. Lev. 18.8–9. The same prohibitions occur in the Law of Holiness in the context of another series (Lev. 18.7–17), the nucleus of which reaches back into the earliest days (rules about living together in the so-called 'extended family' at the nomadic stage).[3] On v. 21 cf. Ex. 22.19; Lev. 18.23; 20.15; on v. 23 cf. Lev. 18.17. On v. 24 cf. Ex. 21.12. On v. 25 cf. Ex. 23.8.

We observe that all the prohibitions set out in the Dodecalogue of Shechem appear also elsewhere in the early Israelite legal traditions. We must conclude from this that we have here a collection of precepts which were significant in forming a pattern for the common life of those who worshipped Yahweh. Nevertheless, this series has a peculiarity which gives it a theological stamp of its own when compared with all similar series; for it condemns practices which could be carried out 'in secret' (vv. 15, 24), that is to say, beyond the control of public opinion. An image set up secretly, a secret murder, a removal of a boundary, the deception of a blind man, or the wide sphere of sexual matters—all these lead into areas upon which as a rule neither a judge nor a complainant turns his eyes. There is something splendid about the way in which Israel on a solemn occasion

---

[1] Von Rad, *Old Testament Theology* I, pp. 215f.
[2] R. Rendtorff, *Kerygma und Dogma*, 1961, pp. 71f.
[3] K. Elliger, 'Das Gesetz Leviticus 18', *ZAW* 67, 1955, pp. 1ff.

acknowledges Yahweh's will expressed as laws for all spheres of life, particularly his will as binding on those occasions when a man believes he is alone by himself. Israel makes itself the agent for carrying out this divine will, by introducing it even into all the secret ramifications of life.

CHAPTER 28.1-68

28 ¹'And if you obey the voice of the LORD your God, being careful to do all his commandments which I command you this day, the LORD your God will set you high above all the nations of the earth. ²And all these blessings shall come upon you and overtake you, if you obey the voice of the LORD your God. ³Blessed shall you be in the city, and blessed shall you be in the field. ⁴Blessed shall be the fruit of your body, and the fruit of your ground, and the fruit of your beasts, the increase of your cattle, and the young of your flock. ⁵Blessed shall be your basket and your kneading-trough. ⁶Blessed shall you be when you come in, and blessed shall you be when you go out.

7 'The LORD will cause your enemies who rise against you to be defeated before you; they shall come out against you one way, and flee before you seven ways. ⁸The LORD will command the blessing upon you in your barns, and in all that you undertake; and he will bless you in the land which the LORD your God gives you. ⁹The LORD will establish you as a people holy to himself, as he has sworn to you, if you keep the commandments of the LORD your God, and walk in his ways. ¹⁰And all the peoples of the earth shall see that you are called by the name of the LORD; and they shall be afraid of you. ¹¹And the LORD will make you abound in prosperity, in the fruit of your body, and in the fruit of your cattle, and in the fruit of your ground, within the land which the LORD swore to your fathers to give you. ¹²The LORD will open to you his good treasury the heavens, to give the rain of your land in its season and to bless all the work of your hands; and you shall lend to many nations, but you shall not borrow. ¹³And the LORD will make you the head, and not the tail; and you shall tend upward only, and not downward; if you obey the commandments of the LORD your God, which I command you this day, being careful to do them, ¹⁴and if you do not turn aside from any of the words which I command you this day, to the right hand or to the left, to go after other gods to serve them.

15 'But if you will not obey the voice of the LORD your God or be careful to do all his commandments and his statutes which I command you this day, then all these curses shall come upon you and overtake you. ¹⁶Cursed shall you be in the city, and cursed shall you be in the

field. [17]Cursed shall be your basket and your kneading-trough. [18]Cursed shall be the fruit of your body, and the fruit of your ground, the increase of your cattle, and the young of your flock. [19]Cursed shall you be when you come in, and cursed shall you be when you go out.

20 'The LORD will send upon you curses, confusion, and frustration, in all that you undertake to do, until you are destroyed and perish quickly, on account of the evil of your doings, because you have forsaken me. [21]The LORD will make the pestilence cleave to you until he has consumed you off the land which you are entering to take possession of it. [22]The LORD will smite you with consumption, and with fever, inflammation, and fiery heat, and with drought, and with blasting, and with mildew; they shall pursue you until you perish. [23]And the heavens over your head shall be brass, and the earth under you shall be iron. [24]The LORD will make the rain of your land powder and dust; from heaven it shall come down upon you until you are destroyed.

25 'The LORD will cause you to be defeated before your enemies; you shall go out one way against them, and flee seven ways before them; and you shall be a horror to all the kingdoms of the earth. [26]And your dead body shall be food for all birds of the air, and for the beasts of the earth; and there shall be none to frighten them away. [27]The LORD will smite you with the boils of Egypt, and with the ulcers and the scurvy and the itch, of which you cannot be healed. [28]The LORD will smite you with madness and blindness and confusion of mind; [29]and you shall grope at noonday, as the blind grope in darkness, and you shall not prosper in your ways; and you shall be only oppressed and robbed continually, and there shall be none to help you. [30]You shall betroth a wife, and another man shall lie with her; you shall build a house, and you shall not dwell in it; you shall plant a vineyard, and you shall not use the fruit of it. [31]Your ox shall be slain before your eyes, and you shall not eat of it; your ass shall be violently taken away before your face, and shall not be restored to you; your sheep shall be given to your enemies, and there shall be none to help you. [32]Your sons and your daughters shall be given to another people, while your eyes look on and fail with longing for them all the day; and it shall not be in the power of your hand to prevent it. [33]A nation which you have not known shall eat up the fruit of your ground and of all your labours; and you shall be only oppressed and crushed continually; [34]so that you shall be driven mad by the sight which your eyes shall see. [35]The LORD will smite you on the knees and on the legs with grievous boils of which you cannot be healed, from the sole of your foot to the crown of your head.

36 'The LORD will bring you, and your king whom you set over you, to a nation that neither you nor your fathers have known; and there you shall serve other gods, of wood and stone. [37]And you shall become a horror, a proverb, and a byword, among all the peoples where the LORD will lead you away. [38]You shall carry much seed into the field, and shall gather little in; for the locust shall consume it. [39]You shall plant vineyards and dress them, but you shall neither drink of the wine nor gather the grapes; for the worm shall eat them. [40]You shall have

olive trees throughout all your territory, but you shall not anoint your-self with the oil; for your olives shall drop off. ⁴¹You shall beget sons and daughters, but they shall not be yours; for they shall go into captivity. ⁴²All your trees and the fruit of your ground the locust shall possess. ⁴³The sojourner who is among you shall mount above you higher and higher; and you shall come down lower and lower. ⁴⁴He shall lend to you, and you shall not lend to him; he shall be the head, and you shall be the tail. ⁴⁵All these curses shall come upon you and pursue you and overtake you, till you are destroyed, because you did not obey the voice of the LORD your God, to keep his commandments and his statutes which he commanded you. ⁴⁶They shall be upon you as a sign and a wonder, and upon your descendants for ever.

47 'Because you did not serve the LORD your God with joyfulness and gladness of heart, by reason of the abundance of all things, ⁴⁸therefore you shall serve your enemies whom the LORD will send against you, in hunger and thirst, in nakedness, and in want of all things; and he will put a yoke of iron upon your neck, until he has destroyed you. ⁴⁹The LORD will bring a nation against you from afar, from the end of the earth, as swift as the eagle flies, a nation whose language you do not understand, ⁵⁰a nation of stern countenance, who shall not regard the person of the old or show favour to the young, ⁵¹and shall eat the off-spring of your cattle and the fruit of your ground, until you are de-stroyed; who also shall not leave you grain, wine, or oil, the increase of your cattle or the young of your flock, until they have caused you to perish. ⁵²They shall besiege you in all your towns, until your high and fortified walls, in which you trusted, come down throughout all your land; and they shall besiege you in all your towns throughout all your land, which the LORD your God has given you. ⁵³And you shall eat the offspring of your own body, the flesh of your sons and daughters, whom the LORD your God has given you, in the siege and in the distress with which your enemies shall distress you. ⁵⁴The man who is the most tender and delicately bred among you will grudge food to his brother, to the wife of his bosom, and to the last of the children who remain to him; ⁵⁵so that he will not give to any of them any of the flesh of his children whom he is eating, because he has nothing left him, in the siege and in the distress with which your enemy shall distress you in all your towns. ⁵⁶The most tender and delicately bred woman among you, who would not venture to set the sole of her foot upon the ground because she is so delicate and tender, will grudge to the husband of her bosom, to her son and to her daughter, ⁵⁷her afterbirth that comes out from between her feet and her children whom she bears, because she will eat them secretly, for want of all things, in the siege and in the distress with which your enemy shall distress you in your towns.

58 'If you are not careful to do all the words of this law which are written in this book, that you may fear this glorious and awful name, the LORD your God, ⁵⁹then the LORD will bring on you and your off-spring extraordinary afflictions, afflictions severe and lasting, and sick-nesses grievous and lasting. ⁶⁰And he will bring upon you again all the

diseases of Egypt, which you were afraid of; and they shall cleave to you. 61Every sickness also, and every affliction which is not recorded in the book of this law, the LORD will bring upon you, until you are destroyed. 62Whereas you were as the stars of heaven for multitude, you shall be left few in number; because you did not obey the voice of the LORD your God. 63And as the LORD took delight in doing you good and multiplying you, so the LORD will take delight in bringing ruin upon you and destroying you; and you shall be plucked off the land which you are entering to take possession of it. 64And the LORD will scatter you among all peoples, from one end of the earth to the other; and there you shall serve other gods, of wood and stone, which neither you nor your fathers have known. 65And among these nations you shall find no ease, and there shall be no rest for the sole of your foot; but the LORD will give you there a trembling heart, and failing eyes, and a languishing soul; 66your life shall hang in doubt before you; night and day you shall be in dread, and have no assurance of your life. 67In the morning you shall say, "Would it were evening!" and at evening you shall say, "Would it were morning!" because of the dread which your heart shall fear and the sights which your eyes shall see. 68And the LORD will bring you back in ships to Egypt, a journey which I promised that you should never make again; and there you shall offer yourselves for sale to your enemies as male and female slaves, but no man will buy you.'

With ch. 28 the last part of Deuteronomy begins. After the obligations of the covenant have been accepted (26.16–19 and 27.9–10) there now follows, according to the ancient pattern, the proclamation of blessing and cursing.[1] On Deuteronomy as a liturgical unit see Introduction (pp. 26ff.). The division between the announcement of the blessings and that of the curses is a natural one. But as regards the analysis of each of the two sections, the commentators have long been occupying themselves with the obviously disproportionate length between the two sections. Verses 1–14 comprise the proclamation of the blessing, vv. 15–68 that of the curses; thus the latter is almost four times as long! That it is precisely the section of curses which has attracted gradual amplifications is easy to understand, when we recall the catastrophe of the exile of 587, regarded by many as the direct fulfilment of the threatened disaster. But it is still not very easy to solve the problem of how we must imagine the original form of the section before its expansion.

It is, in the first place, by no means altogether certain that we should postulate a form of the text in which the number of the

[1] Cf. on this M. Noth, *Leviticus* (OTL), ET 1965, pp. 195ff.

blessings and of the curses corresponds exactly. [1–46] A great help in dividing up the shapeless section of curses is found in vv. 45f., which represent a formal conclusion and summing up. Presumably this was the end of an earlier version of the homily of blessings and curses. We derive additional clues by bringing out the cultic 'formularies' which can be detected behind the individual passages. We know that to bless and to curse was a primaeval cultic operation and therefore it is not surprising if a speech resembling a somewhat disconnected sermon modelled itself from time to time on early forms coined for the cult. A 'formulary' of this kind, particularly easy to recognize because it has not been expanded by any hortatory additions, occurs in vv. 3–6:

Blessed shall you be in the city.
Blessed shall you be in the field.
Blessed shall be the fruit of your body . . .
Blessed shall be your basket and kneading-trough.
Blessed shall you be when you come in.
Blessed shall you be when you go out.

But behind the section immediately following, vv. 7–14, there might also stand stereotyped cultic formulations. These appear perhaps somewhat more clearly still in the negative antitheses in vv. 20–25, 43f.: pestilence, v. 21; corn diseases, v. 22; drought, vv. 23 f.; peril from enemies, v. 25. Compare with this the sequence: death, sword, famine, captivity in Jer. 15.2, or the sequence: hunger, drought, crop diseases, pestilence, sword in Amos 4.6–10 (but for this cf. also Deut. 7.12ff.; 11.13ff., 22ff.). Because the speech is modelled on different early cultic series, the themes dealt with sometimes overlap, for the list of themes of all these formulae of blessings and curses was limited and stereotyped. It is determined by conditions of predominantly rural life, in contrast with those of a nomadic life, or of a specifically urban life, or again those of a merchant's or trader's life. The fact that Baal was completely ousted as the dispenser of blessings from his ancient traditional position of authority in Canaan and far beyond is seldom expressed in the Old Testament in such a comprehensive manner as in the incisive realism of these formal blessings and curses. For it was at this point, when asking himself the simple question about the donor of all that filled basket and kneading-trough, that the peasant arrived at the decision to acknowledge Yahweh as his God.

When attempting to separate the original section of curses from the extensive later amplifications, we must start from the formal symmetry between the words of the blessings and those of the curses. There is a fairly exact correspondence between vv. 3–6 (blessings) and vv. 16–19 (20) (curses); however, vv. 7–13a (blessings) are matched only imperfectly by vv. 21–25a (curses). The section of curses corresponding to vv. 12b–13a occurs only much later in vv. 43–44. These are then followed directly by the concluding formula already mentioned, which must be considered as the end of the earlier version of the section of blessings and curses.

Since the symmetry is disturbed in such a far-reaching manner, it is natural to conjecture a great interpolation (and probably more than one) which interrupted the correspondence of blessings and curses, originally so clearly maintained. For what other reason was the negative counterpart of vv. 12b–13a removed so far away (vv. 43f.)? We should expect it much earlier. We may dispute about the extent of the interpolation, for in the style of an already disconnected homily we must beware of expecting the blessings and curses to be arranged with their parts in an exactly symmetrical pattern. The beginning of the expansion must be in v. 25b, its end not before v. 38, probably not until v. 42. As regards its contents, the section is marked by a definite list of themes. The curse will fall upon Israel in the shape of diseases of the body (v. 27) and the mind (v. 28) and damage to property (vv. 30–33). This series is repeated in vv. 34–42; diseases of the mind and of the body and damage to property. Here the only thing still to be added is the prediction of an exile (vv. 36–37). This last conception has again obviously been discarded from v. 38 onwards; for vv. 38–42 again presuppose Israel in a settled rural condition.

[47–57] But even after the formal ending in vv. 45f. the theme of the curse which has already been introduced is developed further. First come vv. 47–57 standing as a separate unit. In this section v. 47 deserves special attention, because Yahweh's offer is paraphrased in a very pregnant manner; it is stated that this offer would have made it possible for Israel to serve God with joyfulness and gladness! However, the theme of the curse is now developed fully as the pitiless abandonment to cruel enemies. Yahweh himself summons the enemy nation. Here evidently conceptions are employed which the great prophets were the first to set before their hearers (Isa. 5.26ff.; Jer. 5.15). This enemy will strip the countryside, v. 51; he will besiege the towns, v. 52;

hunger will force the beleaguered inhabitants to eat their own children. The curse dwells on this detail with gruesome particulars, vv. 53–57. We may suppose that in this section actual experiences are reproduced which the population of Judah and Jerusalem had endured during the invasion of the neo-Babylonian army in 587 (II Kings 25.1ff.). It must, however, be recalled that the eating of one's own children belongs to the traditional accounts of the horrors conjured up when describing the siege of towns (Lev. 26.29; II Kings 6.26; Jer. 19.9; Lam. 2.20; 4.10; Ezek. 5.10).

[58–68] Verse 58 starts another section with a new introduction. With these verses we enter upon a very late stratum of Deuteronomy, which can be recognized by the fact that it is understood not merely as a living, traditional organism, but as a book, a literary entity complete in itself (vv. 58, 61; Introduction, pp. 29f.). Verses 62–63 stand out again, because they address the readers in the second person plural. Here, and in the last section (vv. 64–68), which turns back to the singular number, the threatening words rise to the highest pitch of horror. It will give Yahweh pleasure to annihilate Israel. But yet even more horrible than final annihilation is the condition of finding no rest, of despair and of never-ending terror into which disobedient Israel is to be thrust. We do not know whether the threat of a final deportation to Egypt is intended to represent an actual contemporary possibility or even one that was in fact realized. Evidently Deuteronomy sees in these events something like a divine liquidation of the whole history of salvation brought about by Yahweh, that is to say, a termination of that road on which, according to the word of Yahweh, already referred to in Deut. 17.16, no return would ever again be made. However, no reference to this word of God can be found outside Deuteronomy.

CHAPTER 29.1 – 29

29 ¹'These are the words of the covenant which the LORD commanded Moses to make with the people of Israel in the land of Moab, besides the covenant which he had made with them at Horeb.

2 And Moses summoned all Israel and said to them: 'You have seen all that the LORD did before your eyes in the land of Egypt, to Pharaoh and to all his servants and to all his land, ³the great trials which your eyes saw, the signs, and those great wonders; ⁴but to this day the LORD has not given you a mind to understand, or eyes to see, or ears to hear. ⁵I have led you forty years in the wilderness; your clothes have not worn out upon you, and your sandals have not worn off your feet; ⁶you have not eaten bread, and you have not drunk wine or strong drink; that you may know that I am the LORD your God. ⁷And when you came to this place, Sihon the king of Heshbon and Og the king of Bashan came out against us to battle, but we defeated them; ⁸we took their land, and gave it for an inheritance to the Reubenites, the Gadites, and the half-tribe of the Manassites. ⁹Therefore be careful to do the words of this covenant, that you may prosper in all that you do.

10 'You stand this day all of you before the LORD your God; the heads of your tribes, your elders, and your officers, all the men of Israel, ¹¹your little ones, your wives, and the sojourner who is in your camp, both he who hews your wood and he who draws your water, ¹²that you may enter into the sworn covenant of the LORD your God, which the LORD your God makes with you this day; ¹³that he may establish you this day as his people, and that he may be your God, as he promised you, and as he swore to your fathers, to Abraham, to Isaac, and to Jacob. ¹⁴Nor is it with you only that I make this sworn covenant, ¹⁵but with him who is not here with us this day as well as with him who stands here with us this day before the LORD our God.

16 'You know how we dwelt in the land of Egypt, and how we came through the midst of the nations through which you passed; ¹⁷and you have seen their detestable things, their idols of wood and stone, of silver and gold, which were among them. ¹⁸Beware lest there be among you a man or woman or family or tribe, whose heart turns away this day from the LORD our God to go and serve the gods of those nations; lest

there be among you a root bearing poisonous and bitter fruit, [19]one who, when he hears the words of this sworn covenant, blesses himself in his heart, saying, "I shall be safe, though I walk in the stubbornness of my heart." This would lead to the sweeping away of moist and dry alike. [20]The LORD would not pardon him, but rather the anger of the LORD and his jealousy would smoke against that man, and the curses written in this book would settle upon him, and the LORD would blot out his name from under heaven. [21]And the LORD would single him out from all the tribes of Israel for calamity, in accordance with all the curses of the covenant written in this book of the law. [22]And the generation to come, your children who rise up after you, and the foreigner who comes from a far land, would say, when they see the afflictions of that land and the sicknesses with which the LORD has made it sick— [23]the whole land brimstone and salt, and a burnt-out waste, unsown, and growing nothing, where no grass can sprout, an over-throw like that of Sodom and Gomorrah, Admah and Zeboiim, which the LORD overthrew in his anger and wrath— [24]yea, all the nations would say, "Why has the LORD done thus to this land? What means the heat of this great anger?" [25]Then men would say, "It is because they forsook the covenant of the LORD, the God of their fathers, which he made with them when he brought them out of the land of Egypt, [26]and went and served other gods and worshipped them, gods whom they had not known and whom he had not allotted to them; [27]therefore the anger of the LORD was kindled against this land, bringing upon it all the curses written in this book; [28]and the LORD uprooted them from their land in anger and fury and great wrath, and cast them into another land, as at this day."

29 'The secret things belong to the LORD our God; but the things that are revealed belong to us and to our children for ever, that we may do all the words of this law.'

[1] It is generally accepted today that this verse which, in German as in Hebrew, is reckoned as the last verse of ch. 28, is to be con-sidered not as the conclusion of what precedes it, but as the heading of what comes next. In this case it only remains to ask about the length of the section which is described by this heading. In my opinion it can hardly have comprised more than chs. 29 and 30.[1] It is very surprising to find here the conception of a covenant made in the land of Moab, which is explicitly distinguished, as an event of a special kind, from the covenant-making at Sinai. Nowhere else in the Old Testament is this mentioned. Indeed, this conception is not

[1] N. Lohfink has a different opinion; he includes under this heading the text right up to Deut. 32.47 (including the Song of Moses) (Der Bundeschluss im Land Moab', Biblische Zeitschrift, N.F.6, 1962, pp. 32ff.).

even the one generally prevailing in Deuteronomy, which considers itself to be in the main only a farewell speech of Moses and an interpretation of the revelation at Sinai. As regards the ceremonial carried out at this 'Moab covenant', the only clear statement is to the effect that at this covenant to be made by Moses 'with the people of Israel' at Yahweh's command, Moses himself is again (cf. 26.17–19) said to have acted as the mediator of the covenant.

[2–9] Now, it is not too easy to find one's way about the text which is included under this heading. On the one hand it is quite easy for an impartial reader to use caesuras or awkward transitions in order to separate the units into sections according to their meaning. But the more he identifies units, which are, in fact, units of very diverse character, the more forcibly does the problem of the meaning of the whole present itself. In this perplexity the 'covenant pattern' offers us some help, because its subdivisions enable us to recognize the cultic sequence of a sacral and legal ritual (see Introduction, pp. 21f.). Thus in vv. 2–8 'the previous history' can certainly be recognized without difficulty. This is followed by the 'declaration of basic principle' which can be seen again in v. 9. 'Blessing and curse' occur in 30.16–18, and finally even the customary 'invocation of witnesses'. In between these items other units are interspersed which certainly for their part, too, contain allusions to the covenant pattern, as especially in 29.16–21.

The historical retrospect in vv. 2–8 recalls in particular that of 8.2–4, because it understands the adversities experienced whilst in the desert and the help in overcoming them as having been brought about by God in order to test Israel. But the idea that Israel could not yet at all grasp then what was troubling it, and that all this is only now becoming intelligible to the present age is quite new. The apocalyptic writings are the first to attribute fundamental significance to the idea that not until the hour of a great crisis do the old traditions reveal themselves to the understanding. With the help of this conception a bridge can without difficulty be built between the past and the present, and the contemporary quality of the old be demonstrated; only now can its full range be understood. In v. 5 the style of the speech changes into words spoken by God in the first person singular.

[10–15] This section is quite different, not at all like a homily. It gives the impression of being a kind of official record, as Lohfink suggests. The cultic community assembled for the making of the covenant is named accurately according to its classes. Then Yahweh's purpose in making the covenant is defined, namely, the establishment of Israel as God's people (v. 13). It is very interesting to note how in conclusion those who are not yet present are also drawn into the sphere of salvation created by this covenant. This was, of course, the most important statement for those who were born later; for now they could apply the making of this covenant to themselves as well. We must pay particular attention to the phrase 'this day', emphasized so strongly in this section. In vv. 2–15 it occurs six times.

[16–21] This short section, as Lohfink says, contains as in a microcosm the subsections of the covenant formula: 'previous history', vv. 16f.; 'declaration of basic principle', namely the prohibition of any worship of idols, v. 18; 'threat of the curse' in the event of disobedience, vv. 19–21. Here, too, (cf. 28.58, 61), Deuteronomy already appears as a book (vv. 20f.) an indication that this tradition must be ascribed to its latest stratum. It is typical of the shift towards a legal interpretation in the understanding of the Sinai revelation that in vv. 12 and 19 the Hebrew word means 'curse'. It has nearly taken over the function of the word 'covenant'. In vv. 12 and 14 the two expressions appear side by side with the same meaning[1] (cf. for this v. 20). In v. 21 even 'the curses of the covenant' are mentioned. It almost seems as if the writer of this stratum, which, as we have explained, is very late, considered this curse on disobedience to be the real purport of Deuteronomy.

[22–29] These verses are described by Lohfink as a magnificent piece of rhetoric. The preacher achieves his peculiar effect by directing the eyes of his hearers to the future and by describing the imaginary case of the curse already in operation. Moreover, he does so in a remarkably indirect manner, namely as if what has happened is reflected in the mirror of the surrounding nations shocked by the catastrophe. Then they will begin to inquire into the cause of this alarming catastrophe, and they will discover that Yahweh himself has cursed his idol-worshipping people. Verse 29, however, is best understood as the conclusion of the sermon. The sentence sounds like a proverbial maxim which once dealt pithily with man's general relationship to what is secret and to what is manifest. Since the words (nistarot, niglot) are quite untheological, this maxim is concerned in the main simply with the relationship of man to what he can and cannot perceive, and hence with the often raised problem of the

---

[1] The RSV "sworn covenant' is a conflation of the two Hebrew expressions. Translator.

limits of all human wisdom. The former is at man's disposal, the latter rests in God's hand, a notion which was very important to teachers of wisdom. By using the words 'of this law', the maxim has been somewhat altered to mean: Yahweh's will expressed in the law is manifest; it is this which belongs to Israel for all time, and for which it is accountable; all else lies in God's hand.

CHAPTER 30.1-20

30 ¹'And when all these things come upon you, the blessing and the curse, which I have set before you, and you call them to mind among all the nations where the LORD your God has driven you, ²and return to the LORD your God, you and your children, and obey his voice in all that I command you this day, with all your heart and with all your soul; ³then the LORD your God will restore your fortunes, and have compassion upon you, and he will gather you again from all the peoples where the LORD your God has scattered you. ⁴If your outcasts are in the uttermost parts of heaven, from there the LORD your God will gather you, and from there he will fetch you; ⁵and the LORD your God will bring you into the land which your fathers possessed, that you may possess it; and he will make you more prosperous and numerous than your fathers. ⁶And the LORD your God will circumcise your heart and the heart of your offspring, so that you will love the LORD your God with all your heart and with all your soul, that you may live. ⁷And the LORD your God will put all these curses upon your foes and enemies who persecuted you. ⁸And you shall again obey the voice of the LORD, and keep all his commandments which I command you this day. ⁹The LORD your God will make you abundantly prosperous in all the work of your hand, in the fruit of your body, and in the fruit of your cattle, and in the fruit of your ground; for the LORD will again take delight in prospering you, as he took delight in your fathers, ¹⁰if you obey the voice of the LORD your God, to keep his commandments and his statutes which are written in this book of the law, if you turn to the LORD your God with all your heart and with all your soul.

11 'For this commandment which I command you this day is not too hard for you, neither is it far off. ¹²It is not in heaven, that you should say, "Who will go up for us to heaven, and bring it to us, that we may hear it and do it?" ¹³Neither is it beyond the sea, that you should say, "Who will go over the sea for us, and bring it to us, that we may hear it and do it?" ¹⁴But the word is very near you; it is in your mouth and in your heart, so that you can do it.

15 'See, I have set before you this day life and good, death and evil. ¹⁶If you obey the commandments of the LORD your God which I com-

mand you this day, by loving the LORD your God, by walking in his ways, and by keeping his commandments and his statutes and his ordinances, then you shall live and multiply, and the LORD your God will bless you in the land which you are entering to take possession of it. [17]But if your heart turns away, and you will not hear, but are drawn away to worship other gods and serve them, [18]I declare to you this day, that you shall perish; you shall not live long in the land which you are going over the Jordan to enter and possess. [19]I call heaven and earth to witness against you this day, that I have set before you life and death, blessing and curse; therefore choose life, that you and your descendants may live, [20]loving the LORD your God, obeying his voice, and cleaving to him; for that means life to you and length of days, that you may dwell in the land which the LORD swore to your fathers, to Abraham, to Isaac, and to Jacob, to give them.'

[1–10] These verses turn our eyes to the future and, like 29.20–29, assume that the threatened judgment has already been carried out. However our text starts from the assumption that Israel has taken this punishment to heart and is 'turning' to Yahweh. In this case Yahweh will have compassion upon his people, will gather it from its dispersion and bring it back to its own land, in order to bestow upon it greater blessings than ever. It is surely beyond question that the speaker of this section is himself living in the period of the exile, and that he is therefore addressing a word of immediate importance to his hard-pressed contemporaries who were likely to be somewhat far removed from taking the punishment quite personally. In that case this section is more or less in line with the passage in 4.29–31 which speaks similarly out of the situation of the exile. In both of them the concept of returning to Yahweh is central. Now the Great Deuteronomistic historical work makes the theme of Israel's return to Yahweh the culmination of its message. It is therefore actually possible, in view of the peculiarities of this section in particular, that 30.1–10 no longer belongs to Deuteronomy, but is already a part of the structure of that great historical and theological work which encloses Deuteronomy as if within a frame.[1] In fact, our text can no longer be called an exhortation; it contains no admonitions, but, with regard to Israel's future, simple affirmative propositions, that is, it is clothed altogether in the style of prophetic predictions. The

---

[1] On the theme of repentance ('turning') in the Deuteronomistic historical work see H. W. Wolff, 'Das Kerygma des deuteronomistischen Geschichtswerk', *ZAW* 73, 1961, pp. 180ff.

saying about circumcising the heart recalls, of course, Jer. 4.4. But since our text supposes that God himself will carry out this inward renewal in man, it approaches more closely to Jer. 31.31ff.; 32.39–41 or Ezek. 36.24ff. The saying about Yahweh's delight in 'prospering' Israel (v. 9) reappears in, in fact, in Jer. 32.41. Altogether the whole picture of the future of God's people healed and blessed by God himself resembles completely that in Jer. 32. Thus the situation of Israel is very different when compared with that in the earlier parts of Deuteronomy; behind the speaker there lies the period of disobedience and of judgment. The curses in Deuteronomy, which is here understood predominantly as law, have been fulfilled. From this standpoint the speaker looks to the future and announces a redemptive activity by which God himself creates for his people the prerequisites for complete obedience.

[11–14] It is much more difficult to assign a place in the history of the tradition to vv. 11–14. The thoughts suggested here concerning 'this commandment', that is, the whole revelation in Deuteronomy of the divine will, are almost unique. What misconceptions need the assurance that this command is not 'too hard', 'too strange' and not 'too far'? Who supposes that he must 'go up to heaven' and bring it down? (This remarkable phrase occurs earlier in quite a different context in an Amarna Letter, in the Babylonian Dialogue of Master and Servant, and also in Ps. 139.8)[1]. The concept of the nearness or remoteness of the divine command seems to have been a regular formula used as a maxim, but it is not unequivocal for us. The preacher seems to be wishing to emphasize that this word of Yahweh to Israel is in every respect something ultimate and all-sufficing. It is something that is evident; it can be comprehended and talked about. It never requires an effort on man's part to fetch it from some distant place and set it actually before his eyes. In this respect Yahweh has done all that is necessary; he has placed it on Israel's lips and in its heart (cf. with this Jer. 31.33). Moreover, this conception of the all-sufficiency of the divine call to Israel also includes the fact that this command is easy to obey and does not raise fresh problems between Israel and its God.

[15–20] This last unit of the tradition of the Moab covenant, probably the very end of the Deuteronomic text, brings us back again to the covenant formula which, even if only in a fragmentary

[1] J. A. Knudzton, Die El-Amarna Tafeln (1915), 264, 14–19; A Pessimistic Dialogue between Master and Servant XII, 5 (ANET, p. 438).

manner, forms the framework of this Moab-covenant tradition. The covenant, when it has finally been made, opens up two possibilities, of blessing or of curse, of life or of death. The appeal to the gods, as witnesses that the covenant has been made, even though it has been demythologized, has become part of the Israelite ceremonial. Heaven and earth must take over the function of witnesses. It is true that we cannot indeed call this section an unimpaired text of the ceremonial; it is permeated too strongly with the Deuteronomic phraseology for that. But we can still recognize clearly the fundamental features of the ceremonial elements of the covenant formula.

CHAPTER 31.1-30

31 1"So Moses continued to speak these words to all Israel. 2And he said to them, "I am a hundred and twenty years old this day; I am no longer able to go out and come in. The LORD has said to me, "You shall not go over this Jordan." 3The LORD your God himself will go over before you; he will destroy these nations before you, so that you shall dispossess them; and Joshua will go over at your head, as the LORD has spoken. 4And the LORD will do to them as he did to Sihon and Og, the kings of the Amorites, and to their land, when he destroyed them. 5And the LORD will give them over to you, and you shall do to them according to all the commandment which I have commanded you. 6Be strong and of good courage, do not fear or be in dread of them: for it is the LORD your God who goes with you; he will not fail you or forsake you.'

7 Then Moses summoned Joshua, and said to him in the sight of all Israel, 'Be strong and of good courage; for you shall go with this people into the land which the LORD has sworn to their fathers to give them; and you shall put them in possession of it. 8It is the LORD who goes before you; he will be with you, he will not fail you or forsake you; do not fear or be dismayed.'

9 And Moses wrote this law, and gave it to the priests the sons of Levi, who carried the ark of the covenant of the LORD, and to all the elders of Israel. 10And Moses commanded them, 'At the end of every seven years, at the set time of the year of release, at the feast of booths, 11when all Israel comes to appear before the LORD your God at the place which he will choose, you shall read this law before all Israel in their hearing. 12Assemble the people, men, women, and little ones, and the sojourner within your towns, that they may hear and learn to fear the LORD your God, and be careful to do all the words of this law, 13and that their children, who have not known it, may hear and learn to fear the LORD your God, as long as you live in the land which you are going over the Jordan to possess.'

14 And the LORD said to Moses, 'Behold, the days approach when you must die; call Joshua, and present yourselves in the tent of meeting, that I may commission him.' And Moses and Joshua went and presented themselves in the tent of meeting. 15And the LORD appeared in

the tent in a pillar of cloud; and the pillar of cloud stood by the door of the tent.

16 And the LORD said to Moses, 'Behold, you are about to sleep with your fathers; then this people will rise and play the harlot after the strange gods of the land, where they go to be among them, and they will forsake me and break my covenant which I have made with them. ¹⁷Then my anger will be kindled against them in that day, and I will forsake them and hide my face from them, and they will be devoured; and many evils and troubles will come upon them, so that they will say in that day, "Have not these evils come upon us because our God is not among us?" ¹⁸And I will surely hide my face in that day on account of all the evil which they have done, because they have turned to other gods. ¹⁹Now therefore write this song, and teach it to the people of Israel; put it in their mouths, that this song may be a witness for me against the people of Israel. ²⁰For when I have brought them into the land flowing with milk and honey, which I swore to give to their fathers, and they have eaten and are full and grown fat, they will turn to other gods and serve them, and despise me and break my covenant. ²¹And when many evils and troubles have come upon them, this song shall confront them as a witness (for it will live unforgotten in the mouths of their descendants); for I know the purposes which they are already forming, before I have brought them into the land that I swore to give.' ²²So Moses wrote this song the same day, and taught it to the people of Israel.

23 And the LORD commissioned Joshua the son of Nun and said, 'Be strong and of good courage; for you shall bring the children of Israel into the land which I swore to give them: I will be with you.'

24 When Moses had finished writing the words of this law in a book, to the very end, ²⁵Moses commanded the Levites who carried the ark of the covenant of the LORD, ²⁶'Take this book of the law, and put it by the side of the ark of the covenant of the LORD your God, that it may be there for a witness against you. ²⁷For I know how rebellious and stubborn you are; behold, while I am yet alive with you, today you have been rebellious against the LORD; how much more after my death! ²⁸Assemble to me all the elders of your tribes, and your officers, that I may speak these words in their ears and call heaven and earth to witness against them. ²⁹For I know that after my death you will surely act corruptly, and turn aside from the way which I have commanded you; and in the days to come evil will befall you, because you will do what is evil in the sight of the LORD, provoking him to anger through the work of your hands.'

30 Then Moses spoke the words of this song until they were finished, in the ears of all the assembly of Israel:

The units comprised in Deut. 31 confront the commentator who seeks to analyse it with a thoroughly complicated state of affairs.

Yet all the individual subdivisions have, after all, one thing in common, namely that the matters with which they deal lie more or less outside the range of subjects with which Deuteronomy has occupied itself hitherto. These matters are the appointment of Joshua (vv. 1–8, 23), a theophany at the tent of meeting (vv. 14–15), a preparatory approach to the Song of Moses (vv. 16–22), directions to read aloud and to deposit the book of Deuteronomy (vv. 9–13, 24–29). But the different character of the traditions making their appearance in ch. 31 can be clearly recognized, and, in fact, more especially by the prevalence of the narrative style in the past tense (vv. 1f., 7, 9f., 14–15, 16, 22–25, 30). For this is well known to be alien to the hortatory manner of speaking in Deuteronomy, except for some historical retrospects—just as alien as the style of the direct speech of God which occurs here twice close together (vv. 14, 16ff.). Thus the method of presentation has abandoned the fiction that Moses is speaking in the land of Moab. It is looking back from a later point of time on the events immediately before the death of Moses.

The tradition of the Moab covenant must probably be considered as the most recent tradition and the last to be attached to the great structure of Deuteronomy. If this is so, it becomes a very likely hypothesis, in view of the narrative style which begins here, that the material from ch. 31 onwards does not in any way belong to Deuteronomy any longer, but belongs instead to the great historical work into which Deuteronomy itself was aborted as a literary unit (see Introduction, p. 12). From the point of view of form the transition in ch. 31 is not smooth, as will soon appear; but it is not unusual for such large aggregates of tradition to show unevennesses and cracks at the seams.

[1–8] The contents of this first unit follow directly on the situation described in Deut. 3.23–29. Moses has learned that he is not allowed to enter the land of promise. Hence he must commission Joshua, who will take over the leadership of Israel from now on. Moses is here carrying out this commission, after concluding 'these words', that is, the farewell speech of Deuteronomy. He begins by informing all Israel of the imminent end of his service as leader, which has lasted up till now. (The sermon attached to it in vv. 3–6 must be judged to be a later amplification of the text.) Then there follows the appointment of Joshua as leader with the statement that Yahweh himself will go before his people. If we ask about the image of

Moses which this section projects, it is that of a leader in holy wars.

[9–13] This next section changes over apparently without difficulty to a different image of Moses. For now he acts as the mediator of Yahweh's great revelation. His personal service as a mediator has, in fact, come to an end. Thus care must be taken to provide for another form in which to preserve and to mediate Yahweh's revelation. What Moses had till then carried in his mind and handed on by word of mouth is now transmitted to the priests in the form of a book, which they must read out from time to time to the assembled community. Here we have the first beginnings of the canon. The idea of reading aloud the whole of Deuteronomy before the great assembly at a festival presents difficulties. But the author of this section by no means invented the custom, assumed here, of a recital of the law at the culmination of a cultic celebration. It had long been customary in Israel (see what was said above about the Decalogue). Our author only modified the custom so far as to claim to know that from now on Deuteronomy was included in the reading.

[14–15, 23] In these verses we have not a speech by Moses, but a narrative of events instead. Nothing more is said about the recital of the law, but Yahweh draws Moses' attention to his imminent end. He is therefore to bring Joshua to the tent of revelation in order that Yahweh may commission him for his new office. Hence this passage does not quite agree in some respects with the situation presumed in vv. 1–8. For this reason these verses have long been thought to be a tradition from the Elohist, and so from a written source of the Pentateuch, fitted in here as well as could be managed. No mention is made of this tent anywhere else in Deuteronomy, nor is its existence assumed in any other passage. However we appear to have here one of the few places where mention is made of the 'tent of meeting', a cultic object which evidently lost its significance soon after Israel's entry into Canaan (Ex. 33.7ff.; Num. 11–12; cf. II Sam. 7.6). This tent was not understood, like the holy ark, to be the place of Yahweh's permanent presence, but as the place of intercourse with Yahweh, who under the cover of an enveloping cloud descended to it from heaven on each occasion. Verses 14–15 are a mere fragment. Joshua's actual commissioning for his office follows only in v. 23 in the words of v. 7, of which the style has been changed for this purpose into the direct speech of God. This verse has subsequently been displaced from its place after v. 15 by Yahweh's great speech in vv. 16–21 (22).

[16–22] The purpose of the speech by God in vv. 16ff. is to induce Moses to write down a song, the contents of which are imparted afterwards. The purpose of writing it down is that this song can rise up later on when Israel shall have broken the covenant as a witness against it (the interesting concept of *yēṣer* (v. 21) which can be rendered by 'tendency', 'disposition', 'nature' is already approaching here closely to the late-Jewish *theologumenon* of the 'evil impulse'). It is very perplexing that in this speech God talks of the people partly in the singular number, partly in the plural.[1] In other respects, too, the language is awkward, especially in v. 21. There follows in vv. 24–29 Moses' address to the Levites after he had handed over the written law for them to preserve. At a later time, when Israel shall have become rebellious, this law will rise against them as a witness. It is obvious how close a parallel this is to the speech in vv. 16ff. Many commentators have therefore in v. 24 replaced the word 'Torah' by *šira* = song and contented themselves with the statement that the transition to the song in Deut. 32 appears in a twofold form. But the position is not like this. It is not the reference to the law in vv. 24–29 which is secondary, but the reference to the song in vv. 16–22. After all, the stereotyped phraseology of the speech in vv. 16ff. 'write', 'teach', 'put in their mouths', 'may be a witness' is not applicable to a song but to a legal document. Therefore, one can hardly agree to eliminate the undoubtedly original reference of the speech in vv. 24ff. to 'this law' by an emendation. In vv. 16–21, too, there is nothing to emend. All that can be said is that whoever wanted to establish the Song of Moses securely as part of this block of traditions adapted for his purpose a form of words which treated originally of writing down the law.[2]

The relationship between the two speeches to the Levites in vv. 9–13 and 24ff. can hardly be understood as that of two commissions following upon each other in time, but rather as that of doublets. In fact the whole chapter contains debris of traditions rather than a real advance in the narrative. So far as the somewhat involved approach to Moses' Song is concerned, it offers a perfect example of a subsequent interpretation of a text arising out of a quite definite situation. This interpreta-

---

[1] In the RSV the plural is used throughout. Translator.

[2] A different view is expressed by O. Eissfeldt, 'Das Lied Moses Dt. 32, 1–43 und das Lehrgedicht Asaphs Ps. 78 samt einer Analyse der Umgebung des Mose-Liedes', *Berichte über die Verhandlangen der Sächsischen Akademie der Wissenschaften zu Leipzig*, 1958, pp. 43ff.

tion of the Song as issuing out of the state of penitence (Israel is accused by the words of the Song) is a very arbitrary one, and it must be said that it diminishes to some extent the purport of the Song. For the comforting statements in the Song (vv. 36, 40ff.), if interpreted in this way, no longer come to fruition.

CHAPTER 32.1–52

32 ¹'Give ear, O heavens, and I will speak;
and let the earth hear the words of my mouth.
² May my teaching drop as the rain,
my speech distil as the dew,
as the gentle rain upon the tender grass,
and as the showers upon the herb.
³ For I will proclaim the name of the LORD.
Ascribe greatness to our God!

⁴ 'The Rock, his work is perfect;
for all his ways are justice.
A God of faithfulness and without iniquity,
just and right is he.
⁵ They have dealt corruptly with him,
they are no longer his children because of their blemish;
they are a perverse and crooked generation.
⁶ Do you thus requite the LORD,
you foolish and senseless people?
Is not he your father, who created you,
who made you and established you?
⁷ Remember the days of old,
consider the years of many generations;
ask your father, and he will show you;
your elders, and they will tell you.
⁸ When the Most High gave to the nations their inheritance,
when he separated the sons of men,
he fixed the bounds of the peoples
according to the number of the sons of God.
⁹ For the LORD's portion is his people,
Jacob his allotted heritage.

¹⁰ 'He found him in a desert land,
and in the howling waste of the wilderness;
he encircled him, he cared for him,
he kept him as the apple of his eye.

11 Like an eagle that stirs up its nest,
    that flutters over its young,
  spreading out its wings, catching them,
    bearing them on its pinions,
12 the LORD alone did lead him,
    and there was no foreign god with him.
13 He made him ride on the high places of the earth,*
    and he ate the produce of the field;
  and he made him suck honey out of the rock,
    and oil out of the flinty rock.
14 Curds from the herd, and milk from the flock,
    with fat of lambs and rams,
    herds of Bashan and goats,
  with the finest of the wheat—
    and of the blood of the grape you drank wine.

15 'But Jeshurun waxed fat, and kicked;
    you waxed fat, you grew thick, you became sleek;
  then he forsook God who made him,
    and scoffed at the Rock of his salvation.
16 They stirred him to jealousy with strange gods;
    with abominable practices they provoked him to anger.
17 They sacrificed to demons which were no gods,
    to gods they had never known,
  to new gods that had come in of late,
    whom your fathers had never dreaded.
18 You were unmindful of the Rock that begot you,
    and you forgot the God who gave you birth.

19 'The LORD saw it, and spurned them,
    because of the provocation of his sons and his daughters.
20 And he said, "I will hide my face from them,
    I will see what their end will be,
  for they are a perverse generation,
    children in whom is no faithfulness.
21 They have stirred me to jealousy with what is no god;
    they have provoked me with their idols.
  So I will stir them to jealousy with those who are no people;
    I will provoke them with a foolish nation.
22 For a fire is kindled by my anger,
    and it burns to the depths of Sheol,
  devours the earth and its increase,
    and sets on fire the foundations of the mountains.

23 ' "And I will heap evils upon them;
    I will spend my arrows upon them;

* As suggested by W. L. Moran, 'Some Remarks on the Song of Moses',
Biblica 43.3, 1962, pp. 323ff.

24 they shall be wasted with hunger,
and devoured with burning heat
and poisonous pestilence;
and I will send the teeth of beasts against them,
with venom of crawling things of the dust.
25 In the open the sword shall bereave,
and in the chambers shall be terror,
destroying both young man and virgin,
the sucking child with the man of grey hairs.
26 I would have said, 'I will scatter them afar,
I will make the remembrance of them cease from among men',
27 had I not feared provocation by the enemy,
lest their adversaries should judge amiss,
lest they should say, 'Our hand is triumphant,
the LORD has not wrought all this.' "

28 'For they are a nation void of counsel,
and there is no understanding in them.
29 If they are wise, they would understand this,
they would discern their latter end!
30 How should one chase a thousand,
and two put ten thousand to flight,
unless their Rock had sold them,
and the LORD had given them up?
31 For their rock is not as our Rock,
even our enemies themselves being judges.
32 For their vine comes from the vine of Sodom,
and from the fields of Gomorrah;
their grapes are grapes of poison,
their clusters are bitter;
33 their wine is the poison of serpents,
and the cruel venom of asps.

34 'Is not this laid up in store with me,
sealed up in my treasuries?
35 Vengeance is mine, and recompense,
for the time when their foot shall slip;
for the day of their calamity is at hand,
and their doom comes swiftly.
36 For the LORD will vindicate his people
and have compassion on his servants,
when he sees that their power is gone,
and there is none remaining, bond or free.
37 Then he will say, "Where are their gods,
the rock in which they took refuge,
38 who ate the fat of their sacrifices,
and drank the wine of their drink offering?
Let them rise up and help you,
let them be your protection!

39 ' "See now that I, even I, am he,
and there is no god beside me;
I kill and I make alive;
I wound and I heal;
and there is none that can deliver out of my hand.
40 For I lift up my hand to heaven,
and swear, As I live for ever,
41 if I whet my glittering sword,
and my hand takes hold on judgment,
I will take vengeance on my adversaries,
and will requite those who hate me.
42 I will make my arrows drunk with blood,
and my sword shall devour flesh—
with the blood of the slain and the captives,
from the long-haired heads of the enemy."

43 'Praise his people, O you nations;
for he avenges the blood of his servants,
and takes vengeance on his adversaries,
and makes expiation for the land of his people.'

44 Moses came and recited all the words of this song in the hearing of the people, he and Joshua the son of Nun. 45And when Moses had finished speaking all these words to all Israel, 46he said to them, 'Lay to heart all the words which I enjoin upon you this day, that you may command them to your children, that they may be careful to do all the words of this law. 47For it is no trifle for you, but it is your life, and thereby you shall live long in the land which you are going over the Jordan to possess.'

48 And the LORD said to Moses that very day, 49'Ascend this mountain of the Abarim, Mount Nebo, which is in the land of Moab, opposite Jericho; and view the land of Canaan, which I give to the people of Israel for a possession; 50and die on the mountain which you ascend, and be gathered to your people, as Aaron your brother died in Mount Hor and was gathered to his people; 51because you broke faith with me in the midst of the people of Israel at the waters of Meri-bath-kadesh, in the wilderness of Zin; because you did not revere me as holy in the midst of the people of Israel. 52For you shall see the land before you; but you shall not go there, into the land which I give to the people of Israel.'

The so-called Song of Moses is a long widely ranging poem which came into existence quite independently of Deuteronomy. In consequence its nature and origin can be determined only by internal evidence. The outline of its arrangement is as follows:

vv. 1–2   a didactic opening summons
vv. 3–7   the subject of the poem, Yahweh's perfect ways
vv. 8–14   Yahweh's redemptive acts
vv. 15–18   Israel's backsliding
vv. 19–25   the judgment
vv. 26–35   God's argument with himself
vv. 36–38   announcement of Yahweh's imminent coming to succour his people
vv. 39–42   Yahweh's concluding words
v. 43   a hymn-like ending.

[1–7] The 'didactic opening summons', in the main elaborately worked up and consisting here of four parts, is particularly frequent in Wisdom poems (Ps. 49.2ff.; 78.1f.; Isa. 28.23 etc.).[1] The words 'teaching' (*leqaḥ*) and 'speech' (*imrā*) also belong preponderantly to the language of the Wisdom sayings (in that case we must, of course, also consider the opening words in Gen. 4.23 or in Judg. 5.3 to be Wisdom formulae in the wider sense). In v. 3 the poet passes on to announce his theme; Yahweh's Name, that is, Yahweh as he has become manifest to Israel; the Rock, the faithful God against whom Israel has sinned. Here the poem introduces one of its great themes, Israel's denial of God. Verse 7 is very typical; it reminds us that Yahweh is known from history. We need only ask our elders. By this means the poem has skilfully prepared the transition to its first main part, which treats of the history of God and his people.

[8–14] The beginning of this history, which elsewhere in Israel is paraphrased in terms such as 'election', is here presented in a way unique in the whole Old Testament. [2]At that time, that is, at the beginning of all history, when Yahweh was fixing the boundaries of all peoples, he divided up the nations according to the number of the sons of God; i.e. he subordinated one nation to each of the heavenly beings who had to take care of it, like a guardian angel. He departed from

---

[1] On the didactic opening summons see H. W. Wolff, *Hosea*, pp. 122f.

[2] The Massoretic Text in v. 8b reads: 'he fixed the bounds of the people according to the number of the sons of Israel.' This text has long been suspect, because the LXX reads 'according to the number of the sons of God'. Now a fragment from Cave Four at Qumran has made it as good as certain that the Massoretic Text cannot be the original one. This text modified the conception so as to mean that there exists a relationship ordained by God which makes the number of the nations correspond to that of the sons of Israel. Cf. R. Meyer, 'Die Bedeutung von Dt. 32.8f., 43 (IV Q) für die Auslegung des Moseliedes', in *Verbannung und Heimkehr, Festschrift für W. Rudolph*, pp. 197ff.

this general arrangement in one case alone: Israel was chosen by Yahweh for himself and subordinated directly to himself. Thus it was in this way, as a great King subordinates the provinces of his universal empire to his satraps, that God at the beginning carried out the division of the world according to its nations (so R. Meyer). But he excepted Israel from this arrangement, because he claimed it for his own immediate possession. The peculiarity of this passage is not the fact that it mentions yet other heavenly beings beside Yahweh (this conception is not rare in the Old Testament) but that it confers on them such an important place in the government of the world. Nevertheless, the conception resembles Ps. 82, according to which it was the task of these heavenly beings to provide for justice and order amongst the nations. We might also recall I Kings 22.19, where the sons of God have a place and a voice in the heavenly deliberations. Our passage in vv. 8–9 is unmistakably intended to be aetiological; it is asking how the direct relationship between Yahweh, the God of the whole world, and Israel came about? What is the explanation of the fact that Israel is subordinated not, like all other nations, to one of these sons of God but to Yahweh directly? This must be traced back to a particular decision of Yahweh himself, who at the division of the world claimed Israel for himself. Cf. for this Ecclus. 17.17.

The story passes from this event which took place in the divine council before all history to the first encounter between Yahweh and Israel. The strange conception that Yahweh 'found' Israel in the wilderness cannot be attributed simply to the freedom of poetic expression. The conception of the finding occurs equally clearly once more in Hos. 9.10 and probably in Jer. 31.2f. as well. There is much to be said for the hypothesis that we must consider this 'tradition of the finding' to be an old tradition, by this time half-forgotten, about the origins of Israel, which had, in fact, been almost completely pushed aside and overlaid by the other traditions of the election (the Exodus tradition, the patriarchal tradition).[1] The Song then goes on to dwell with impressive comparisons upon the protection and sheltering control which followed, yet without referring to any precise historical situation.

[15–18] The next section of the Song, in vv. 15–18, turns to Yahweh's partner, who has been so much sheltered and pampered. The effect of these benefits was a quite unexpected one. Israel became weary

[1] R. Bach, 'Die Erwählung Israels in der Wüste', *TLZ*, 1953, col. 687.

of Yahweh and turned aside to other gods. It is significant as showing the historical awareness of the religion of Yahweh that these gods are called 'new gods that have come in of late', who could therefore not boast of a relationship to Israel determined by a long history. In this account of the history disloyalty to Yahweh, which in fact took very many forms, is reduced in a striking manner to the one sin against the first commandment. It thus reveals an obvious dependence on a view of history already much subordinated to theology. In my opinion no other view than the Deuteronomistic one can be considered, and this is supported by some of the phraseology used in this section. The word 'Jeshurun' which is rare in the Old Testament (cf. Deut. 33.5, 26) has still not yet been sufficiently elucidated. Only one point is evident, namely that it was an honourable title for Israel. The whole section speaks of Israel in the third person, but occasionally it drops, apparently by chance, into the second person singular (vv. 14b, 15aβ, 18), which makes the whole appear as a prophetic indictment.

[19–25] These verses now describe the outburst of divine wrath. God called up against Israel 'those who are no people', and also famine, pestilence and beasts of prey. All attempts to interpret the chastisements by this 'no-people' as referring to a definite historical calamity remain uncertain. Usually the Babylonians have been suggested. The latest interpretation, proposed by Eissfeldt, is that the Philistines are meant, but this would involve a barely defensible early dating for the Song. Does not v. 25 recall certain descriptions in the Lamentations of Jeremiah (e.g. 2.21)?

[26–35] This section is particularly important for understanding the whole. The Hebrew word ('āmartî) must be understood in the sense of 'Then I thought'. Thus the section introduces something quite new, a detailed deliberation in the heart of God. The description of historical events continuous from v. 8 onwards breaks off. A new description of coming events does not start again until v. 36. This section is therefore an interlude which takes us out of the turmoil of historical processes and allows us to overhear a soliloquy within the depths of the divine heart. Yahweh was firmly resolved to annihilate Israel completely, and to blot out its memory from amongst mankind. But now he fears he will be humiliated by his enemies, who would certainly attribute the annihilation of Israel to their own strength and fail to recognize in it the hand of Yahweh. They are, after all, without understanding of the dispensations of history (vv.

28–30 must refer to these enemies). From the overthrow of Israel they will conclude that they themselves are strong; they do not know that Yahweh has abandoned Israel to them. Such deliberations within himself on the part of God, which almost indicate something like lack of resolution, are not altogether rare in the Old Testament (Gen. 6.5–7; Hos. 6.4; 11.8f.). They occur in just those cases where a decision for salvation or for judgment is at stake. Here we are told about this deliberation for a definitely aetiological purpose. It is concerned with answering the question, why then has Yahweh in spite of such grievous offences nevertheless not cast off his people? The reply given here does the poem no dishonour. It states that this did not happen for Israel's sake, but for the sake of Yahweh's honour, which ought not to be exposed to any humiliation from the nations (for this cf. also Ezek. 20.21f.; 36.22). After Yahweh has pictured to himself in vv. 32–33 the complete wickedness in which these people lived, he announces solemnly and formally the result of his deliberations (vv. 34–35). It consists in his remembering his office of judge and avenger which pertains to him alone, and by virtue of which he will shortly advance against the nations. This brings the soliloquy to an end.

[36–38] Here we seem to hear a prophetic message of salvation, that is, the voice of a messenger who is informed of the result of God's deliberation (he speaks of Yahweh in the third person) and hurries to hand it on. The synonymous parallelism of 'vindicate' and 'have compassion' in v. 36 is interesting: it is a question of a legal act of deliverance. In thus turning in favour to his people, Yahweh indeed humbles them, too; he does not refrain from reproaching them about their idols, to whom they offered their trust and their sacrifices. The failure of their idols, which in the opinion of our Song can already be perceived within history, sweeps the poem on to its real culmination in a splendid testimony by Yahweh to his own all-sufficient being as God. The statements in v. 39a have close parallels in Deutero-Isaiah (cf. Isa. 43.11), those in 39b are paralleled in I Sam. 2.6. This means that in both cases the poem depends on hymn-like language originally derived from the cult. There is, of course, no thought of an awakening from physical death. According to the ideas of early Israel man entered the domain of death even in sickness or in captivity, in fact in every condition seriously prejudicial to his life.[1]

[39–43] In vv. 39–42 Yahweh himself now announces with great

[1] Chr. Barth, *Die Errettung vom Tode*, 1947, pp. 53ff.

solemnity the resolve formed during his deliberations (in vv. 26–35). Yahweh swears by his everlasting life that he will destroy these nations. As in the old days, Yahweh will slay them in a warlike action in which he actually rises in person against his foes. The Song closes with a hymn which replies to this divine resolve (for the invocation to the heavenly beings to join in the hymn, cf. Ps. 29.1; 148.1). The reference to an imminent expiation for the land is remarkable. Had it become necessary owing to a hostile invasion? It is more likely due to Israel's cultic aberrations.

It is not easy to determine the time and the theological position of the author of this swan-song of Moses. In our opinion it originated in a period in which it was already known how to combine poetically, with great freedom and effect, extreme heterogeneous formal elements originally alien to each other. Cf. the didactic opening summons reminiscent of Wisdom literature, in vv. 1ff., the prophetic style of the announcements in vv. 36ff., 39ff., hymn-like matter in vv. 3f., 43f., etc. The Song of Moses is in every way a poem with literary pretensions. By a certain strong individuality in the choice of words, but also by harking back to ancient and unfamiliar conceptions (vv. 8f., 10), the poem gives the impression of being something uncommon. As far as its religious purport is concerned there can hardly be any question of any early date.[1] The nearness to Deutero-Isaiah and Ezekiel or the occasional changeover into Deuteronomistic phraseology suggest possibly the period of the exile. It is at that time that we meet with the first reflections on the conceivable psychological effect on the nations of Israel's rejection (cf. v. 27 with Ezek. 20.9, 14, 22; 36.20) and also with the remarkable conception of Yahweh as the creator of the people. This represents a mingling of the beliefs concerning creation and salvation (vv. 6, 15b, 18; cf. on this Isa. 43.1; 44.2, 24). That it was later thought to be a document of the so-called testamentary literature is certain; but ought it to be ascribed to this type? It is, after all, not really didactic enough in character for this. Nevertheless we must look for the origin of the poem in the sphere of Wisdom literature. Perhaps that is one of the reasons why it could not be quite successful in giving a really graphic description of historical events.

[1] In an exhaustive form-historical analysis G. E. Wright suggests the hypothesis that the Song is based on the framework of a divine lawsuit against Israel ('The Lawsuit of God: A Form-critical Study of Deuteronomy 32', *Israel's Prophetic Heritage*, Essays in honour of James Muilenburg, ed. B. W. Anderson and W. Harrelson, 1962, pp. 26ff.).

[44–47] With these verses we reach once more the prose framework of the narrative which has surrounded the Song, and we are thus confronted once more, as in vv. 16ff., by that double train of thought which speaks on the one hand of the Song (v. 44), on the other of the law (v. 46). It seems as if this can only be explained by the fact that a text originally treating of the law was by a rather superficial revision applied to the Song. It is noteworthy that the religion of Yahweh was so closely bound up with history that even a poem like the Song of Moses was not accepted simply for its content, but only when it was clearly embedded in the history of salvation. In the statement that Yahweh's offer is 'no empty word',[1] but implies Israel's life, an important fact, realized by early Israel, has found expression in a pregnant phrase rarely equalled. There stands behind the sentence a long, mainly prophetic experience of the creative power of Yahweh's Word. The almost contemporary Deutero-Isaiah, basing himself on the same principle, asserts that Yahweh's word shall not return to him empty (Isa. 55.11).[2]

[48–52] This section contains the summons to Moses to ascend Mount Nebo in order to die there. It belongs neither to the tradition of Deuteronomy nor to that of the Deuteronomic history, but to that of the Priestly Writings, where it could, in fact, be read already in a very similar version (Num. 27.12–14). Has it been put in again at this point after the summons to ascend the mountain has been separated altogether too far from the event of Moses' death by the great interpolation of Deuteronomy? This is conjectured by Noth. We would be more ready to agree with this hypothesis, if it were a question of an actual repetition, and so of a simple copy of the first text. Yet the text in vv. 48–52 reads more like a variant. In both versions the death of Moses in sight of the land of promise is brought into connexion with a sin on the part of Moses himself (cf. on this Num. 20.1ff.). In the tradition of Deuteronomy and that of the Deuteronomic history this fate was accounted for in quite a different way, namely that Moses had to die vicariously for the sake of Israel's sin (Deut. 4.21; 1.37. On the subject of surveying the land (v. 52), see below on ch. 34.

---

[1] RSV: 'no trifle'. Translator.
[2] On this theology of the Word see von Rad, *Old Testament Theology* II, pp. 80ff., 91ff.

33 ¹This is the blessing with which Moses the man of God blessed the children of Israel before his death. ²He said,
'The LORD came from Sinai,
    and dawned from Seir upon us;
    he shone forth from Mount Paran,
he came from the ten thousands of holy ones,
    with flaming fire at his right hand.
³ Yea, he loved his people;
    all those consecrated to him were in his hand;
so they followed in thy steps,
    receiving direction from thee,
⁴ when Moses commanded us a law,
    as a possession for the assembly of Jacob.
⁵ Thus the LORD became king in Jeshurun,
    when the heads of the people were gathered,
    all the tribes of Israel together.

⁶ 'Let Reuben live, and not die,
    nor let his men be few.'

⁷ And this he said of Judah:
    'Hear, O LORD, the voice of Judah,
    and bring him in to his people.
With thy hands contend for him,
    and be a help against his adversaries.'

⁸ And of Levi he said,
    'Give to Levi thy Thummim,
    and thy Urim to thy godly one,
whom thou didst test at Massah,
    with whom thou didst strive at the waters of Meribah;
⁹ who said of his father and mother,
    "I regard them not";

he disowned his brothers,
    and ignored his children.
For they observed thy word,
    and kept thy covenant.
10 They shall teach Jacob thy ordinances,
    and Israel thy law;
they shall put incense before thee,
    and whole burnt offering upon thy altar.
11 Bless, O LORD, his substance,
    and accept the work of his hands;
crush the loins of his adversaries,
    of those that hate him, that they rise not again.'

12 Of Benjamin he said,
'The beloved of the LORD,
    he dwells in safety by him;
he encompasses him all the day long,
    and makes his dwelling between his shoulders.'

13 And of Joseph he said,
'Blessed by the LORD be his land,
    with the choicest gifts of heaven above,
    and of the deep that couches beneath,
14 with the choicest fruits of the sun,
    and the rich yield of the months,
15 with the finest produce of the ancient mountains,
    and the abundance of the everlasting hills,
16 with the best gifts of the earth and its fulness,
    and the favour of him that dwelt in the bush.
Let these come upon the head of Joseph,
    and upon the crown of the head of him that is prince among his
      brothers.
17 His firstling bull has majesty,
    and his horns are the horns of a wild ox;
with them he shall push the peoples,
    all of them, to the ends of the earth;
such are the ten thousands of Ephraim,
    and such are the thousands of Manasseh.'

18 And of Zebulun he said,
'Rejoice, Zebulun, in your going out;
    and Issachar, in your tents.
19 They shall call peoples to their mountain;
    there they offer right sacrifices;
for they suck the affluence of the seas
    and the hidden treasures of the sand.'

20 And of Gad he said,
  'Blessed be he who enlarges Gad!
    Gad couches like a lion,
    he tears the arm, and the crown of the head.
21 He chose the best of the land for himself,
    for there a commander's portion was reserved;
  and he came to the heads of the people,
    with Israel he executed the commands
    and just decrees of the LORD.'

22 And of Dan he said,
  'Dan is a lion's whelp,
    that leaps forth from Bashan.'

23 And of Naphtali he said,
  'O Naphtali, satisfied with favour,
    and full of the blessing of the LORD
    possess the lake and the south.'

24 And of Asher he said,
  'Blessed above sons be Asher;
    let him be the favourite of his brothers, and let him dip his foot
    in oil.
25 Your bars shall be iron and bronze;
    and as your days, so shall your strength be.

26 'There is none like God, O Jeshurun,
    who rides through the heavens to your help,
    and in his majesty through the skies.
27 The eternal God is your dwelling place,
    and underneath are the everlasting arms.
  And he thrust out the enemy before you,
    and said, Destroy.
28 So Israel dwelt in safety,
    the fountain of Jacob alone,
  in a land of grain and wine;
    yea, his heavens drop down dew.
29 Happy are you, O Israel! Who is like you,
    a people saved by the LORD,
  that shield of your help,
    and the sword of your triumph!
  Your enemies shall come fawning to you;
    and you shall tread upon their high places.'

Yet another poem, the 'Blessing of Moses', was inserted later into
Deuteronomy. Moses is understood here to be a 'man of God', that is,

a prophet, who as he contemplates his imminent death utters predictions concerning the future of the individual tribes. The blessing by such a mighty man is much more than merely an empty wish. It contains creative words which are able to shape the future. It is from this point of view, that is to say, as a prediction of the dying Moses, that according to the present text the sayings about the tribes are intended to be understood. But, of course, this does not imply that the poem in itself suggests this interpretation of it. The problem of understanding it is complicated still further by the fact that the actual collection of sayings about the tribes in vv. 6–25 is set in the frame of a psalm-like poem which, it is usually assumed, must have existed formerly by itself.

[2–5, 26–29] To judge by its type, this poem can be claimed as an 'informative psalm of praise' in so far as it sings of historical events: Yahweh's coming from Sinai and the protection he bestows upon his people. If with the majority of the commentators v. 5 is applied to Yahweh, then the main idea of the Song is that Yahweh has come from Sinai in order to enter upon his kingly power in Israel (on Jeshurun see 32.15). But it is very doubtful if this idea could be expressed in such terms, and besides, was Yahweh really king in 'Israel'? Elsewhere the conception of Yahweh as king is understood to be confined to a kingdom over the gods and the nations (Pss. 95–99). Probably the sentence is to be applied to the rise of the earthly kingdom in Israel. The conception in v. 26 (cf. Pss. 68.4; 104.3) is borrowed from the Canaanite religion. The view that Israel dwells by itself 'alone' (v. 28) reveals already an awareness of Israel's special position amongst the nations (more clearly in Num. 23.9).

Our comments on many details of the sayings about the tribes cannot go beyond conjectures. Much help is given by a comparison with the sayings on the same subject in Gen. 49, and also with the exhortations addressed to individual tribes in Judg. 5. Moreover, it is important to determine their peculiarities from the form-critical point of view. The proper form of such sayings is that in which the characteristics and distinctive features of a tribe are conveyed in general sayings of praise or blame. It will appear that this form is by no means predominant in the collection of Deut. 33. [6] Thus, to begin with, the saying concerning Reuben is shaped as a wish. The tribe of Reuben must have lost its political importance earlier than this. The small amount of information which we can infer from v. 6

is that at the time of the saying probably only a few members who claimed descent from the former tribe were still living.

[7] The saying about Judah is actually framed as a prayer, more precisely as an intercession for Judah. The request 'to bring him in to his people' might refer to the division of the kingdom, and in that case the political position of the speaker should be sought in the Northern Kingdom, where Judah was considered to be the rebel. But this interpretation, too, is not quite certain. The sentence has also been applied to a much earlier situation and taken as a rebuke for the attachment of this southern tribe to the sanctuary of Mamre and not to that of Shechem, an attachment which had an isolating effect. In fact, the omission of any mention of the monarchy is striking.

[8–11] The saying about Levi too, is addressed to Yahweh somewhat in the style of a prayer. We find it difficult to understand, because we know so very little about the history and official duties of the tribe of Levi and hence, too, about the particular situation which this saying concerning Levi takes for granted. We can only express conjectures. If Urim and Thummim, that is, the oracle by lot, are requested for Levi, this implies a claim to the office of priest. Was this office at that time new or perhaps in danger? According to v. 10 the office has two distinct prerogatives: the first consists in guarding the sacral traditions and in exercising the authority derived from them to 'teach thy law', the second has to do with the performance and supervision of the cult and its sacrifices. Certain events which lie in the distant past, because they evidently serve to provide Levi with legitimate authority to perform this important office, are now recalled in the saying. As long ago as in the time of the desert wanderings (in the region of the oases of Kadesh) Yahweh put Levi to the test; indeed, he actually set in motion legal proceedings against him. For the sake of an unqualified bond with Yahweh (we may complete the meaning in this way) this Levi set aside all obligations of loyalty to his own kindred—a most unusual way of behaving in the ancient East. (Underlying the statement in v. 9 an archaic legal formula has rightly been conjectured.)

We need not be surprised that these allusions to historical happenings cannot be made completely consistent with any of the accounts in the Pentateuch; reminiscences are revived here which were still current in Israel when the saying was composed. Nevertheless, v. 9 recalls Ex. 32.26–29 while in v. 8 allusions have been found to Ex. 17.1–7 and Num. 20.1–13. The request to appoint Levi to the office of priest, the eagerness to make him play a full legitimate part in the history of salvation, and now in addition the request to protect him from his enemies—all this suggests the thought that at the time of the saying this office was not yet in the case of Levi and old well-established one, or at any rate not yet a secure one, but that it was possibly being disputed in some way.

[12] The saying concerning Benjamin seems to be composed as a simple statement. In v. 12b some commentators apply the phrase 'between his shoulders' to Yahweh, on whose shoulders Benjamin sits like a favourite child. But the Hebrew word can also mean 'hill-side'.

[13-17] The saying for Joseph is very comprehensive. Its first part in vv. 13-16 is really a blessing, and its peculiarly elevated style is determined by its being recited in the ritual. Thus it is a fertility blessing, and its parts are constructed with strict symmetry (cf. Gen. 49.25). The reference to 'him that dwelt in the bush' can doubtless only be explained by reference to Ex. 3.2ff. But it is a strange one. Did Yahweh 'dwell' in the bush? Joseph is the Nazirite, the consecrated one, the one singled out from amongst his brethren, evidently by his being placed in a superior political position. Verse 17 passes into the descriptive style. For the 'horns of a wild ox' cf. Num. 23.22. The mention of Ephraim and Manasseh in v. 17b might be understood as a later amplification, identifying the more ancient 'house of Joseph' with these two tribes.

[18-19] The neighbouring tribes of Zebulun and Issachar get only one saying, this time in the form of personal address. Their particular responsibility is the cult on Mount Tabor, which attracted a large number of participants, as was usual in such cases.[1] The 'affluence of the sea' probably refers to import trade; 'the treasures of the sand' has been held to mean the purple mollusc. [20-21] Such meaning as can be given to the largely obscure saying for Gad seems to refer to his expansion by violence in the area of east of Jordan. On the conception of God 'who enlarges Gad' Israelite colonization compare Gen. 9.27.[2] The juxtaposition of Gad and Israel in v. 21 is remarkable. Was the tribe perhaps considered, on account of its exposed position on the east, rather more as a tribe standing outside Israel (cf. on this Josh. 22.19, 24ff.)? The rest is now barely intelligible.

[1] O. Eissfeldt, 'Der Gott des Tabor und seine Verbreitung', *Kleine Schriften* II, 1963, pp. 29ff.
[2] Von Rad, *Genesis*, pp. 133f.

[22–25] The sayings concerning Dan and Naphtali are genuine tribal sayings in the form of aphorisms, rather colourless as regards content. The lake mentioned in the obscure v. 23b is probably the Lake of Gennesaret. The saying about Asher begins with a wish. As in Gen. 49.20, so here, too, the fertility of his territory is praised. It is hard to see what it has to do with iron and bronze bars.

An opinion on the Blessing of Moses could only be based on some knowledge of its literary development. But in this respect only very little can be ascertained. Is it true that originally the collection of sayings followed immediately after the introduction in v. 1, and that it was therefore not inserted into the 'psalm' until later? It is true that the language and ideas of the psalm give the impression of being very primitive. But does this not also apply to Hab. 3? So far as the corpus of sayings is concerned, we are inclined to agree with those commentators who make a clear distinction between the sayings in Gen. 49 and these, which they ascribe to a considerably later period. The latter reflect a state of greater security. The political conditions of the tribes have been stabilized. There is now hardly any question of tension between the tribes; every kind of censure is entirely lacking. With this in mind, we might perhaps think of a date in the ninth or early eighth century.

Moreover, it is noticeable that the Blessing of Moses is more 'religious'. In it the tribes are much more closely associated (often by the language of prayer) with Yahweh. In the sayings in the Blessing of Jacob the name of Yahweh did not occur at all. But we need to know more about the setting and use of such series of sayings. Where, when and for what purpose did the custom come into use of coining sayings about the individual tribes of the amphictyonic league, collecting them and perhaps even proclaiming them? If the form of the Saying in the narrower sense of the word is really to be regarded as the original form of such sayings (but we do not know this), then this form is already in a state of partial disintegration in the Blessing of Jacob. In the Blessing of Moses it recedes completely into the background. As a form of expression its place is taken by prayer.

CHAPTER 34.1–12

34 ¹And Moses went up from the plains of Moab to Mount Nebo, to the top of Pisgah, which is opposite Jericho. And the LORD showed him all the land, Gilead as far as Dan, ²all Naphtali, the land of Ephraim and Manasseh, all the land of Judah as far as the Western Sea, ³the Negeb, and the Plain, that is, the valley of Jericho the city of palm trees, as far as Zoar. ⁴And the LORD said to him, 'This is the land of which I swore to Abraham, to Isaac, and to Jacob, "I will give it to your descendants." I have let you see it with your eyes, but you shall not go over there.' ⁵So Moses the servant of the LORD died there in the land of Moab, according to the word of the LORD, ⁶and he buried him in the valley in the land of Moab opposite Beth-peor; but no man knows the place of his burial to this day. ⁷Moses was a hundred and twenty years old when he died; his eye was not dim, nor his natural force abated. ⁸And the people of Israel wept for Moses in the plains of Moab thirty days; then the days of weeping and mourning for Moses were ended.

9 And Joshua the son of Nun was full of the spirit of wisdom, for Moses had laid his hands upon him; so the people of Israel obeyed him, and did as the LORD had commanded Moses. ¹⁰And there has not arisen a prophet since in Israel like Moses, whom the LORD knew face to face, ¹¹none like him for all the signs and the wonders which the LORD sent him to do in the land of Egypt, to Pharaoh and to all his servants and to all his land, ¹²and for all the mighty power and all the great and terrible deeds which Moses wrought in the sight of all Israel.

[1–12] The reader must think of the narrative about Moses' death as the immediate continuation of 32.48–52. This connexion has been loosened by the great interpolation of the Song and Blessing of Moses. A considerable part (vv. 1, 7–9) of this text belongs to the Priestly source, the rest to the Deuteronomistic historical narrative. The

reader knows from Deut. 1.37 and 4.21 that in the view of this historical work the death of Moses is regarded as a vicarious act for the
sins of the people. The narrator certainly does not attempt to tell us
anything about his own feelings, still less about those of Moses in the
face of such an event. The facts soberly imparted tell the reader
enough.

But the account of the death of this great and lonely figure is not
composed in narrative form simply for the sake of its undoubtedly
incomparable emotional value. Probably primitive legal conceptions
also play their part in it. For instance, the 'mountain survey', with the
invitation to scan the land (cf. Deut. 3.27) was considered originally
to be a legal act, by means of which the conveyance of the land in
question was carried out (cf. for this Gen. 13.14ff.).[1] The view from
Nebo certainly does not stretch over the hills of Judah as far as the
sea. Since Moses is not likely to have climbed the mountain without
companions, it is more natural in v. 6 to translate as 'he was buried'
(in the preceding sentence Yahweh was not the subject either). The
note 'In the valley opposite Bethpeor' gives the impression that
Moses' grave was probably still well known in earlier days, but that
in course of time the knowledge of it was lost and that in the opinion
of the narrator the grave ought never to be known to men.[2]

The reference to Joshua, his charisma and his office refers to Num.
27.18ff. (P). The verdict on Moses as a prophet, indeed as a prophet
without an equal, is, of course, again Deuteronomistic. The reader
must know that the Deuteronomistic account of the history follows
on from here without a break to Josh. 1 and to the description of the
events in the period of Joshua.

[1] D. Daube, *Studies in Biblical Law*, p. 24, and 'Von Ugarit nach Qumran',
Festschrift für O. Eissfeldt, 1958, p. 35.
[2] M. Noth, *Überlieferungsgeschichte des Pentateuch*, 1948, pp. 186ff.

INDEX OF MODERN AUTHORS